THE
INDIVIDUAL
AND
COMMUNITY

A HERITAGE READER

Selected by
**The Heritage Studies Program Faculty
Carthage College**

Jeffrey L. Roberg
Director of the Heritage Studies Program

Including Selections from
A WORLD OF IDEAS:
ESSENTIAL READINGS FOR COLLEGE WRITERS
Sixth Edition
Lee A. Jacobus, *University of Connecticut*

BEDFORD/ST. MARTIN'S
Boston ◆ *New York*

Manufactured in the United States of America.

8   7   6   5
f   e   d   c

For information, write: Bedford/St. Martin's, 75 Arlington Street, Boston, MA 02116
(617-399-4000)

ISBN: 0–312–41985–6

Acknowledgments
Acknowledgments and copyrights are appear at the back of the book, which constitutes
an extension of the copyright page.

CONTENTS

EVALUATING IDEAS
An Introduction
to Critical Reading

The selections in this book demand a careful and attentive reading. The authors, whose works have changed the way we view our world, our institutions, and ourselves, make every effort to communicate their views with clarity and style. But their views are complex and subtle, and we must train ourselves to read them sensitively, responsively, and critically. Critical reading is basic for approaching the essays in this book. Indeed, it is fundamental for approaching any reading material that deserves serious attention.

Reading critically means reading actively: questioning the premises of the argument, speculating on the ways in which evidence is used, comparing the statements of one writer with those of another, and holding an inner dialogue with the author. These skills differ from the passive reception we employ when we watch television or read lightweight materials. Being an active, participating reader makes it possible for us to derive the most from good books.

Critical reading involves most of the following processes:

- *Prereading*   Developing a sense of what the piece is about and what its general purposes seem to be.

- *Annotating*   Using a pencil or a pen to mark those passages that seem important enough to return to later. Annotations establish a dialogue between you and the author.

- *Questioning*   Raising issues that you feel need to be taken into consideration. These may be issues that you believe the author has treated either well or badly and that you feel are important. Questioning can be part of the annotation process.

- *Reviewing*   Rereading your annotations and underlinings in order to grasp the entire "picture" of what you've just read.

Sometimes writing a summary of the piece as you review makes the meaning even clearer.

* *Forming your own ideas*   Reviewing what you have read, evaluating the way that the writer presents the issues, and developing your own views on the issues. This is the final step.

THE PROCESS OF CRITICAL READING

Prereading

Begin any selection in this book by reading its headnote. Each headnote supplies historical background on the writer, sets the intellectual stage for the ideas discussed in the selection, and comments on the writer's main points. The second part of each headnote also introduces the main rhetorical or stylistic methods that the writer uses to communicate his/her thoughts. In the process of reading the headnote, you will develop an overview that helps prepare you for reading the selection.

This kind of preparation is typical of critical reading. It makes the task of reading more delightful, more useful, and much easier. A review of the headnote and the selection will illustrate the usefulness of such preparation. Thus, as a critical reader, you will be well advised to keep track of the headnote's basic statements. You need not accept all of them, but you should certainly be alert to the issues that will probably be central to your experience of the essay. Remember: it is just as reasonable to question the headnote as it is to question the selection itself.

Before reading the selection in detail, you might develop an overview of its meaning by scanning it quickly. Checking each of the subheadings before you read the entire piece might provide you with a map or guide to the selction.

Most passages are preceded by two or three prereading questions. These are designed to keep two or three points in mind as you read. Each of these questions focuses your attention on an important idea or interpretation in the passage.

Annotating and Questioning

As you read a text, your annotations establish a dialogue between you and the author. You can underline or highlight important statements that you feel help clarify the author's position. They may be statements to which you will want to refer later. Think of them as serving one overriding purpose: to make it possible for you to review the piece and understand its key points without having to reread it entirely.

Your dialogue with the author will be most visible in the margins of the selection, which is one reason the margins in this book are so generous. Take issue with key points or note your assent—the more you annotate, the more you free your imagination to develop your own ideas. My own methods involve notating both agreement and disagreement. I annotate thoroughly, so that after a quick second glance I know what the author is saying as well as what I thought of the essay when I read it closely. My annotations help me keep the major points fresh in my mind.

Annotation keeps track both of what the author says and of what our responses are. No one can reduce annotation to a formula—we all do it differently—but it is not a passive act. Reading with a pencil or a pen in hand should become second nature. Without annotations, you often have to reread entire sections of an essay to remember an argument that once was clear and understandable but after time has become part of the fabric of the prose and thus "invisible." Annotation is the conquest of the invisible; it provides a quick view of the main points.

When you annotate,

- Read with a pen or a pencil.
- Underline key sentences—for example, definitions and statements of purpose.
- Underline key words that appear often.
- Note the topic of paragraphs in the margins.
- Ask questions in the margins.
- Make notes in the margins to remind yourself to develop ideas later.
- Mark passages you might want to quote later.
- Keep track of points with which you disagree.

Some sample annotations follow from Niccolò Machiavelli's "The Qualities of the Prince." A sixteenth-century text in translation,

The Prince is challenging to work with. My annotations appear in the form of underlinings and marginal comments and questions. Only the first few paragraphs appear here.

A Prince's Duty Concerning Military Matters

The prince's profession should be war.

A prince, therefore, must not have any other object nor any other thought, nor must he take anything as his profession but war, its institutions, and its discipline; because that is the only profession which befits one who commands; and it is of such importance that not only does it maintain those who were born princes, but many times it enables men of private station to rise to that position; and, on the other hand, it is evident that when princes have given more thought to personal luxuries than to arms, they have lost their state. And the first way to lose it is to neglect this art; and the way to acquire it is to be well versed in this art.

Examples

Francesco Sforza became Duke of Milan from being a private citizen because he was armed; his sons, since they avoided the inconveniences of arms, became private citizens after having been dukes. For, among the other bad effects it causes, being dis-

Being disarmed makes you despised. Is this true?

armed makes you despised; this is one of those infamies a prince should guard himself against, as will be treated below: for between an armed and an unarmed man there is no comparison whatsoever, and it is not reasonable for an armed man to obey an unarmed man willingly, nor that an unarmed man should be safe among armed servants; since, when the former is suspicious and the latter are contemptuous, it is impossible for them to work well together. And therefore, a prince who does not understand military matters, besides the other misfortunes already noted, cannot be esteemed by his own soldiers, nor can he trust them.

Training: action/mind

He must, therefore, never raise his thought from this exercise of war, and in peacetime he must train himself more than in time of war; this can be done in two ways: one by action, the other by the mind. And as far as actions are concerned, besides keeping his soldiers well disciplined and trained,

*Knowledge of
terrain*

Two benefits

he must always be out hunting, and must accustom his body to hardships in this manner; and he must also learn the nature of the terrain, and know how mountains slope, how valleys open, how plains lie, and understand the nature of rivers and swamps; and he should devote much attention to such activities. Such knowledge is useful in two ways: first, one learns to know one's own country and can better understand how to defend it; second, with the knowledge and experience of the terrain, one can easily comprehend the characteristics of any other terrain that it is necessary to explore for the first time; for the hills, valleys, plains, rivers, and swamps of Tuscany, for instance, have certain similarities to those of other provinces; so that by knowing the lay of the land in one province one can easily understand it in others. And a prince who lacks this ability lacks the most important quality in a leader; because this skill teaches you to find the enemy, choose a campsite, lead troops, organize them for battle, and besiege towns to your own advantage.

[There follow the examples of Philopoemon, who was always observing terrain for its military usefulness, and a recommendation that princes read histories and learn from them. Three paragraphs are omitted.]

On Those Things for Which Men, and Particularly Princes, Are Praised or Blamed

Now there remains to be examined what should be the methods and procedures of a prince in dealing with his subjects and friends. And because I know that many have written about this, I am afraid that writing about it again I shall be thought of as presumptuous, since in discussing this material I depart radically from the procedures of others. But since my intention is to write something useful for anyone who understands it, it seemed more suitable to me to search after the effectual truth of the matter rather than its imagined

Those who are good at all times come to ruin among those who are not good.

one. And many writers have imagined for themselves republics and principalities that have never been seen nor known to exist in reality; for there is such a gap between how one lives and how one ought to live that anyone who abandons what is done for what ought to be done learns his ruin rather than his preservation: for a man who wishes to make a vocation of being good at all times will come to ruin among so many who are not good.

Prince must learn how not to be good.

Hence it is necessary for a prince who wishes to maintain his position to learn how not to be good, and to use this knowledge or not to use it according to necessity.

Leaving aside, therefore, the imagined things concerning a prince, and taking into account those that are true, I say that all men, when they are spoken of, and particularly princes, since they are placed on a higher level, are judged by some of

Note the prince's reputation.

these qualities which bring them either blame or praise. And this is why one is considered generous, another miserly (to use a Tuscan word, since "avaricious" in our language is still used to mean one who wishes to acquire by means of theft; we call "miserly" one who excessively avoids using what he has); one is considered a giver, the other rapacious; one cruel, another merciful; one treacherous, another faithful; one effeminate and cowardly, another bold and courageous; one humane, another haughty; one lascivious, another chaste; one trustworthy, another cunning; one harsh, another lenient; one serious, another frivolous; one religious, another unbelieving; and the like. And I know that everyone will admit that it would be a very praiseworthy thing to find in a prince, of the qualities mentioned above, those that are held to

Prince must avoid reputation for the worst vices.

be good, but since it is neither possible to have them nor to observe them all completely, because human nature does not permit it, a prince must be prudent enough to know how to escape the bad reputation of those vices that would lose the state

Some vices may be needed to hold the state. True?

for him, and must protect himself from those that will not lose it for him, if this is possible; but if he cannot, he need not concern himself unduly if he ignores these less serious vices. And, moreover,

he need not worry about incurring the bad reputation of those vices without which it would be difficult to hold his state; since, carefully taking
everything into account, one will discover that

**Some virtues
may end in
destruction.**

something which appears to be a virtue, if pursued,
will end in his destruction; while some other thing
which seems to be a vice, if pursued, will result in
his safety and his well-being.

Reviewing

The process of review, which takes place after a careful reading,
is much more useful if you have annotated and underlined the text
well. To a large extent, the review process can be devoted to ac-
counting for the primary ideas that have been uncovered by your
annotations and underlinings. For example, reviewing the Machiavelli annotations shows that the following ideas are crucial to
Machiavelli's thinking:

- The prince's profession should be war, so the most successful
  princes are probably experienced in the military.
- If they do not pay attention to military matters, princes will lose
  their power.
- Being disarmed makes the prince despised.
- The prince should be in constant training.
- The prince needs a sound knowledge of terrain.
- Machiavelli says he tells us what is true, not what ought to be true.
- Those who are always good will come to ruin among those who
  are not good.
- To remain in power, the prince must learn how not to be good.
- The prince should avoid the worst vices in order not to harm
  his reputation.
- To maintain power, some vices may be necessary.
- Some virtues may end in destruction.

Putting Machiavelli's ideas in this raw form does an injustice
to his skill as a writer, but annotation is designed to result in such
summary statements. We can see that there are some constant
themes, such as the insistence that the prince be a military person.
In Machiavelli's day Italy was a group of rival city-states, and
France, a larger, united nation, was invading these states one by

one. Machiavelli dreamed that one powerful prince, such as his favorite, Cesare Borgia, could fight the French and save Italy. He
emphasized the importance of the military because he lived in an
age in which war was a constant threat.

Machiavelli anticipates the complaints of pacifists—those who
argue against war—by telling us that those who remain unarmed
are despised. To demonstrate his point, he gives us examples of
those who lost their positions as princes because they avoided being
armed. He clearly expects these examples to be persuasive.

A second important theme pervading Machiavelli's essay is his
view on moral behavior. For Machiavelli, being in power is much
more important than being virtuous. He is quick to admit that vice is
not desirable and that the worst vices will harm the prince's reputation. But he also says that the prince need not worry about the "less serious" vices. Moreover, the prince need not worry about incurring a
bad reputation by practicing vices that are necessary if he wishes to
hold his state. In the same spirit, Machiavelli tells us that there are
some virtues that might lead to the destruction of the prince.

Forming Your Own Ideas

One of the most important reasons for reading the texts in this
book critically is to enable you to develop your own positions on issues that these writers raise. Identifying and clarifying the main
ideas is only the first step; the next step in critical reading is evaluating those ideas.

For example, you might ask whether Machiavelli's ideas have
any relevance for today. After all, he wrote nearly five hundred years
ago and times have changed. You might feel that Machiavelli was
relevant strictly during the Italian Renaissance or, alternatively, that
his principles are timeless and have something to teach every age.
For most people, Machiavelli is a political philosopher whose views
are useful anytime and anywhere.

If you agree with the majority, then you may want to examine
Machiavelli's ideas to see whether you can accept them. Consider
just two of those ideas and their implications:

- Should rulers always be members of the military? Should they
  always be armed? Should the ruler of a nation first demonstrate
  competence as a military leader?

- Should rulers ignore virtue and practice vice when it is convenient?

If we were to follow Machiavelli's advice, then we would choose presidents on the basis of whether or not they had been good military leaders. Among those we would not have chosen from American history might be Thomas Jefferson, Abraham Lincoln, and Franklin Delano Roosevelt. Those who were high-ranking military men include George Washington, Ulysses S. Grant, and Dwight D. Eisenhower. If you followed Machiavelli's rhetorical technique of using examples to convince your audience, you could choose from either group to prove your case.

Of course, there are examples from other nations. It has been common since the 1930s to see certain leaders dressed in their military uniforms: Benito Mussolini (Italy), Adolf Hitler (Germany), Joseph Stalin (Russia), Idi Amin (Uganda), Muammar al-Qaddafi (Libya). These are all tyrants who have tormented their citizens and their neighbors. That gives us something to think about. Should a president dress in full military regalia all the time? Is that a good image for the ruler of a free nation to project?

Do you want a ruler, then, who is usually virtuous but embraces vice when it is necessary? This is a very difficult question to answer. When Jimmy Carter swore to the American people that he would never lie to them, many Americans were skeptical. They thought that politics was essentially a game of careful and judicious lying — at least at times. In other words, these Americans were already committed to Machiavelli's position.

These are only a few of the questions that are raised by my annotations in the brief excerpt from Machiavelli examined here. Many other issues could be uncovered by these annotations, and many more from subsequent pages of the essay. Critical reading can be a powerful means by which to open what you read to discovery and discussion.

Once you begin a line of questioning, the ways in which you think about a passage begin expanding. You find yourself with more ideas of your own that have grown in response to those you have been reading about. Reading critically, in other words, gives you an enormous return on your investment of time. If you have the chance to investigate your responses to the assumptions and underlying premises of passages such as Machiavelli's, you will be able to refine your thinking even further. For example, if you agree with Machiavelli that rulers should be successful military leaders for whom small vices may be useful at times, and you find yourself in a position to argue with someone who feels Machiavelli is mistaken in this view, then you will have a good opportunity to evaluate the soundness of your thinking. You will have a chance to see your own assumptions and arguments tested.

In many ways, this entire book is about such opportunities. The essays and plays that follow offer you powerful ideas from great thinkers. They invite you to participate in their thoughts, exercise your own knowledge and assumptions, and arrive at your own conclusions. Basically, that is the meaning of education.

THE INDIVIDUAL
IN
COMMUNITY
AND CULTURE

FRANCIS BACON
The Four Idols

FRANCIS BACON, Lord Verulam (1561–1626), lived during one of the most exciting times in history. Among his contemporaries were the essayist Michel de Montaigne; the playwrights Christopher Marlowe and William Shakespeare; the adventurer Sir Francis Drake; and Queen Elizabeth I, in whose reign Bacon held several high offices. He became lord high chancellor of England in 1618 but fell from power in 1621 through a complicated series of events, among which was his complicity in a bribery scheme. His so-called crimes were minor, but he paid dearly for them. His book *Essayes* (1597) was exceptionally popular during his lifetime, and when he found himself without a proper job, he devoted himself to what he declared to be his own true work: writing about philosophy and science.

His purpose in *Novum Organum* (The new organon), published in 1620, was to replace the old organon, or instrument of thought, Aristotle's treatises on logic and thought. Despite Aristotle's pervasive influence on sixteenth- and seventeenth-century thought—his texts were used in virtually all schools and colleges—Bacon thought that Aristotelian deductive logic produced error. In *Novum Organum* he tried to set the stage for a new attitude toward logic and scientific inquiry. He proposed a system of reasoning usually referred to as induction. This quasi-scientific method involves collecting and listing observations from nature. Once a mass of observations is gathered and organized, Bacon believed, the truth about what is observed will become apparent.

Bacon is often mistakenly credited with having invented the scientific method of inquiring into nature; but although he was right about the need for collecting and observing, he was wrong

---

From *Novum Organum.* Translated by Francis Headlam and R. L. Ellis.

about the outcome of such endeavors. After all, one could watch an infinite number of apples (and oranges, too) fall to the ground without ever having the slightest sense of why they do so. What Bacon failed to realize—and he died before he could become scientific enough to realize it—is the creative function of the scientist as expressed in the hypothesis. The hypothesis—an educated guess about why something happens—must be tested by the kinds of observations Bacon recommended.

Nonetheless, "The Four Idols" is a brilliant work. It does establish the requirements for the kind of observation that produces true scientific knowledge. Bacon despaired of any thoroughly objective inquiry in his own day, in part because no one paid attention to the ways in which the idols, limiting preconceptions, strangled thought, observation, and imagination. He realized that the would-be natural philosopher was foiled even before he began. Bacon was a farsighted man. He was correct about the failures of science in his time; and he was correct, moreover, in his assessment that advancement would depend on sensory perception and on aids to perception, such as microscopes and telescopes. The real brilliance of "The Four Idols" lies in Bacon's focus not on what is observed but on the instrument of observation—the human mind. Only when the instrument is freed of error can we rely on its observations to reveal the truth.

Bacon's Rhetoric

Bacon was trained during the great age of rhetoric, and his prose (even though in this case it is translated from Latin) shows the clarity, balance, and organization that characterize the prose writing of seventeenth-century England. The most basic device Bacon uses is enumeration: stating clearly that there are four idols and implying that he will treat each one in turn.

Enumeration is one of the most common and most reliable rhetorical devices. The listener hears a speaker say "I have only three things I want to say today" and is alerted to listen for all three, while feeling secretly grateful that there are only three. When encountering complex material, the reader is always happy to have such "road signs" as "The second aspect of this question is . . ."

"The Four Idols," after a three-paragraph introduction, proceeds with a single paragraph devoted to each idol, so that we have an early definition of each and a sense of what to look for. Paragraphs 8 to 16 cover only the issues related to the Idols of the Tribe: the problems all people have simply because they are peo-

ple. Paragraphs 17 to 22 consider the Idols of the Cave: those particular fixations individuals have because of their special back-
grounds or limitations. Paragraphs 23 to 26 address the questions
related to Idols of the Marketplace, particularly those that deal
with the way people misuse words and abuse definitions. The re-
mainder of the selection treats the Idols of the Theater, which relate entirely to philosophic systems and preconceptions—all of
which tend to narrow the scope of research and understanding.

Enumeration is used within each of these groups of paragraphs
as well. Bacon often begins a paragraph with such statements as
"There is one principal . . . distinction between different minds"
(para. 19). Or he says, "The idols imposed by words on the understanding are of two kinds" (para. 24). The effect is to ensure clarity
where confusion could easily reign.

As an added means of achieving clarity, Bacon sets aside a single paragraph—the last—to summarize the main points that he
has made, in the order in which they were made.

Within any section of this selection, Bacon depends on observation, example, and reason to make his points. When he speaks of
a given idol, he defines it, gives several examples to make it clearer,
discusses its effects on thought, and then dismisses it as dangerous. He then goes on to the next idol. Where appropriate, in some
cases he names those who are victims of a specific idol. In each
case he tries to be thorough, explanatory, and convincing.

Not only is this work a landmark in thought; it is also, because
of its absolute clarity, a beacon. We can still profit from its light.

PREREADING QUESTIONS:
WHAT TO READ FOR

The following prereading questions may help you anticipate key issues
in the discussion on Francis Bacon's "The Four Idols." Keeping them in
mind during your first reading of the selection should help focus your
reactions.

- What are the four idols?
- Why do the four idols make it difficult for us to see the truth?
- What are some chief characteristics of human understanding?

The Four Idols

The idols[1] and false notions which are now in possession of the   1
human understanding, and have taken deep root therein, not only
so beset men's minds that truth can hardly find entrance, but even
after entrance obtained, they will again in the very instauration[2] of
the sciences meet and trouble us, unless men being forewarned of
the danger fortify themselves as far as may be against their assaults.

There are four classes of idols which beset men's minds. To   2
these for distinction's sake I have assigned names—calling the first
class *Idols of the Tribe*; the second, *Idols of the Cave*; the third, *Idols of
the Marketplace*; the fourth, *Idols of the Theater*.

The formation of ideas and axioms by true induction[3] is no   3
doubt the proper remedy to be applied for the keeping off and clearing away of idols. To point them out, however, is of great use; for
the doctrine of idols is to the interpretation of nature what the doctrine of the refutation of sophisms[4] is to common logic.

The *Idols of the Tribe* have their foundation in human nature it-   4
self, and in the tribe or race of men. For it is a false assertion that the
sense of man is the measure of things. On the contrary, all perceptions as well of the sense as of the mind are according to the measure of the individual and not according to the measure of the universe. And the human understanding is like a false mirror, which,
receiving rays irregularly, distorts and discolors the nature of things
by mingling its own nature with it.

The *Idols of the Cave* are the idols of the individual man. For   5
everyone (besides the errors common to human nature in general)
has a cave or den of his own, which refracts[5] and discolors the light
of nature; owing either to his own proper and peculiar nature; or to
his education and conversation with others; or to the reading of
books, and the authority of those whom he esteems and admires; or

---

[1] **idols** By this term Bacon means phantoms or illusions. The Greek philosopher Democritus spoke of *eidola*, tiny representations of things that impressed themselves on the mind (see note 21).

[2] **instauration** Institution.

[3] **induction** Bacon championed induction as the method by which new knowledge is developed. As he saw it, induction involved a patient gathering and categorizing of facts in the hope that a large number of them would point to the truth. As a
process of gathering evidence from which inferences are drawn, induction is con-
trasted with Aristotle's method, *deduction,* according to which a theory is established
and the truth deduced. Deduction places the stress on the authority of the expert;
induction places the stress on the facts themselves.

[4] **sophisms** Apparently intelligent statements that are wrong; false wisdom.

[5] **refracts** Deflects, bends back, alters.

to the differences of impressions, accordingly as they take place in a mind preoccupied and predisposed or in a mind indifferent and settled; or the like. So that the spirit of man (according as it is meted out to different individuals) is in fact a thing variable and full of perturbation,[6] and governed as it were by chance. Whence it was well observed by Heraclitus[7] that men look for sciences in their own lesser worlds, and not in the greater or common world.

There are also idols formed by the intercourse and association of men with each other, which I call *Idols of the Marketplace,* on account of the commerce and consort of men there. For it is by discourse that men associate; and words are imposed according to the apprehension of the vulgar.[8] And therefore the ill and unfit choice of words wonderfully obstructs the understanding. Nor do the definitions or explanations wherewith in some things learned men are wont[9] to guard and defend themselves, by any means set the matter right. But words plainly force and overrule the understanding, and throw all into confusion and lead men away into numberless empty controversies and idle fancies.

Lastly, there are idols which have immigrated into men's minds from the various dogmas of philosophies, and also from wrong laws of demonstration.[10] These I call *Idols of the Theater;* because in my judgment all the received systems[11] are but so many stage-plays, representing worlds of their own creation after an unreal and scenic fashion. Nor is it only of the systems now in vogue, or only of the ancient sects and philosophies, that I speak; for many more plays of the same kind may yet be composed and in like artificial manner set forth; seeing that errors the most widely different have nevertheless causes for the most part alike. Neither again do I mean this only of entire systems, but also of many principles and axioms in science, which by tradition, credulity, and negligence, have come to be received.

But of these several kinds of idols I must speak more largely and exactly, that the understanding may be duly cautioned.

---

[6] **perturbation** Uncertainty, disturbance. In astronomy, the motion caused by the gravity of nearby planets.

[7] **Heraclitus (535?–475? B.C.)** Greek philosopher who believed that there was no reality except in change; all else was illusion. He also believed that fire was the basis of all the world and that everything we see is a transformation of it.

[8] **vulgar** Common people.

[9] **wont** Accustomed.

[10] **laws of demonstration** Bacon may be referring to Aristotle's logical system of syllogism and deduction.

[11] **received systems** Official or authorized views of scientific truth.

The human understanding is of its own nature prone to suppose   9
the existence of more order and regularity in the world than it finds.
And though there be many things in nature which are singular and
unmatched, yet it devises for them parallels and conjugates and relatives[12] which do not exist. Hence the fiction that all celestial bodies
move in perfect circles; spirals and dragons being (except in name)
utterly rejected. Hence too the element of fire with its orb is brought
in, to make up the square with the other three which the sense perceives. Hence also the ratio of density[13] of the so-called elements is
arbitrarily fixed at ten to one. And so on of other dreams. And these
fancies affect not dogmas only, but simple notions also.

The human understanding when it has once adopted an opin-   10
ion (either as being the received opinion or as being agreeable to itself) draws all things else to support and agree with it. And though
there be a greater number and weight of instances to be found on
the other side, yet these it either neglects and despises, or else by
some distinction sets aside and rejects; in order that by this great
and pernicious predetermination the authority of its former conclusions may remain inviolate. And therefore it was a good answer that
was made by one who when they showed him hanging in a temple a
picture of those who had paid their vows as having escaped ship-
wreck, and would have him say whether he did not now acknowledge the power of the gods — "Ay," asked he again, "but where are
they painted that were drowned after their vows?" And such is the
way of all superstition, whether in astrology, dreams, omens, divine
judgments, or the like; wherein men having a delight in such vani-
ties, mark the events where they are fulfilled, but where they fail,
though this happen much oftener, neglect and pass them by. But
with far more subtlety does this mischief insinuate itself into philosophy and the sciences; in which the first conclusion colors and
brings into conformity with itself all that come after, though far
sounder and better. Besides, independently of that delight and vanity which I have described, it is the peculiar and perpetual error of
the human intellect to be more moved and excited by affirmatives
than by negatives; whereas it ought properly to hold itself indiffer-
ently disposed towards both alike. Indeed, in the establishment of
any true axiom, the negative instance is the more forcible of the two.

---

[12] **parallels and conjugates and relatives** A reference to the habit of assuming that phenomena are regular and ordered, consisting of squares, triangles, circles,
and other regular shapes.
[13] **ratio of density** The false assumption that the relationship of mass or weight
to volume was ten to one. This is another example of Bacon's complaint, establishing
a convenient regular "relative," or relationship.

The human understanding is moved by those things most   11
which strike and enter the mind simultaneously and suddenly, and
so fill the imagination; and then it feigns and supposes all other
things to be somehow, though it cannot see how, similar to those
few things by which it is surrounded. But for that going to and fro to
remote and heterogeneous instances, by which axioms are tried as in
the fire,[14] the intellect is altogether slow and unfit, unless it be
forced thereto by severe laws and overruling authority.

The human understanding is unquiet; it cannot stop or rest, and   12
still presses onward, but in vain. Therefore it is that we cannot conceive of any end or limit to the world, but always as of necessity it
occurs to us that there is something beyond. Neither again can it be
conceived how eternity has flowed down to the present day; for that
distinction which is commonly received of infinity in time past and
in time to come can by no means hold; for it would thence follow
that one infinity is greater than another, and that infinity is wasting
away and tending to become finite. The like subtlety arises touching
the infinite divisibility of lines,[15] from the same inability of thought
to stop. But this inability interferes more mischievously in the discovery of causes:[16] for although the most general principles in nature ought to be held merely positive, as they are discovered, and
cannot with truth be referred to a cause; nevertheless, the human
understanding being unable to rest still seeks something prior in the
order of nature. And then it is that in struggling towards that which
is further off, it falls back upon that which is more nigh at hand;
namely, on final causes: which have relation clearly to the nature of
man rather than to the nature of the universe, and from this source

----

[14] **tried as in the fire** Trial by fire is a figure of speech representing thorough,
rigorous testing even to the point of risking what is tested. An axiom is a statement
of apparent truth that has not yet been put to the test of examination and investigation.

[15] **infinite divisibility of lines** This gave rise to the paradox of Zeno, the Greek
philosopher of the fifth century B.C. who showed that it was impossible to get from
one point to another because one had to pass the midpoint of the line determined by
the two original points, and then the midpoint of the remaining distance, and then
of that remaining distance, down to an infinite number of points. By using accepted
truths to "prove" an absurdity about motion, Zeno actually hoped to prove that motion itself did not exist. This is the "subtlety," or confusion, Bacon says is produced
by the "inability of thought to stop."

[16] **discovery of causes** Knowledge of the world was based on four causes: effi-
cient (who made it?), material (what is it made of?), formal (what is its shape?),
and final (what is its purpose?). The scholastics concentrated their thinking on the
first and last, whereas the "middle causes," related to matter and shape, were the
proper subject matter of science because they alone yielded to observation. (See
para. 34.)

have strangely defiled philosophy. But he is no less an unskilled and shallow philosopher who seeks causes of that which is most general, than he who in things subordinate and subaltern[17] omits to do so.

The human understanding is no dry light, but receives an   13
infusion from the will and affections;[18] whence proceed sciences which may be called "sciences as one would." For what a man had rather were true he more readily believes. Therefore he rejects difficult things from impatience of research; sober things, because they narrow hope; the deeper things of nature, from superstition; the light of experience, from arrogance and price, lest his mind should seem to be occupied with things mean and transitory; things not commonly believed, out of deference to the opinion of the vulgar. Numberless in short are the ways, and sometimes imperceptible, in which the affections color and infect the understanding.

But by far the greatest hindrance and aberration of the human   14
understanding proceeds from the dullness, incompetency, and deceptions of the senses; in that things which strike the sense outweigh things which do not immediately strike it, though they be more important. Hence it is that speculation commonly ceases where sight ceases; insomuch that of things invisible there is little or no observation. Hence all the working of the spirits[19] enclosed in tangible bodies lies hid and unobserved of men. So also all the more subtle changes of form in the parts of coarser substances (which they commonly call alteration, though it is in truth local motion through exceedingly small spaces) is in like manner unobserved. And yet unless these two things just mentioned be searched out and brought to light, nothing great can be achieved in nature, as far as the production of works is concerned. So again the essential nature of our common air, and of all bodies less dense than air (which are very many) is almost unknown. For the sense by itself is a thing infirm and erring; neither can instruments for enlarging or sharpening the senses do much; but all the truer kind of interpretation of nature is effected by instances and experiments fit and apposite;[20] wherein the sense decides touching the experiment only, and the experiment touching the point in nature and the thing itself.

---

[17] **subaltern** Lower in status.
[18] **will and affections** Human free will and emotional needs and responses.
[19] **spirits** The soul or animating force.
[20] **apposite** Appropriate; well related.

The human understanding is of its own nature prone to abstractions and gives a substance and reality to things which are fleeting. But to resolve nature into abstractions is less to our purpose than to dissect her into parts; as did the school of Democritus,[21] which went further into nature than the rest. Matter rather than forms should be the object of our attention, its configurations and changes of configuration, and simple action, and law of action or motion; for forms are figments of the human mind, unless you will call those laws of action forms. 15

Such then are the idols which I call *Idols of the Tribe;* and which take their rise either from the homogeneity of the substance of the human spirit,[22] or from its preoccupation, or from its narrowness, or from its restless motion, or from an infusion of the affections, or from the incompetency of the senses, or from the mode of impression. 16

The *Idols of the Cave* take their rise in the peculiar constitution, mental or bodily, of each individual; and also in education, habit, and accident. Of this kind there is a great number and variety; but I will instance those the pointing out of which contains the most important caution, and which have most effect in disturbing the clearness of the understanding. 17

Men become attached to certain particular sciences and speculations, either because they fancy themselves the authors and inventors thereof, or because they have bestowed the greatest pains upon them and become most habituated to them. But men of this kind, if they betake themselves to philosophy and contemplations of a general character, distort and color them in obedience to their former fancies; a thing especially to be noticed in Aristotle,[23] who made his natural philosophy[24] a mere bondservant to his logic, thereby rendering it contentious and well nigh useless. The race of chemists[25] 18

---

[21] **Democritus (460?–370? B.C.)** Greek philosopher who thought the world was composed of atoms. Bacon felt such "dissection" to be useless because it was impractical. Yet Democritus's concept of the *eidola,* the mind's impressions of things, may have contributed to Bacon's idea of "the idol."

[22] **human spirit** Human nature.

[23] **Aristotle (384–322 B.C.)** Greek philosopher whose *Organon* (system of logic) dominated the thought of Bacon's time. Bacon sought to overthrow Aristotle's hold on science and thought.

[24] **natural philosophy** The scientific study of nature in general—biology, zoology, geology, etc.

[25] **chemists** Alchemists had developed a "fantastic philosophy" from their experimental attempts to transmute lead into gold.

again out of a few experiments of the furnace have built up a fantastic philosophy, framed with reference to a few things; and Gilbert[26] also, after he had employed himself most laboriously in the study and observation of the loadstone, proceeded at once to construct an entire system in accordance with his favorite subject.

There is one principal and, as it were, radical distinction be-   19
tween different minds, in respect of philosophy and the sciences, which is this: that some minds are stronger and apter to mark the differences of things, others to mark their resemblances. The steady and acute mind can fix its contemplations and dwell and fasten on the subtlest distinctions: the lofty and discursive mind recognizes and puts together the finest and most general resemblances. Both kinds however easily err in excess, by catching the one at gradations, the other at shadows.

There are found some minds given to an extreme admiration of   20
antiquity, others to an extreme love and appetite for novelty; but few so duly tempered that they can hold the mean, neither carping at what has been well laid down by the ancients, nor despising what is well introduced by the moderns. This however turns to the great injury of the sciences and philosophy; since these affectations of antiquity and novelty are the humors[27] of partisans rather than judgments; and truth is to be sought for not in the felicity of any age, which is an unstable thing, but in the light of nature and experience, which is eternal. These factions therefore must be abjured,[28] and care must be taken that the intellect be not hurried by them into assent.

Contemplations of nature and of bodies in their simple form   21
break up and distract the understanding, while contemplations of nature and bodies in their composition and configuration overpower and dissolve the understanding: a distinction well seen in the school of Leucippus[29] and Democritus as compared with the other philosophies. For that school is so busied with the particles that it hardly attends to the structure; while the others are so lost in admiration of the structure that they do not penetrate to the simplicity of nature. These kinds of contemplation should therefore be alternated and taken by turns; that so the understanding may be rendered at once

---

[26] **William Gilbert (1544–1603)** An English scientist who studied magnetism and codified many laws related to magnetic fields. He was particularly ridiculed by Bacon for being too narrow in his researches.

[27] **humors** Used in a medical sense to mean a distortion caused by imbalance.

[28] **abjured** Renounced, sworn off, repudiated.

[29] **Leucippus (fifth century B.C.)** Greek philosopher; teacher of Democritus and inventor of the atomistic theory. His works survive only in fragments.

penetrating and comprehensive, and the inconveniences above mentioned, with the idols which proceed from them, may be avoided.

Let such then be our provision and contemplative prudence for 22 keeping off and dislodging the *Idols of the Cave*, which grow for the most part either out of the predominance of a favorite subject, or out of an excessive tendency to compare or to distinguish, or out of partiality for particular ages, or out of the largeness or minuteness of the objects contemplated. And generally let every student of nature take this as a rule — that whatever his mind seizes and dwells upon with peculiar satisfaction is to be held in suspicion, and that so much the more care is to be taken in dealing with such questions to keep the understanding even and clear.

But the *Idols of the Marketplace* are the most troublesome of all: 23 idols which have crept into the understanding through the alliances of words and names. For men believe that their reason governs words; but it is also true that words react on the understanding; and this it is that has rendered philosophy and the sciences sophistical and inactive. Now words, being commonly framed and applied according to the capacity of the vulgar, follow those lines of division which are most obvious to the vulgar understanding. And whenever an understanding of greater acuteness or a more diligent observation would alter those lines to suit the true divisions of nature, words stand in the way and resist the change. Whence it comes to pass that the high and formal discussions of learned men end oftentimes in disputes about words and names; with which (according to the use and wisdom of the mathematicians) it would be more prudent to begin, and so by means of definitions reduce them to order. Yet even definitions cannot cure this evil in dealing with natural and material things; since the definitions themselves consist of words, and those words beget others: so that it is necessary to recur to individual instances, and those in due series and order; as I shall say presently when I come to the method and scheme for the formation of notions and axioms.[30]

The idols imposed by words on the understanding are of two 24 kinds. They are either names of things which do not exist (for as there are things left unnamed through lack of observation, so likewise are there names which result from fantastic suppositions and to which nothing in reality responds), or they are names of things which exist, but yet confused and ill-defined, and hastily and irregularly derived from realities. Of the former kind are Fortune, the Prime Mover, Planetary Orbits, Element of Fire, and like fictions

---

[30] **notions and axioms** Conceptions and definitive statements of truth.

which owe their origin to false and idle theories.[31] And this class of idols is more easily expelled, because to get rid of them it is only necessary that all theories should be steadily rejected and dismissed as obsolete.

But the other class, which springs out of a faulty and unskillful 25 abstraction, is intricate and deeply rooted. Let us take for example such a word as *humid;* and see how far the several things which the word is used to signify agree with each other; and we shall find the word *humid* to be nothing else than a mark loosely and confusedly applied to denote a variety of actions which will not bear to be reduced to any constant meaning. For it both signifies that which easily spreads itself round any other body; and that which in itself is indeterminate and cannot solidize; and that which readily yields in every direction; and that which easily divides and scatters itself; and that which easily unites and collects itself; and that which readily flows and is put in motion; and that which readily clings to another body and wets it; and that which is easily reduced to a liquid, or being solid easily melts. Accordingly when you come to apply the word — if you take it in one sense, flame is humid; if in another, air is not humid; if in another, fine dust is humid; if in another, glass is humid. So that it is easy to see that the notion is taken by abstraction only from water and common and ordinary liquids, without any due verification.

There are however in words certain degrees of distortion and 26 error. One of the least faulty kinds is that of names of substances, especially of lowest species and well-deduced (for the notion of *chalk* and of *mud* is good, of *earth* bad);[32] a more faulty kind is that of actions, as *to generate, to corrupt, to alter;* the most faulty is of qualities (except such as are the immediate objects of the sense), as *heavy, light, rare, dense,* and the like. Yet in all these cases some notions are of necessity a little better than others, in proportion to the greater variety of subjects that fall within the range of the human sense.

But the *Idols of the Theater* are not innate, nor do they steal into 27 the understanding secretly, but are plainly impressed and received into the mind from the play-books of philosophical systems and the

---

[31] **idle theories** These are things that cannot be observed and thus do not exist. Fortune is fate; the Prime Mover is God or some "first" force; the notion that planets orbited the sun was considered as "fantastic" as these others or as the idea that everything was made up of fire and its many permutations.
  [32] ***earth* bad** Chalk and mud were useful in manufacture; hence they were terms of approval. *Earth* is used here in the sense we use *dirt,* as in "digging in the dirt."

perverted rules of demonstration.[33] To attempt refutations in this case would be merely inconsistent with what I have already said: for since we agree neither upon principles nor upon demonstrations, there is no place for argument. And this is so far well, inasmuch as it leaves the honor of the ancients untouched. For they are no wise disparaged—the question between them and me being only as to the way. For as the saying is, the lame man who keeps the right road outstrips the runner who takes a wrong one. Nay, it is obvious that when a man runs the wrong way, the more active and swift he is the further he will go astray.

But the course I propose for the discovery of sciences is such as 28 leaves but little to the acuteness and strength of wits, but places all wits[34] and understandings nearly on a level. For as in the drawing of a straight line or perfect circle, much depends on the steadiness and practice of the hand, if it be done by aim of hand only, but if with the aid of rule or compass, little or nothing; so is it exactly with my plan. But though particular confutations[35] would be of no avail, yet touching the sects and general divisions of such systems I must say something; something also touching the external signs which show that they are unsound; and finally something touching the causes of such great infelicity and of such lasting and general agreement in error; that so the access to truth may be made less difficult, and the human understanding may the more willingly submit to its purgation and dismiss its idols.

Idols of the Theater, or of systems, are many, and there can be 29 and perhaps will be yet many more. For were it not that now for many ages men's minds have been busied with religion and theology; and were it not that civil governments, especially monarchies, have been averse to such novelties, even in matters speculative; so that men labor therein to the peril and harming of their fortunes— not only unrewarded, but exposed also to contempt and envy; doubtless there would have arisen many other philosophical sects like to those which in great variety flourished once among the Greeks. For as on the phenomena of the heavens many hypotheses may be constructed, so likewise (and more also) many various dogmas may be set up and established on the phenomena of philosophy. And in the plays of this philosophical theater you may

---

[33] **perverted rules of demonstration** Another complaint against Aristotle's logic as misapplied in Bacon's day.

[34] **wits** Intelligence, powers of reasoning.

[35] **confutations** Specific counterarguments. Bacon means that he cannot offer particular arguments against each scientific sect; thus he offers a general warning.

observe the same thing which is found in the theater of the poets, that stories invented for the stage are more compact and elegant, and more as one would wish them to be, than true stories out of history.

In general, however, there is taken for the material of philoso- 30 phy either a great deal out of a few things, or a very little out of many things; so that on both sides philosophy is based on too narrow a foundation of experiment and natural history, and decides on the authority of too few cases. For the rational school of philosophers[36] snatches from experience a variety of common instances, neither duly ascertained nor diligently examined and weighed, and leaves all the rest to meditation and agitation of wit.

There is also another class of philosophers,[37] who having be- 31 stowed much diligent and careful labor on a few experiments, have thence made bold to educe and construct systems; wresting all other facts in a strange fashion to conformity therewith.

And there is yet a third class,[38] consisting of those who out of 32 faith and veneration mix their philosophy with theology and traditions; among whom the vanity of some has gone so far aside as to seek the origin of sciences among spirits and genii.[39] So that this parent stock of errors—this false philosophy—is of three kinds; the sophistical, the empirical, and the superstitious. . . .

But the corruption of philosophy by superstition and an admix- 33 ture of theology is far more widely spread, and does the greatest harm, whether to entire systems or to their parts. For the human understanding is obnoxious to the influence of the imagination no less than to the influence of common notions. For the contentious and sophistical kind of philosophy ensnares the understanding; but this kind, being fanciful and tumid[40] and half poetical, misleads it more

---

[36] **rational school of philosophers** Platonists who felt that human reason alone could discover the truth and that experiment was unnecessary. Their observation of experience produced only a "variety of common instances" from which they reasoned.

[37] **another class of philosophers** William Gilbert (1544–1603) experimented tirelessly with magnetism, from which he derived numerous odd theories. Though Gilbert was a true scientist, Bacon thought of him as limited and on the wrong track.

[38] **a third class** Pythagoras (580?–500? B.C.) was a Greek philosopher who experimented rigorously with mathematics and a tuned string. He is said to have developed the musical scale. His theory of reincarnation, or the transmigration of souls, was somehow based on his travels in India and his work with scales. The superstitious belief in the movement of souls is what Bacon complains of.

[39] **genii** Oriental demons or spirits; a slap at Pythagoras, who traveled in the Orient.

[40] **tumid** Overblown, swollen.

by flattery. For there is in man an ambition of the understanding, no less than of the will, especially in high and lofty spirits.

Of this kind we have among the Greeks a striking example in 34 Pythagoras, though he united with it a coarser and more cumbrous superstition; another in Plato and his school,[41] more dangerous and subtle. It shows itself likewise in parts of other philosophies, in the introduction of abstract forms and final causes and first causes, with the omission in most cases of causes intermediate, and the like. Upon this point the greatest caution should be used. For nothing is so mischievous as the apotheosis of error; and it is a very plague of the understanding for vanity to become the object of veneration. Yet in this vanity some of the moderns have with extreme levity indulged so far as to attempt to found a system of natural philosophy on the first chapter of Genesis, on the book of Job, and other parts of the sacred writings; seeking for the dead among the living: which also makes the inhibition and repression of it the more important, because from this unwholesome mixture of things human and divine there arises not only a fantastic philosophy but also an heretical religion. Very meet it is therefore that we be sober-minded, and give to faith that only which is faith's. . . .

So much concerning the several classes of Idols, and their 35 equipage: all of which must be renounced and put away with a fixed and solemn determination, and the understanding thoroughly freed and cleansed; the entrance into the kingdom of man, founded on the sciences, being not much other than the entrance into the kingdom of heaven, whereunto none may enter except as a little child.

QUESTIONS FOR CRITICAL READING

1. Which of Bacon's idols is the most difficult to understand? Do your best to define it.
2. Which of these idols do we still need to worry about? Why? What dangers does it present?
3. What does Bacon mean by implying that our senses are weak (para. 14)? In what ways do you agree or disagree with that opinion?
4. Occasionally Bacon says something that seems a bit like an aphorism. Find at least one such expression in this selection. On examination, does the expression have as much meaning as it seems to have?

---

[41] **Plato and his school** Plato's religious bent was further developed by Plotinus (A.D. 205–270) in his *Enneads*. Although Plotinus was not a Christian, his Neoplatonism was welcomed as a philosophy compatible with Christianity.

5. What kind of readers did Bacon expect for this piece? What clues does his way of communicating provide regarding the nature of his anticipated readers?

SUGGESTIONS FOR WRITING

1. Which of Bacon's idols most seriously affects the way you as a person observe nature? Using enumeration, arrange the idols in order of their effect on your own judgment. If you prefer, you may write about the idol you believe is most effective in slowing investigation into nature.

2. Is it true, as Bacon says in paragraph 10, that people are in general "more moved and excited by affirmatives than by negatives"? Do we really stress the positive and deemphasize the negative in the conduct of our general affairs? Find at least three instances in which people seem to gravitate toward the positive or the negative in everyday situations. Try to establish whether Bacon has, in fact, described what is a habit of mind.

3. In paragraph 13, Bacon states that the "will and affections" enter into matters of thought. By this he means that our understanding of what we observe is conditioned by what we want and what we feel. Thus, when he says, "For what a man had rather were true he more readily believes," he tells us that people tend to believe what they want to believe. Test this statement by means of observation. Find out, for example, how many older people are convinced that the world is deteriorating, how many younger people feel that there is a plot on the part of older people to hold them back, how many women feel that men consciously oppress women, and how many men feel that feminists are not as feminine as they should be. What other beliefs can you discover that seem to have their origin in what people want to believe rather than in what is true?

4. Bacon's views on religion have always been difficult to define. He grew up in a very religious time, but his writings rarely discuss religion positively. In this work he talks about giving "to faith that only which is faith's" (para. 34). He seems to feel that scientific investigation is something quite separate from religion. Examine the selection carefully to determine what you think Bacon's view on this question is. Then take a stand on the issue of the relationship between religion and science. Should science be totally independent of religious concerns? Should religious issues control scientific experimentation? What does Bacon mean when he complains about the vanity of founding "a system of natural philosophy on the first chapter of Genesis, on the book of Job, and other parts of the sacred writings" (para. 34)? "Natural philosophy" means biology, chemistry, physics, and science in general. Are Bacon's complaints justified? Would his complaints be relevant today?

CHARLES DARWIN
Natural Selection

CHARLES DARWIN (1809–1882) was trained as a minister in the Church of England, but he was also the grandson of one of England's greatest horticulturists, Erasmus Darwin. Partly as a way of putting off ordination in the church and partly because of his natural curiosity, Darwin found himself performing the functions of a naturalist on HMS *Beagle*, which was engaged in scientific explorations around South America during the years 1831 to 1836. Darwin's book *Journal of Researches into the Geology and Natural History of the Various Countries Visited by H. M. S. Beagle, 1832–36* (1839) details the experiences he had and offers some views of his self-education as a naturalist.

His journeys on the *Beagle* led him to note variations in species of animals he found in various separate locales, particularly between remote islands and the mainland. Varieties—his term for any visible (or invisible) differences in markings, coloration, size or shape of appendages, organs, or bodies—were of some peculiar use, he believed, for animals in the environment in which he found them. He was not certain about the use of these varieties, and he did not know whether the changes that created the varieties resulted from the environment or from some chance operation of nature. Ultimately, he concluded that varieties in nature were caused by three forces: (1) natural selection, in which varieties occur spontaneously by chance but are then "selected for" because they are aids to survival; (2) direct action of the environment, in which

---

From *On the Origin of Species by Means of Natural Selection*. This text is from the first edition, published in 1859. In the five subsequent editions, Darwin hedged more and more on his theory, often introducing material in defense against objections. The first edition is vigorous and direct; this edition jolted the worlds of science and religion out of their complaisance. In later editions, this chapter was titled "Natural Selection; or, Survival of the Fittest."

nonadaptive varieties do not survive because of climate, food conditions, or the like; and (3) the effects of use or disuse of a variation (for example, the short beak of a bird mentioned in para. 9). Darwin later regarded sexual selection, which figures prominently in this work, as less significant.

The idea of evolution—the gradual change of species through some kind of modification of varieties—had been in the air for many years when Darwin began his work. The English scientists W. C. Wells in 1813 and Patrick Matthew in 1831 had both proposed theories of natural selection, although Darwin was unaware of their work. Alfred Russel Wallace (1823–1913), a younger English scientist, revealed in 1858 that he was about to propose the same theory of evolution as was Darwin. They jointly published brief versions of their theories in 1858, and the next year Darwin rushed the final version of his book *On the Origin of Species by Means of Natural Selection* to press.

Darwin did not mention human beings as part of the evolutionary process in *On the Origin of Species;* because he was particularly concerned about the probable adverse reactions of theologians, he merely promised later discussion of that subject. It came in *The Descent of Man and Selection in Relation to Sex* (1871), the companion to *On the Origin of Species.*

When Darwin returned to England after completing his research on the *Beagle,* he supplemented his knowledge with information gathered from breeders of pigeons, livestock, dogs, and horses. This research, it must be noted, involved relatively few samples and was conducted according to comparatively unscientific practices. Yet although limited, it corresponded with his observations of nature. Humans could and did cause changes in species; Darwin's task was to show that nature—through the process of natural selection—could do the same thing.

The Descent of Man stirred up a great deal of controversy between the church and Darwin's supporters. Not since the Roman Catholic Church denied the fact that the earth went around the sun, which Galileo proved scientifically by 1632 (and was placed under house arrest for his pains), had there been a more serious confrontation between science and religion. Darwin was ridiculed by ministers and doubted by older scientists; but his views were stoutly defended by younger scientists, many of whom had arrived at similar conclusions. In the end, Darwin's views were accepted by the Church of England, and when he died in 1882 he was lionized and buried at Westminster Abbey in London. Only recently has controversy concerning his work arisen again.

Darwin's Rhetoric

Despite the complexity of the material it deals with, Darwin's writing is fluent, smooth, and stylistically sophisticated and keeps the reader engaged. Darwin's rhetorical method depends entirely on the yoking of thesis and demonstration. He uses definition frequently, but most often he uses testimony, gathering information and instances, both real and imaginary, from many different sources.

Interestingly enough, Darwin claimed that he used Francis Bacon's method of induction in his research, gathering evidence of many instances of a given phenomenon, from which the truth—or a natural law—emerges. In fact, Darwin did not quite follow this path. Like most modern scientists, he established a hypothesis after a period of observation, and then he looked for evidence that confirmed or refuted the hypothesis. He was careful to include examples that argued against his view, but like most scientists, he emphasized the importance of the supportive samples.

Induction plays a part in the rhetoric of this selection in that it is dominated by examples from bird breeding, birds in nature, domestic farm animals and their breeding, and botany, including the breeding of plants and the interdependence of certain insects and certain plants. Erasmus Darwin was famous for his work with plants, and it is natural that such observations would play an important part in his grandson's thinking.

The process of natural selection is carefully discussed, particularly in paragraph 8 and thereafter. Darwin emphasizes its positive nature and its differences from selection by human breeders. The use of comparison, which appears frequently in the selection, is most conspicuous in these paragraphs. He postulates a nature in which the fittest survive because they are best adapted for survival, but he does not dwell on the fate of those who are unfit individuals. It was left to later writers, often misapplying his theories, to do that.

PREREADING QUESTIONS: WHAT TO READ FOR

The following prereading questions may help you anticipate key issues in the discussion on Charles Darwin's "Natural Selection." Keeping them in mind during your first reading of the selection should help focus your reactions.

• What is the basic principle of natural selection?

• How does "human" selection differ from nature's selection?

Natural Selection

How will the struggle for existence . . . act in regard to varia-   1
tion? Can the principle of selection, which we have seen is so potent
in the hands of man, apply in nature? I think we shall see that it can
act most effectually. Let it be borne in mind in what an endless
number of strange peculiarities our domestic productions, and, in a
lesser degree, those under nature, vary; and how strong the heredi-
tary tendency is. Under domestication, it may be truly said that the
whole organization becomes in some degree plastic.[1] Let it be borne
in mind how infinitely complex and close-fitting are the mutual relations of all organic beings to each other and to their physical conditions of life. Can it, then, be thought improbable, seeing that
variations useful to man have undoubtedly occurred, that other variations useful in some way to each being in the great and complex
battle of life, should sometimes occur in the course of thousands of
generations? If such do occur, can we doubt (remembering that
many more individuals are born than can possibly survive) that individuals having any advantage, however slight, over others, would
have the best chance of surviving and or procreating their kind? On
the other hand, we may feel sure that any variation in the least degree injurious would be rigidly destroyed. This preservation of favorable variations and the rejection of injurious variations, I call
Natural Selection. Variations neither useful nor injurious would not
be affected by natural selection, and would be left a fluctuating element, as perhaps we see in the species called polymorphic.[2]

We shall best understand the probable course of natural selec-   2
tion by taking the case of a country undergoing some physical
change, for instance, of climate. The proportional numbers of its inhabitants would almost immediately undergo a change, and some
species might become extinct. We may conclude, from what we
have seen of the intimate and complex manner in which the inhabitants of each country are bound together, that any change in the numerical proportions of some of the inhabitants, independently of the
change of climate itself, would most seriously affect many of the others. If the country were open on its borders, new forms would certainly immigrate, and this also would seriously disturb the relations
of some of the former inhabitants. Let it be remembered how powerful the influence of a single introduced tree or mammal has been

---

[1] **plastic** Capable of being shaped and changed.
[2] **species called polymorphic** Species that have more than one form over the
course of their lives, such as butterflies.

shown to be. But in the case of an island, or of a country partly surrounded by barriers, into which new and better adapted forms
could not freely enter, we should then have places in the economy
of nature which would assuredly be better filled up, if some of the
original inhabitants were in some manner modified; for, had the
area been open to immigration, these same places would have been
seized on by intruders. In such case, every slight modification,
which in the course of ages chanced to arise, and which in any way
favored the individuals of any of the species, by better adapting
them to their altered conditions, would tend to be preserved; and
natural selection would thus have free scope for the work of improvement.

We have reason to believe . . . that a change in the conditions of   3
life, by specially acting on the reproductive system, causes or increases variability; and in the foregoing case the conditions of life are
supposed to have undergone a change, and this would manifestly be
favorable to natural selection, by giving a better chance of profitable
variations occurring; and unless profitable variations do occur, natural selection can do nothing. Not that, as I believe, any extreme
amount of variability is necessary; as man can certainly produce
great results by adding up in any given direction mere individual
differences, so could Nature, but far more easily, from having incomparably longer time at her disposal. Nor do I believe that any
great physical change, as of climate, or any unusual degree of isolation to check immigration, is actually necessary to produce new and
unoccupied places for natural selection to fill up by modifying and
improving some of the varying inhabitants. For as all the inhabitants
of each country are struggling together with nicely balanced forces,
extremely slight modifications in the structure or habits of one in-
habitant would often give it an advantage over others; and still
further modifications of the same kind would often still further increase the advantage. No country can be named in which all the native inhabitants are now so perfectly adapted to each other and to
the physical conditions under which they live, that none of them
could anyhow be improved; for in all countries, the natives have
been so far conquered by naturalized productions, that they have allowed foreigners to take firm possession of the land. And as foreigners have thus everywhere beaten some of the natives, we may safely
conclude that the natives might have been modified with advantage,
so as to have better resisted such intruders.

As man can produce and certainly has produced a great result   4
by his methodical and unconscious means of selection, what may
not nature effect? Man can act only on external and visible characters; nature cares nothing for appearances, except in so far as they

may be useful to any being. She can act on every internal organ, on every shade of constitutional difference, on the whole machinery of life. Man selects only for his own good; Nature only for that of the being which she tends. Every selected character is fully exercised by her; and the being is placed under well-suited conditions of life. Man keeps the natives of many climates in the same country; he seldom exercises each selected character in some peculiar and fitting manner; he feeds a long and a short beaked pigeon on the same food; he does not exercise a long-backed or long-legged quadruped in any peculiar manner; he exposes sheep with long and short wool to the same climate. He does not allow the most vigorous males to struggle for the females. He does not rigidly destroy all inferior animals, but protects during each varying season, as far as lies in his power, all his productions. He often begins his selection by some half-monstrous form; or at least by some modification prominent enough to catch the eye, or to be plainly useful to him. Under nature, the slightest difference of structure or constitution may well turn the nicely balanced scale in the struggle for life, and so be preserved. How fleeting are the wishes and efforts of man! how short his time! and consequently how poor will his products be, compared with those accumulated by nature during whole geological periods. Can we wonder, then, that nature's productions should be far "truer" in character than man's productions; that they should be infinitely better adapted to the most complex conditions of life, and should plainly bear the stamp of far higher workmanship?

It may be said that natural selection is daily and hourly scruti- 5 nizing, throughout the world, every variation, even the slightest; rejecting that which is bad, preserving and adding up all that is good; silently and insensibly working, whenever and wherever opportunity offers, at the improvement of each organic being in relation to its organic and inorganic conditions of life. We see nothing of these slow changes in progress, until the hand of time has marked the long lapse of ages, and then so imperfect is our view into long past geological ages, that we only see that the forms of life are now different from what they formerly were.

Although natural selection can act only through and for the 6 good of each being, yet characters and structures, which we are apt to consider as of very trifling importance, may thus be acted on. When we see leaf-eating insects green, and bark-feeders mottled-grey; the alpine ptarmigan white in winter, the red-grouse the color of heather, and the black-grouse that of peaty earth, we must believe that these tints are of service to these birds and insects in preserving them from danger. Grouse, if not destroyed at some period of their lives, would increase in countless numbers; they are known to suffer largely from birds of prey; and hawks are guided by eyesight to their prey—so much so that on parts of the Continent[3] persons are warned not to keep white pigeons, as being the most liable to destruction. Hence I can see no reason to doubt that natural selection might be most effective in giving the proper color to each kind of grouse, and in keeping that color, when once acquired, true and constant. Nor ought we to think that the occasional destruction of an animal of any particular color would produce little effect; we should remember how essential it is in a flock of white sheep to destroy every lamb with the faintest trace of black. In plants, the down on the fruit and the color of the flesh are considered by botanists as characters of the most trifling importance; yet we hear from an excellent horticulturist, Downing,[4] that in the United States, smooth-skinned fruits suffer far more from a beetle, a curculio,[5] than those with down; that purple plums suffer far more from a certain disease than yellow plums; whereas another disease attacks yellow-fleshed peaches far more than those with other colored flesh. If, with all the aids of art, these slight differences make a great difference in cultivating the several varieties, assuredly, in a state of nature, where the trees would have to struggle with other trees and with a host of enemies, such differences would effectually settle which variety, whether a smooth or downy, a yellow or purple fleshed fruit, should succeed.

In looking at many small points of difference between species, which, as far as our ignorance permits us to judge, seem to be quite unimportant, we must not forget that climate, food, etc., probably produce some slight and direct effect. It is, however, far more necessary to bear in mind that there are many unknown laws of correlation[6] of growth, which, when one part of the organization is modified through variation and the modifications are accumulated by natural selection for the good of the being, will cause other modifications, often of the most unexpected nature. 7

As we see that those variations which under domestication appear at any particular period of life, tend to reappear in the offspring at the same period—for instance, in the seeds of the many varieties 8

---

[3] **Continent** European continent; the contiguous land mass of Europe, which excludes the British Isles.

[4] **Andrew Jackson Downing (1815–1852)** American horticulturist and specialist in fruit and fruit trees.

[5] **curculio** A weevil.

[6] **laws of correlation** In certain plants and animals, one condition relates to another, as in the case of blue-eyed white cats, which are often deaf; the reasons are not clear but have to do with genes and their locations.

of our culinary and agricultural plants; in the caterpillar and cocoon stages of the varieties of the silkworm; in the eggs of poultry, and in the color of the down of their chickens; in the horns of our sheep and cattle when nearly adult—so in a state of nature, natural selection will be enabled to act on and modify organic beings at any age, by the accumulation of profitable variations at that age, and by their inheritance at a corresponding age. If it profit a plant to have its seeds more and more widely disseminated by the wind, I can see no greater difficulty in this being effected through natural selection than in the cotton-planter increasing and improving by selection the down in the pods on his cotton-trees. Natural selection may modify and adapt the larva of an insect to a score of contingencies, wholly different from those which concern the mature insect. These modifications will no doubt effect, through the laws of correlation, the structure of the adult; and probably in the case of those insects which live only for a few hours, and which never feed, a large part of their structure is merely the correlated result of successive changes in the structure of their larvae. So, conversely, modifications in the adult will probably often affect the structure of the larva; but in all cases natural selection will ensure that modifications consequent on other modifications at a different period of life, shall not be in the least degree injurious: for if they became so, they would cause the extinction of the species.

Natural selection will modify the structure of the young in rela-   9
tion to the parent, and of the parent in relation to the young. In social animals it will adapt the structure of each individual for the benefit of the community, if each in consequence profits by the selected change. What natural selection cannot do is to modify the structure of one species, without giving it any advantage, for the good of another species; and though statements to this effect may be found in works of natural history, I cannot find one case which will bear investigation. A structure used only once in an animal's whole life, if of high importance to it, might be modified to any extent by natural selection; for instance, the great jaws possessed by certain insects, and used exclusively for opening the cocoon—or the hard tip to the beak of nestling birds, used for breaking the egg. It has been asserted that of the best short-beaked tumbler-pigeons, more perish in the egg than are able to get out of it; so that fanciers[7] assist in the act of hatching. Now, if nature had to make the beak of a full-grown pigeon very short for the bird's own advantage, the process of modification would be very slow, and there would be simultaneously the

---

[7]**fanciers** Amateurs who raise and race pigeons.

most rigorous selection of the young birds within the egg, which had the most powerful and hardest beaks, for all with weak beaks would inevitably perish; or, more delicate and more easily broken shells might be selected, the thickness of the shell being known to vary like every other structure.

Sexual Selection

Inasmuch as peculiarities often appear under domestication in   10 one sex and become hereditarily attached to that sex, the same fact probably occurs under nature, and if so, natural selection will be able to modify one sex in its functional relations to the other sex, or in relation to wholly different habits of life in the two sexes, as is sometimes the case with insects. And this leads me to say a few words on what I call Sexual Selection. This depends, not on a struggle for existence, but on a struggle between the males for possession of the females; the result is not death to the unsuccessful competitor, but few or no offspring. Sexual selection is, therefore, less rigorous than natural selection. Generally, the most vigorous males, those which are best fitted for their places in nature, will leave most progeny. But in many cases, victory will depend not on general vigor, but on having special weapons, confined to the male sex. A hornless stag or spurless cock would have a poor chance of leaving offspring. Sexual selection by always allowing the victor to breed might surely give indomitable courage, length to the spur, and strength to the wing to strike in the spurred leg, as well as the brutal cock fighter,[8] who knows well that he can improve his breed by careful selection of the best cocks. How low in the scale of nature this law of battle descends, I know not; male alligators have been described as fighting, bellowing, and whirling round, like Indians in a wardance, for the possession of the females; male salmons have been seen fighting all day long; male stag-beetles often bear wounds from the huge mandibles[9] of other males. The war is, perhaps, severest between the males of polygamous animals,[10] and these seem oftenest provided with special weapons. The males of carnivorous animals are already well armed; though to them and to others, special means of defense may be given through means of sexual selection, as the

---

   [8] **brutal cock fighter** Cockfights were a popular spectator sport in England, especially for gamblers, but many people considered them a horrible brutality.

   [9] **mandibles** Jaws.

   [10] **polygamous animals** Animals that typically have more than one mate.

mane to the lion, the shoulder-pad to the boar, and the hooked jaw to the male salmon; for the shield may be as important for victory as the sword or spear.

Among birds, the contest is often of a more peaceful character. 11 All those who have attended to the subject believe that there is the severest rivalry between the males of many species to attract, by singing, the females. The rock-thrush of Guiana,[11] birds of paradise, and some others, congregate; and successive males display their gorgeous plumage and perform strange antics before the females, which standing by as spectators, at last choose the most attractive partner. Those who have closely attended to birds in confinement well know that they often take individual preferences and dislikes: thus Sir R. Heron[12] has described how one pied peacock was eminently attractive to all his hen birds. It may appear childish to attribute any effect to such apparently weak means: I cannot here enter on the details necessary to support this view; but if man can in a short time give elegant carriage and beauty to his bantams,[13] according to his standard of beauty, I can see no good reason to doubt that female birds, by selecting, during thousands of generations, the most melodious or beautiful males, according to their standard of beauty, might produce a marked effect. I strongly suspect that some well-known laws with respect to the plumage of male and female birds, in comparison with the plumage of the young, can be explained on the view of plumage having been chiefly modified by sexual selection, acting when the birds have come to the breeding age or during the breeding season; the modifications thus produced being inherited at corresponding ages or seasons, either by the males alone, or by the males and females; but I have not space here to enter on this subject.

Thus it is, as I believe, that when the males and females of any 12 animal have the same general habits of life, but differ in structure, color, or ornament, such differences have been mainly caused by sexual selection; that is, individual males have had, in successive generations, some slight advantage over other males, in their weapons, means of defense, or charms; and have transmitted these advantages to their male offspring. Yet, I would not wish to attribute all such sexual differences to this agency: for we see peculiarities arising and becoming attached to the male sex in our domestic

---

[11] **Guiana** Formerly British Guiana, now Guyana, on the northeast coast of South America.
[12] **Sir Robert Heron (1765–1854)** English politician who maintained a menagerie of animals.
[13] **bantams** Cocks bred for fighting.

animals (as the wattle in male carriers, horn-like protuberances in the cocks of certain fowls, etc.), which we cannot believe to be either useful to the males in battle, or attractive to the females. We see analogous cases under nature, for instance, the tuft of hair on the breast of the turkey-cock, which can hardly be either useful or ornamental to this bird; indeed, had the tuft appeared under domestication, it would have been called a monstrosity.

Illustrations of the Action of Natural Selection

In order to make it clear how, as I believe, natural selection acts, I must beg permission to give one or two imaginary illustrations. Let us take the case of a wolf, which preys on various animals, securing some by craft, some by strength, and some by fleetness; and let us suppose that the fleetest prey, a deer for instance, had from any change in the country increased in numbers, or that other prey had decreased in numbers, during that season of the year when the wolf is hardest pressed for food. I can under such circumstances see no reason to doubt that the swiftest and slimmest wolves would have the best chance of surviving, and so be preserved or selected, provided always that they retained strength to master their prey at this or at some other period of the year, when they might be compelled to prey on other animals. I can see no more reason to doubt this, than that man can improve the fleetness of his greyhounds by careful and methodical selection, or by that unconscious selection which results from each man trying to keep the best dogs without any thought of modifying the breed. 13

Even without any change in the proportional numbers of the animals on which our wolf preyed, a cub might be born with an innate tendency to pursue certain kinds of prey. Nor can this be thought very improbable; for we often observe great differences in the natural tendencies of our domestic animals; one cat, for instance, taking to catch rats, another mice; one cat, according to Mr. St. John,[14] bringing home winged game, another hares or rabbits, and another hunting on marshy ground and almost nightly catching woodcocks or snipes. The tendency to catch rats rather than mice is known to be inherited. Now, if any slight innate change of habit or of structure benefited an individual wolf, it would have the best chance of surviving and of leaving offspring. Some of its young 14

---

[14] **Charles George William St. John (1809–1856)** An English naturalist whose book *Wild Sports and Natural History of the Highlands* was published in 1846.

would probably inherit the same habits or structure, and by the repetition of this process, a new variety might be formed which would either supplant or coexist with the parent-form of wolf. Or, again, the wolves inhabiting a mountainous district, and those frequenting the lowlands, would naturally be forced to hunt different prey; and from the continued preservation of the individuals best fitted for the two sites, two varieties might slowly be formed. These varieties would cross and blend where they met; but to this subject of intercrossing we shall soon have to return. I may add, that, according to Mr. Pierce,[15] there are two varieties of the wolf inhabiting the Catskill Mountains in the United States, one with a light greyhound-like form, which pursues deer, and the other more bulky, with shorter legs, which more frequently attacks the shepherd's flocks.

Let us now take a more complex case. Certain plants excrete a   15
sweet juice, apparently for the sake of eliminating something injurious from their sap; this is effected by glands at the base of the stipules[16] in some Leguminosæ, and at the back of the leaf of the common laurel. This juice, though small in quantity, is greedily sought by insects. Let us now suppose a little sweet juice or nectar to be excreted by the inner bases of the petals of a flower. In this case insects in seeking the nectar would get dusted with pollen, and would certainly often transport the pollen from one flower to the stigma of another flower. The flowers of two distinct individuals of the same species would thus get crossed; and the act of crossing, we have good reason to believe (as will hereafter be more fully alluded to), would produce very vigorous seedlings, which consequently would have the best chance of flourishing and surviving. Some of these seedlings would probably inherit the nectar-excreting power. Those individual flowers which had the largest glands or nectaries, and which excreted most nectar, would be oftenest visited by insects, and would be oftenest crossed; and so in the long-run would gain the upper hand. Those flowers, also, which had their stamens and pistils[17] placed, in relation to the size and habits of the particular insects which visited them, so as to favor in any degree the transportal of their pollen from flower to flower, would likewise be favored or selected. We might have taken the case of insects visiting flowers for the sake of collecting pollen instead of nectar; and as pollen is formed for the sole object of fertilization, its destruction appears a simple loss to the plant; yet if a little pollen were carried, at first oc-

---

[15] **Pierce** Unidentified.

[16] **stipules** Spines at the base of a leaf.

[17] **stamens and pistils** Sexual organs of plants. The male and female organs appear together in the same flower.

casionally and then habitually, by the pollen-devouring insects from flower to flower, and a cross thus effected, although nine-tenths of the pollen were destroyed, it might still be a great gain to the plant; and those individuals which produced more and more pollen, and had larger and larger anthers,[18] would be selected.

When our plant, by this process of the continued preservation or natural selection of more and more attractive flowers, had been rendered highly attractive to insects, they would, unintentionally on their part, regularly carry pollen from flower to flower; and that they can most effectually do this, I could easily show by many striking instances. I will give only one — not as a very striking case, but as likewise illustrating one step in the separation of the sexes of plants, presently to be alluded to. Some holly-trees bear only male flowers, which have four stamens producing rather a small quantity of pollen, and a rudimentary pistil; other holly-trees bear only female flowers; these have a full-sized pistil, and four stamens with shrivelled anthers, in which not a grain of pollen can be detected. Having found a female tree exactly sixty yards from a male tree, I put the stigmas[19] of twenty flowers, taken from different branches, under the microscope, and on all, without exception, there were pollen-grains, and on some a profusion of pollen. As the wind had set for several days from the female to the male tree, the pollen could not thus have been carried. The weather had been cold and boisterous, and therefore not favorable to bees; nevertheless every female flower which I examined had been effectually fertilized by the bees, accidentally dusted with pollen, having flown from tree to tree in search of nectar. But to return to our imaginary case: as soon as the plant had been rendered so highly attractive to insects that pollen was regularly carried from flower to flower, another process might commence. No naturalist doubts the advantage of what has been called the "physiological division of labor"; hence we may believe that it would be advantageous to a plant to produce stamens alone in one flower or on one whole plant, and pistils alone in another flower or on another plant. In plants under culture and placed under new conditions of life, sometimes the male organs and sometimes the female organs become more or less impotent; now if we suppose this to occur in ever so slight a degree under nature, then as pollen is already carried regularly from flower to flower, and as a more complete separation of the sexes of our plant would be advantageous on the principle of the division of labor, individuals with this tendency

16

---

[18] **anthers** An anther is that part of the stamen that contains pollen.
[19] **stigmas** Where the plant's pollen develops.

more and more increased, would be continually favored or selected, until at last a complete separation of the sexes would be effected.

Let us now turn to the nectar-feeding insects in our imaginary   17
case: we may suppose the plant of which we have been slowly increasing the nectar by continued selection, to be a common plant; and that certain insects depended in main part on its nectar for food. I could give many facts, showing how anxious bees are to save time; for instance, their habit of cutting holes and sucking the nectar at the bases of certain flowers, which they can, with a very little more trouble, enter by the mouth. Bearing such facts in mind, I can see no reason to doubt that an accidental deviation in the size and form of the body, or in the curvature and length of the proboscis,[20] etc., far too slight to be appreciated by us, might profit a bee or other insect, so that an individual so characterized would be able to obtain its food more quickly, and so have a better chance of living and leaving descendants. Its descendants would probably inherit a tendency to a similar slight deviation of structure. The tubes of the corollas[21] of the common red and incarnate clovers (Trifolium pratense and incarnatum) do not on a hasty glance appear to differ in length; yet the hive-bee can easily suck the nectar out of the incarnate clover, but not out of the common red clover, which is visited by humble-bees[22] alone; so that whole fields of the red clover offer in vain an abundant supply of precious nectar to the hive-bee. Thus it might be a great advantage to the hive-bee to have a slightly longer or differently constructed proboscis. On the other hand, I have found by experiment that the fertility of clover greatly depends on bees visiting and moving parts of the corolla, so as to push the pollen on to the stigmatic surface. Hence, again, if humble-bees were to become rare in any country, it might be a great advantage to the red clover to have a shorter or more deeply divided tube to its corolla, so that the hive-bee could visit its flowers. Thus I can understand how a flower and a bee might slowly become, either simultaneously or one after the other, modified and adapted in the most perfect manner to each other, by the continued preservation of individuals presenting mutual and slightly favorable deviations of structure.

I am well aware that this doctrine of natural selection, exempli-   18
fied in the above imaginary instances, is open to the same objections which were at first urged against Sir Charles Lyell's noble views[23] on

---

[20] **proboscis** Snout.

[21] **corollas** Inner set of floral petals.

[22] **humble-bees** Bumblebees.

[23] **Sir Charles Lyell's noble views** Lyell (1797–1875) was an English geologist whose landmark work, *Principles of Geology* (1830–1833), Darwin read while on the *Beagle*. The book inspired Darwin, and the two scientists became friends. Lyell was shown portions of *On the Origin of Species* while Darwin was writing it.

"the modern changes of the earth, as illustrative of geology"; but we now very seldom hear the action, for instance, of the coast-waves, called a trifling and insignificant cause, when applied to the excavation of gigantic valleys or to the formation of the longest lines of inland cliffs. Natural selection can act only by the preservation and accumulation of infinitesimally small inherited modifications, each profitable to the preserved being; and as modern geology has almost banished such views as the excavation of a great valley by a single diluvial[24] wave, so will natural selection, if it be a true principle, banish the belief of the continued creation of new organic beings, or of any great and sudden modification in their structure.

QUESTIONS FOR CRITICAL READING

1. Darwin's metaphor "battle of life" (para. 1) introduces issues that might be thought extraneous to a scientific inquiry. What is the danger of using such a metaphor? What is the advantage of doing so?
2. Many religious groups reject Darwin's concept of natural selection, but they heartily accept human selection in the form of controlled breeding. Why would there be such a difference between the two?
3. Do you feel that the theory of natural selection is a positive force? Could it be directed by divine power?
4. In this work, there is no reference to human beings in terms of the process of selection. How might the principles at work on animals also work on people? Do you think that Darwin assumes this?
5. When this chapter was published in a later edition, Darwin added to its title "Survival of the Fittest." What issues or emotions does that new title raise that "Natural Selection" does not?

SUGGESTIONS FOR WRITING

1. In paragraph 13, Darwin uses imaginary examples. Compare the value of his genuine examples and these imaginary ones. How effective is the use of imaginary examples in an argument? What requirements should an imaginary example meet to be forceful in an argument? Do you find Darwin's imaginary examples to be strong or weak?

---

[24] **diluvial** Pertaining to a flood. Darwin means that geological changes, such as those that caused the Grand Canyon, were no longer thought of as occurring instantly by flood (or other catastrophes) but were considered to have developed over a long period of time, as he imagines happened in the evolution of the species.

2. From paragraph 14 on, Darwin discusses the process of modification of a species through its beginning in the modification of an individual. Explain, insofar as you understand the concept, how a species could be modified by a variation occurring in just one individual. In your explanation, use Darwin's rhetorical technique of the imaginary example.

3. Write an essay that takes as its thesis statement the following sentence from paragraph 18: "Natural selection can act only by the preservation and accumulation of infinitesimally small inherited modifications, each profitable to the preserved being." Be sure to examine the work carefully for other statements by Darwin that add strength, clarity, and meaning to this one. You may also employ the Darwinian device of presenting imaginary instances in your essay.

4. A controversy exists concerning the Darwinian theory of evolution. Explore the *Readers' Guide to Periodical Literature* (a reference book you can find at your local or college library), and the Internet for up-to-date information on the creationist-evolutionist conflict in schools. Look up either or both terms to see what articles you can find. Define the controversy and take a stand on it. Use your knowledge of natural selection gained from this piece. Remember, too, that Darwin was trained as a minister of the church and was concerned about religious opinion.

5. When Darwin wrote this piece, he believed that sexual selection was of great importance in evolutionary changes in species. Assuming that this belief is true, establish the similarities between sexual selection in plants and animals and sexual selection, as you have observed it, in people. Paragraphs 10 to 12 discuss this issue. Darwin does not discuss selection in human beings, but it is clear that physical and stylistic distinctions between the sexes have some bearing on selection. Assuming that to be true, what qualities in people (physical and mental) are likely to survive? Why?

PLATO

The Allegory of the Cave

PLATO (428–347 B.C.) was born into an aristocratic, probably
Athenian, family and educated according to the best precepts available. He eventually became a student of Socrates and later involved
himself closely with Socrates' work and teaching. Plato was not
only Socrates' finest student but also the one who immortalized
Socrates in his works. Most of Plato's works are philosophical essays in which Socrates speaks as a character in a dialogue with one
or more students or listeners.

Both Socrates and Plato lived in turbulent times. In 404 B.C.
Athens was defeated by Sparta and its government was taken over
by tyrants. Political life in Athens became dangerous. Plato felt,
however, that he could effect positive change in Athenian politics
until Socrates was tried unjustly for corrupting the youth of Athens
and sentenced to death in 399 B.C. After that, Plato withdrew from
public life and devoted himself to writing and to the Academy he
founded in an olive grove in Athens. The Academy endured for almost a thousand years, which tells us how greatly Plato's thought
was valued.

Although it is not easy to condense Plato's views, he may be
said to have held the world of sense perception to be inferior to the
world of ideal entities that exist only in a pure spiritual realm.
These ideals, or forms, Plato argued, are perceived directly by
everyone before birth and then dimly remembered here on earth.
But the memory, dim as it is, enables people to understand what
the senses perceive, despite the fact that the senses are unreliable
and their perceptions imperfect.

This view of reality has long been important to philosophers
because it gives a philosophical basis to antimaterialistic thought.

From *The Republic.* Translated and glossed by Benjamin Jowett.

It values the spirit first and frees people from the tyranny of sensory perception and sensory reward. In the case of love, Plato held that Eros leads individuals to revere the body and its pleasures; but the thrust of his teaching is that the body is a metaphor for spiritual delights. Plato maintains that the body is only a starting point, which eventually can lead to both spiritual fulfillment and the appreciation of true beauty.

On the one hand, "The Allegory of the Cave" is a discussion of politics: *The Republic,* from which it is taken, is a treatise on justice and the ideal government. On the other hand, it has long stood as an example of the notion that if we rely on our perceptions to know the truth about the world, then we will know very little about it. In order to live ethically, it is essential to know what is true and, therefore, what is important beyond the world of sensory perception.

Plato's allegory has been persuasive for centuries and remains at the center of thought that attempts to counter the pleasures of the sensual life. Most religions aim for spiritual enlightenment and praise the qualities of the soul, which lies beyond perception. Thus, it comes as no surprise that Christianity and other religions have developed systems of thought that bear a close resemblance to Plato's. Later refinements of his thought, usually called Neo-Platonism, have been influential even into modern times.

Plato's Rhetoric

Two important rhetorical techniques are at work in the following selection. The first and more obvious—at least on one level—is the device of the allegory, a story in which the characters and situations actually represent people and situations in another context. It is a difficult technique to sustain, although Aesop's fables were certainly successful in using animals to represent people and their foibles. The advantage of the technique is that a complex and sometimes unpopular argument can be fought and won before the audience realizes that an argument is under way. The disadvantage of the technique is that the terms of the allegory may only approximate the situation it represents; thus, the argument may fail to be convincing.

The second rhetorical technique Plato uses is the dialogue. In fact, this device is a hallmark of Plato's work; indeed, most of his writings are called dialogues. The *Symposium, Apology, Phaedo, Crito, Meno,* and most of his famous works are written in dialogue form. Usually in these works Socrates is speaking to a student or a friend about highly abstract issues, asking questions that require simple answers. Slowly, the questioning proceeds to elucidate the answers to complex issues.

This question-and-answer technique basically constitutes the Socratic method. Socrates analyzes the answer to each question, examines its implications, and then asserts the truth. The method works partly because Plato believes that people do not learn things but remember them. That is, people originate from heaven, where they knew the truth; they already possess knowledge and must recover it by means of the dialogue. Socrates' method is ideally suited to that purpose.

Beyond these techniques, however, we must look at Plato's style. It is true that he is working with difficult ideas, but his style is so clear, simple, and direct that few people would have trouble understanding what he is saying at any given moment. Considering the influence this work has had on world thought and the reputation Plato had earned by the time he wrote *The Republic,* its style is remarkably plain and accessible. Plato's respect for rhetoric and its proper uses is part of the reason he can express himself with such impressive clarity.

PREREADING QUESTIONS:
WHAT TO READ FOR

The following prereading questions may help you anticipate key issues in the discussion on Plato's "The Allegory of the Cave." Keeping them in mind during your first reading of the selection should help focus your reactions.

- In what ways are we like the people in the cave looking at shadows?

- Why is the world of sensory perception somewhat illusory?

- For Plato, what is the difference between the upper world and the lower world?

The Allegory of the Cave

SOCRATES,
GLAUCON. *The*
den, the prison-
ers: the light at
a distance;

And now, I said, let me show in a figure how   1
far our nature is enlightened or unenlightened: —
Behold! human beings living in an underground
den, which has a mouth open towards the light

and reaching all along the den; here they have been from their childhood, and have their legs and necks chained so that they cannot move, and can only see before them, being prevented by the chains from turning round their heads. Above and behind them a fire is blazing at a distance, and between the fire and the prisoners there is a raised way; and you will see, if you look, a low wall built along the way, like the screen which marionette players have in front of them, over which they show the puppets.

I see.   2

the low wall, and the moving figures of which the shadows are seen on the opposite wall of the den.

And do you see, I said, men passing along the   3 wall carrying all sorts of vessels, and statues and figures of animals made of wood and stone and various materials, which appear over the wall? Some of them are talking, others silent.

You have shown me a strange image, and they   4 are strange prisoners.

Like ourselves, I replied; and they see only   5 their own shadows, or the shadows of one another, which the fire throws on the opposite wall of the cave?

True, he said; how could they see anything but   6 the shadows if they were never allowed to move their heads?

And of the objects which are being carried in   7 like manner they would only see the shadows?

Yes, he said.   8

And if they were able to converse with one an-   9 other, would they not suppose that they were naming what was actually before them?

Very true.   10

The prisoners would mistake the shadows for realities.

And suppose further that the prison had an   11 echo which came from the other side, would they not be sure to fancy when one of the passers-by spoke that the voice which they heard came from the passing shadow?

No question, he replied.   12

To them, I said, the truth would be literally   13 nothing but the shadows of the images.

That is certain.   14

And now look again, and see what will natu-   15 rally follow if the prisoners are released and disabused of their error. At first, when any of them is liberated and compelled suddenly to stand up and turn his neck round and walk and look towards the light, he will suffer sharp pains; the glare will distress him, and he will be unable to see the realities of which in his former state he had seen the shadows; and then conceive someone saying to him, that what he saw before was an illusion, but that now, when he is approaching nearer to being and his eye is turned towards more real existence, he has a clearer vision—what will be his reply? And you may further imagine that his instructor is pointing to the objects as they pass and requiring him to name them,—will he not be perplexed? Will he not fancy that the shadows which he formerly saw are truer than the objects which are now shown to him?

And when released, they would still persist in maintaining the superior truth of the shadows.

Far truer.   16

And if he is compelled to look straight at the 17
light, will he not have a pain in his eyes which will make him turn away to take refuge in the objects of vision which he can see, and which he will conceive to be in reality clearer than the things which are now being shown to him?

True, he said.   18

And suppose once more, that he is reluctantly 19
dragged up a steep and rugged ascent, and held fast until he is forced into the presence of the sun himself, is he not likely to be pained and irritated? When he approaches the light his eyes will be dazzled, and he will not be able to see anything at all of what are now called realities.

When dragged upwards, they would be dazzled by excess of light.

Not all in a moment, he said.   20

He will require to grow accustomed to the 21
sight of the upper world. And first he will see the shadows best, next the reflections of men and other objects in the water, and then the objects themselves; then he will gaze upon the light of the moon and the stars and the spangled heaven; and he will see the sky and the stars by night better than the sun or the light of the sun by day?

Certainly.   22

Last of all he will be able to see the sun, and 23
not mere reflections of him in the water, but he

*At length
they will see
the sun and
understand
his nature.*

will see him in his own proper place, and not in another; and he will contemplate him as he is.

Certainly. 24

He will then proceed to argue that this is he 25 who gives the season and the years, and is the guardian of all that is in the visible world, and in a certain way the cause of all things which he and his fellows have been accustomed to behold?

Clearly, he said, he would first see the sun and 26 then reason about him.

And when he remembered his old habitation, 27 and the wisdom of the den and his fellow prison-

*They would then
pity their old
companions
of the den.*

ers, do you not suppose that he would felicitate himself on the change, and pity them?

Certainly, he would. 28

And if they were in the habit of conferring 29 honors among themselves on those who were quickest to observe the passing shadows and to re-mark which of them went before, and which fol-lowed after, and which were together; and who were therefore best able to draw conclusions as to the future, do you think that he would care for such honors and glories, or envy the possessors of them? Would he not say with Homer,

Better to be the poor servant of a poor master,

and to endure anything, rather than think as they do and live after their manner?

Yes, he said, I think that he would rather suffer 30 anything than entertain these false notions and live in this miserable manner.

Imagine once more, I said, such an one coming 31 suddenly out of the sun to be replaced in his old situation; would he not be certain to have his eyes full of darkness?

To be sure, he said. 32

*But when they
returned to the
den, they would
see much worse
than those
who had never
left it.*

And if there were a contest, and he had to 33 compete in measuring the shadows with the pris-oners who had never moved out of the den, while his sight was still weak, and before his eyes had be-come steady (and the time which would be needed to acquire this new habit of sight might be very considerable), would he not be ridiculous? Men would say of him that up he went and down he came without his eyes; and that it was better not even to think of ascending; and if any one tried to loose another and lead him up to the light, let them only catch the offender, and they would put him to death.

No question, he said.   34

The prison is the world of sight, the light of the fire is the sun.

This entire allegory, I said, you may now append, dear Glaucon, to the previous argument; the prison house is the world of sight, the light of the fire is the sun, and you will not misapprehend me if you interpret the journey upwards to be the ascent of the soul into the intellectual world according to my poor belief, which, at your desire, I have expressed—whether rightly or wrongly God knows. But, whether true or false, my opinion is that in the world of knowledge the idea of good appears last of all, and is seen only with an effort; and, when seen, is also inferred to be the universal author of all things beautiful and right, parent of light and of the lord of light in this visible world, and the immediate source of reason and truth in the intellectual; and that this is the power upon which he who would act rationally either in public or private life must have his eye fixed.   35

I agree, he said, as far as I am able to understand you.   36

Moreover, I said, you must not wonder that those who attain to this beatific vision are unwilling to descend to human affairs; for their souls are ever hastening into the upper world where they desire to dwell; which desire of theirs is very natural, if our allegory may be trusted.   37

Yes, very natural.   38

Nothing extraordinary in the philosopher being unable to see in the dark.

And is there anything surprising in one who passes from divine contemplations to the evil state of man, misbehaving himself in a ridiculous manner; if, while his eyes are blinking and before he has become accustomed to the surrounding darkness, he is compelled to fight in courts of law, or in other places, about the images or the shadows of images of justice, and is endeavoring to meet the conceptions of those who have never yet seen absolute justice?   39

Anything but surprising, he replied.   40

The eyes may be blinded in two ways, by excess or by defect of light.

Anyone who has common sense will remem- 41
ber that the bewilderments of the eyes are of two
kinds, and arise from two causes, either from coming out of the light or from going into the light,
which is true of the mind's eye, quite as much as of
the bodily eye; and he who remembers this when
he sees anyone whose vision is perplexed and
weak, will not be too ready to laugh; he will first
ask whether that soul of man has come out of the
brighter life, and is unable to see because unaccus-
tomed to the dark, or having turned from darkness
to the day is dazzled by excess of light. And he will
count the one happy in his condition and state of
being, and he will pity the other; or, if he have a
mind to laugh at the soul which comes from below
into the light, there will be more reason in this
than in the laugh which greets him who returns
from above out of the light into the den.

That, he said, is a very just distinction. 42

The conversion of the soul is the turning round the eye from darkness to light.

But then, if I am right, certain professors of ed- 43
ucation must be wrong when they say that they can
put a knowledge into the soul which was not there
before, like sight into blind eyes.

They undoubtedly say this, he replied. 44

Whereas, our argument shows that the power 45
and capacity of learning exists in the soul already;
and that just as the eye was unable to turn from
darkness to light without the whole body, so too
the instrument of knowledge can only by the
movement of the whole soul be turned from the
world of becoming into that of being, and learn by
degrees to endure the sight of being, and of the
brightest and best of being, or in other words, of
the good.

Very true. 46

And must there not be some art which will ef- 47
fect conversion in the easiest and quickest manner;
not implanting the faculty of sight, for that exists
already, but has been turned in the wrong direction, and is looking away from the truth?

Yes, he said, such an art may be presumed. 48

And whereas the other so-called virtues of the 49
soul seem to be akin to bodily qualities, for even
when they are not originally innate they can be im-

The virtue of wisdom has a divine power which may be turned either towards good or towards evil.

planted later by habit and exercise, the virtue of wisdom more than anything else contains a divine element which always remains, and by this conversion is rendered useful and profitable; or, on the other hand, hurtful and useless. Did you never observe the narrow intelligence flashing from the keen eye of a clever rogue—how eager he is, how clearly his paltry soul sees the way to his end; he is the reverse of blind, but his keen eyesight is forced into the service of evil, and he is mischievous in proportion to his cleverness?

Very true, he said.   50

But what if there had been a circumcision of   51
such natures in the days of their youth; and they had been severed from those sensual pleasures, such as eating and drinking, which, like leaden weights, were attached to them at their birth, and which drag them down and turn the vision of their souls upon the things that are below—if, I say, they had been released from these impediments and turned in the opposite direction, the very same faculty in them would have seen the truth as keenly as they see what their eyes are turned to now.

Very likely.   52

Neither the uneducated nor the over-educated will be good servants of the State.

Yes, I said; and there is another thing which is   53
likely, or rather a necessary inference from what has preceded, that neither the uneducated and uninformed of the truth, nor yet those who never make an end of their education, will be able ministers of State; not the former, because they have no single aim of duty which is the rule of all their actions, private as well as public; nor the latter, because they will not act at all except upon compulsion, fancying that they are already dwelling apart in the islands of the blessed.

Very true, he replied.   54

Then, I said, the business of us who are the   55
founders of the State will be to compel the best minds to attain that knowledge which we have already shown to be the greatest of all—they must continue to ascend until they arrive at the good; but when they have ascended and seen enough we must not allow them to do as they do now.

What do you mean?   56

Men should ascend to the upper world, but they should also return to the lower.

I mean that they remain in the upper world: 57 but this must not be allowed; they must be made to descend again among the prisoners in the den, and partake of their labors and honors, whether they are worth having or not.

But is not this unjust? he said; ought we to give 58 them a worse life, when they might have a better?

You have again forgotten, my friend, I said, the 59 intention of the legislator, who did not aim at making any one class in the State happy above the rest; the happiness was to be in the whole State, and he held the citizens together by persuasion and necessity, making them benefactors of the State, and therefore benefactors of one another; to this end he created them, not to please themselves, but to be his instruments in binding up the State.

True, he said, I had forgotten.   60

The duties of philosophers.

Observe, Glaucon, that there will be no injus- 61 tice in compelling our philosophers to have a care and providence of others; we shall explain to them that in other States, men of their class are not obliged to share in the toils of politics: and this is reasonable, for they grow up at their own sweet will, and the government would rather not have them. Being self-taught, they cannot be expected to show any gratitude for a culture which they have never received. But we have brought you into the world to be rulers of the hive, kings of yourselves and of the other citizens, and have educated you far better and more perfectly than they have been educated, and you are better able to share in the double duty. Wherefore each of you, when his turn comes, must go down to the general underground abode, and get the habit of seeing in the dark.

Their obligations to their country will induce them to take part in her government.

When you have acquired the habit, you will see ten thousand times better than the inhabitants of the den, and you will know what the several images are, and what they represent, because you have seen the beautiful and just and good in their truth. And thus our State, which is also yours, will be a reality, and not a dream only, and will be administered in a spirit unlike that of other States, in which men fight with one another about shadows only and are distracted in the struggle for power, which in their eyes is a great good. Whereas the truth is that the State in which the rulers are most reluctant to govern is always the best and most quietly governed, and the State in which they are most eager, the worst.

Quite true, he replied.   62

And will our pupils, when they hear this,   63 refuse to take their turn at the toils of State, when they are allowed to spend the greater part of their time with one another in the heavenly light?

They will be willing but not anxious to rule.

Impossible, he answered; for they are just   64 men, and the commands which we impose upon them are just; there can be no doubt that every one of them will take office as a stern necessity, and not after the fashion of our present rulers of State.

The statesman must be provided with a better life than that of a ruler; and then he will not covet office.

Yes, my friend, I said; and there lies the point.   65 You must contrive for your future rulers another and a better life than that of a ruler, and then you may have a well-ordered State; for only in the State which offers this, will they rule who are truly rich, not in silver and gold, but in virtue and wisdom, which are the true blessings of life. Whereas if they go to the administration of public affairs, poor and hungering after their own private advantage, thinking that hence they are to snatch the chief good, order there can never be; for they will be fighting about office, and the civil and domestic broils which thus arise will be the ruin of the rulers themselves and of the whole State.

Most true, he replied.   66

And the only life which looks down upon the   67 life of political ambition is that of true philosophy. Do you know of any other?

Indeed, I do not, he said.   68

QUESTIONS FOR CRITICAL READING

1. What is the relationship between Socrates and Glaucon? Are they equal in intellectual authority? Are they concerned with the same issues?

2. How does the allegory of the prisoners in the cave watching shadows on a wall relate to us today? What shadows do we see, and how do they distort our sense of what is real?
3. Are we prisoners in the same sense that Plato's characters are?
4. If Plato is right that the material world is an illusion, how would too great a reliance on materialism affect ethical decisions?
5. What ethical issues, if any, are raised by Plato's allegory?
6. In paragraph 49, Plato states that the virtue of wisdom "contains a divine element." What is "a divine element"? What does this statement seem to mean? Do you agree with Plato?
7. What distinctions does Plato make between the public and the private? Would you make the same distinctions (see paras. 53–55)?

SUGGESTIONS FOR WRITING

1. Analyze the allegory of the cave for its strengths and weaknesses. Consider what the allegory implies for people living in a world of the senses and for what might lie behind that world. To what extent are people like (or unlike) the figures in the cave? To what extent is the world we know like the cave?
2. Socrates ends the dialogue by saying that rulers of the state must be able to look forward to a better life than that of being rulers. He and Glaucon agree that only one life "looks down upon the life of political ambition"—"that of true philosophy" (para. 67). What is the life of true philosophy? Is it superior to that of governing (or anything else)? How would you define its superiority? What would its qualities be? What would its concerns be? Would you be happy leading such a life?
3. In what ways would depending on the material world for one's highest moral values affect ethical behavior? What is the connection between ethics and materialism? Write a brief essay that defends or attacks materialism as a basis for ethical action. How can people aspire to the good if they root their greatest pleasures in the senses? What alternatives do modern people have if they choose to base their actions on nonmaterialistic, or spiritual, values? What are those values? How can they guide our ethical behavior? Do you think they should?
4. In paragraph 61, Socrates outlines a program that would assure Athens of having good rulers and good government. Clarify exactly what the program is, what its problems and benefits are, and how it could be put into action. Then decide whether the program would work. You may consider whether it would work for our time, for Socrates' time, or both. If possible, use examples (hypothetical or real) to bolster your argument.
5. Socrates states unequivocally that Athens should compel the best and the most intelligent young men to be rulers of the state. Review his reasons for saying so, consider what his concept of the state is, and then take a stand on the issue. Is it right to compel the best and most

intelligent young people to become rulers? If so, would it be equally proper to compel those well suited for the professions of law, medicine, teaching, or religion to follow those respective callings? Would an ideal society result if all people were forced to practice the calling for which they had the best aptitude?

COMMUNITIES AND CULTURES: THE IDEAL AND THE REALITY

ARISTOTLE
A Definition of Justice

ARISTOTLE (384–322 B.C.) is the great inheritor of Plato's influence in Greek philosophical thought. A student at the Academy
of Plato in Athens from age seventeen to thirty-seven, he was by all
accounts Plato's most brilliant pupil. He did not agree with Plato
on all issues, however, and seems to have broken with his master's
thinking around the time of Plato's death (347 B.C.). For example,
in Aristotle's comments on justice, drawn from his *Politics,* he
treats matters that Plato addressed as well. In the *Republic,* Plato
explored many issues of justice in the ideal state; Aristotle, however, is unconcerned with ideal states and examines justice only in
oligarchies and democracies, the states with which Athens was
familiar.

When Aristotle himself became a teacher in the Academy his
most distinguished student was Alexander the Great, the youthful
ruler who spread Greek values and laws to the rest of the known
world. There has been much speculation regarding what Aristotle
taught Alexander about justice; the thoroughness of the *Politics* implies that it may have been a great deal. A surviving fragment of a
letter from Aristotle to Alexander suggests that he advised Alexander to become the leader of the Greeks and the master of the so-
called barbarians of other cultures.

Aristotle discusses justice entirely in relation to the state. In
his time the state was a city-state, such as Athens with its surrounding areas. For him, the well-ordered state was the greatest of
human inventions, of such noble value that other ideals must take
second place to it. He did not put divinity or godliness first. A practical man, Aristotle was concerned with the life that human beings
know on earth.

In the passage that follows, which comes from Book III, Chapters 9–12 of the *Politics,* a few issues concerning Greek society
need to be clarified. The most startling information for the modern

reader may be the fact that Aristotle accepted the practice of slavery as the norm. During this era wars were frequent, and the losers were ordinarily killed or placed into slavery. Thus, for powerful and victorious states such as Athens, slaves were abundant. However, the classical Greek institution of slavery was unlike the modern institution in the West during the eighteenth and nineteenth centuries. For example, Greek slaves had some rights and privileges and were not debased as a matter of course.

In this passage Aristotle discusses the rights of the freeborn but not those of slaves, who have, he tells us, no choices in how they are to live. Indeed, Aristotle differed from many of his contemporaries in believing that slaves deserved to be slaves in the same way that prisoners deserved prison. (This view is not acceptable to us today, but it was a widely held belief for thousands of years, and not only in the West. Such a stance was not seriously challenged until the modern period beginning in the seventeenth century.) Justice, therefore, in Aristotle's view, was a question that centered on the relationship of the state to the noble and freeborn, and almost certainly only to the men among them.

At the beginning of the passage Aristotle also makes a distinction concerning how justice functions in two forms of government: oligarchy and democracy. An oligarchy is a government by the few, such as a clique of high-born military men or closely related men. In an oligarchy, justice is based on inequality: the small elite group is superior and all others are inferior. A democracy is a government by the many: the wealthy, the less wealthy, and the poor. For those who champion democracy, everyone is equal; the wealthy have the same vote as lesser property holders. During Aristotle's time, however, women and slaves had no voice in either form of government. Only free men were represented. In an oligarchy, Aristotle argues, justice implies inequality only between those people who are unequal. In other words, the oligarchs cannot declare themselves superior by arbitrary decree. If other people are superior to them, they must be recognized as such.

On the other hand, Aristotle tells us that democrats who say justice lies in equality must also recognize that some people are simply not equal to others. In examining the nature of equality, he points out that most people are "bad judges in their own affairs" (para. 1) because they are primarily concerned with themselves and cannot clearly see themselves in relation to others. Justice exists between equals, he says, but individuals talk holistically about justice when they are actually referring only to a part of it. Aristotle discusses matters of equality of wealth, equality of physiology and beauty, equality of virtue, and equality of talent, demonstrating that there are far too many kinds of equality for anyone to cite only one as the absolute. Consequently, politicians must concern themselves with the kinds of equality that relate to the responsibilities of being part of the state.

In discussing issues of justice, Aristotle also addresses the nature of the state. In an earlier portion of this discussion, Aristotle expresses a principle that would later be stated by Rousseau: the state begins with the family, proceeds to the village and then to the surrounding community, and ends with the city-state. This natural progression implies a very large size for a city-state in which intermarriage within the state is a defining feature. Trade and other interactions with neighboring states follow as a matter of course. Aristotle views these exchanges as based on friendship: "for the will to live together is friendship. The end of the state is the good life, and these are the means towards it" (para. 2).

Aristotle always sought the end consequence of every art he wrote about: "In all sciences and arts the end is a good, and the greatest good and in the highest degree a good in the most authoritative of all [arts] — this is the political science of which the good is justice, in other words, the common interest" (para. 10). This comment implies that the interest of the whole — the commonwealth that comprises the state — is superior to the interest of the individual. Thus, justice is key to the happiness of the community. He says at the end of the passage, "if wealth and freedom are necessary elements, justice and valour are equally so; for without the former qualities a state cannot exist at all, without the latter not well" (para. 10).

Aristotle's Rhetoric

Aristotle's *Rhetoric* is probably the most influential treatise on rhetoric worldwide. Yet this passage from *Politics*, like many of his scholarly discussions, does not use especially rousing or stirring rhetoric. The reason may lie in the fact that this work was meant as a teaching treatise, a document for students of political science. Indeed, the passage is structured as an argument that masquerades as an examination of the facts. Aristotle argues for a state that is democratic in nature, in which the wealthy do not necessarily have the largest say and in which the poor are not encouraged to pillage the rich in the name of equality. Moreover, in this state, the poor have a voice in government, although not at the highest levels. Women and slaves, being unequal, have no voice in government, yet their concerns are expected to be considered in a well-ordered state.

A number of interesting hypothetical questions arise in the course of the discussion. For example, Aristotle imagines a government in which those "who are not rich and have no personal merit" (para. 7) are permitted to share the greatest offices of the state. He sees them as eventually giving in to incompetence and crime. Yet he also believes it is essential to give them some role in government, and he uses the analogy of mixing "impure food" with "pure" to produce an "entire mass more wholesome than a small quantity of the pure would be" (para. 7). This argument is consistent with Aristotle's earlier discussion of who should rule. Should the best person rule? The wealthiest? The most valorous? He discards all these possibilities one by one in favor of democracy, that is, rule by the many. His argument centers on an astonishingly modern hypothesis: that the decisions of the many are less likely to be extreme and more likely to be right than the decisions of the few.

Aristotle is famously methodical in his approach to any question, breaking it down into parts, categorizing the parts, and addressing each in turn. He is careful not to lose the reader in the details, and he stops often to recapitulate the argument. He uses carefully chosen analogies to help his argument along. In the last paragraph, for example, he talks about flute players as analogies for citizens at large. If there are many good flute players and only a few excellent flutes, it is wise to give the best flutes to the best players, not to the wealthiest, the noblest, the most virtuous, or the most valorous. This analogy is an example of justice in relation to inequality. Nevertheless the point is that excellence (in this case, musical excellence) is recognized, and in being recognized justice is done. This forceful and sensible example works in the common interest. Therefore, in a community, proper recognition of equalities and inequalities among people will result in justice. And without justice no state can exist well.

PREREADING QUESTIONS: WHAT TO READ FOR

The following prereading questions may help you anticipate key issues in the discussion on Aristotle's "A Definition of Justice." Keeping them in mind during your first reading of the selection should help focus your reactions.

- How does Aristotle define the state?
- Establish Aristotle's attitude toward the concept of equality and in-equality.

A Definition of Justice

CHAPTER 9

Let us begin by considering the common definitions of oligarchy   1
and democracy,[1] and what is justice oligarchical and democratical. For
all men cling to justice of some kind, but their conceptions are imperfect and they do not express the whole idea. For example, justice is
thought by them to be, and is, equality, not, however, for all, but only
for equals. And inequality is thought to be, and is, justice; neither is
this for all, but only for unequals. When the persons are omitted, then
men judge erroneously. The reason is that they are passing judgement
on themselves, and most people are bad judges in their own case. And
whereas justice implies a relation to persons as well as to things, and a
just distribution, as I have already said in the *Ethics,* implies the same
ratio between the persons and between the things, they agree about
the equality of the things, but dispute about the equality of the persons, chiefly for the reason which I have just given — because they are
bad judges in their own affairs; and secondly, because both the parties
to the argument are speaking of a limited and partial justice, but imagine themselves to be speaking of absolute justice. For the one party, if
they are unequal in one respect, for example wealth, consider themselves to be unequal in all; and the other party, if they are equal in one
respect, for example free birth, consider themselves to be equal in all.
But they leave out the capital point. For if men met and associated out
of regard to wealth only, their share in the state would be propor-
tioned to their property, and the oligarchical doctrine would then
seem to carry the day. It would not be just that he who paid one mina
should have the same share of a hundred minae, whether of the principal or of the profits, as he who paid the remaining ninety-nine. But a
state exists for the sake of a good life, and not for the sake of life only:
if life only were the object, slaves and brute animals might form a state,
but they cannot, for they have no share in happiness or in a life of free
choice. Nor does a state exist for the sake of alliance and security from

---

[1] **oligarchy and democracy** Government by the few and government by the
many, respectively.

injustice, nor yet for the sake of exchange and mutual intercourse; for then the Tyrrhenians and the Carthaginians, and all who have commercial treaties with one another, would be the citizens of one state. True, they have agreements about imports, and engagements that they will do no wrong to one another, and written articles of alliance. But there are no magistracies common to the contracting parties who will enforce their engagements; different states have each their own magistracies. Nor does one state take care that the citizens of the other are such as they ought to be, nor see that those who come under the terms of the treaty do no wrong or wickedness at all, but only that they do no injustice to one another. Whereas, those who care for good government take into consideration virtue and vice in states. Whence it may be further inferred that virtue must be the care of a state which is truly so called, and not merely enjoys the name: for without this end the community becomes a mere alliance which differs only in place from alliances of which the members live apart; and law is only a convention, "a surety to one another of justice," as the sophist[2] Lycophron says, and has no real power to make the citizens good and just.

This is obvious; for suppose distinct places, such as Corinth and   2
Megara, to be brought together so that their walls touched, still they would not be one city, not even if the citizens had the right to intermarry, which is one of the rights peculiarly characteristic of states. Again, if men dwelt at a distance from one another, but not so far off as to have no intercourse, and there were laws among them that they should not wrong each other in their exchanges, neither would this be a state. Let us suppose that one man is a carpenter, another a husbandman, another a shoemaker, and so on, and that their number is ten thousand: nevertheless, if they have nothing in common but exchange, alliance, and the like, that would not constitute a state. Why is this? Surely not because they are at a distance from one another: for even supposing that such a community were to meet in one place, but that each man had a house of his own, which was in a manner his state, and that they made alliance with one another, but only against evil-doers; still an accurate thinker would not deem this to be a state, if their intercourse with one another was of the same character after as before their union. It is clear then that a state is not a mere society, having a common place, established for the prevention of mutual crime and for the sake of exchange. These are conditions without which a state cannot exist; but all of them together do not constitute a state, which is a community of families and aggregations of families in well-being, for the sake of a perfect and self-

---

[2] **sophist:** Teacher of rhetoric.

sufficing life. Such a community can only be established among those who live in the same place and intermarry. Hence arise in cities family connexions, brotherhoods, common sacrifices, amusements which draw men together. But these are created by friendship, for the will to live together is friendship. The end of the state is the good life, and these are the means towards it. And the state is the union of families and villages in a perfect and self-sufficing life, by which we mean a happy and honourable life.

Our conclusion, then, is that political society exists for the sake 3 of noble actions, and not of mere companionship. Hence they who contribute most to such a society have a greater share in it than those who have the same or a greater freedom or nobility of birth but are inferior to them in political virtue; or than those who exceed them in wealth but are surpassed by them in virtue.

From what has been said it will be clearly seen that all the 4 partisans of different forms of government speak of a part of justice only.

CHAPTER 10

There is also a doubt as to what is to be the supreme power in 5 the state: — Is it the multitude? Or the wealthy? Or the good? Or the one best man? Or a tyrant? Any of these alternatives seems to involve disagreeable consequences. If the poor, for example, because they are more in number, divide among themselves the property of the rich — is not this unjust? No, by heaven (will be the reply), for the supreme authority justly willed it. But if this is not injustice, pray what is? Again, when in the first division all has been taken, and the majority divide anew the property of the minority, is it not evident, if this goes on, that they will ruin the state? Yet surely, virtue is not the ruin of those who possess her, nor is justice destructive of a state; and therefore this law of confiscation clearly cannot be just. If it were, all the acts of a tyrant must of necessity be just; for he only coerces other men by superior power, just as the multitude coerce the rich. But is it just then that the few and the wealthy should be the rulers? And what if they, in like manner, rob and plunder the people — is this just? If so, the other case will likewise be just. But there can be no doubt that all these things are wrong and unjust.

Then ought the good to rule and have supreme power? But in 6 that case everybody else, being excluded from power, will be dishonoured. For the offices of a state are posts of honour; and if one set of men always hold them, the rest must be deprived of them. Then will it be well that the one best man should rule? Nay, that is still more oligarchical, for the number of those who are dishonoured is thereby increased. Some one may say that it is bad in any case for a man, subject as he is to all the accidents of human passion, to have the supreme power, rather than the law. But what if the law itself be democratical or oligarchical, how will that help us out of our difficulties? Not at all; the same consequences will follow.

CHAPTER 11

Most of these questions may be reserved for another occasion. 7 The principle that the multitude ought to be supreme rather than the few best is one that is maintained, and, though not free from difficulty, yet seems to contain an element of truth. For the many, of whom each individual is but an ordinary person, when they meet together may very likely be better than the few good, if regarded not individually but collectively, just as a feast to which many contribute is better than a dinner provided out of a single purse. For each individual among the many has a share of virtue and prudence, and when they meet together, they become in a manner one man, who has many feet, and hands, and senses; that is a figure of their mind and disposition. Hence the many are better judges than a single man of music and poetry; for some understand one part, and some another, and among them they understand the whole. There is a similar combination of qualities in good men, who differ from any individual of the many, as the beautiful are said to differ from those who are not beautiful, and works of art from realities, because in them the scattered elements are combined, although, if taken separately, the eye of one person or some other feature in another person would be fairer than in the picture. Whether this principle can apply to every democracy, and to all bodies of men, is not clear. Or rather, by heaven, in some cases it is impossible of application; for the argument would equally hold about brutes; and wherein, it will be asked, do some men differ from brutes? But there may be bodies of men about whom our statement is nevertheless true. And if so, the difficulty which has been already raised, and also another which is akin to it—viz. what power should be assigned to the mass of freemen and citizens, who are not rich and have no personal merit—are both solved. There is still a danger in allowing them to share the great offices of state, for their folly will lead them into error, and their dishonesty into crime. But there is a danger also in not letting them share, for a state in which many poor men are excluded from office will necessarily be full of enemies. The only way of escape is to assign to them some deliberative and judicial functions. For this reason Solon[3] and certain other legislators give them

---

[3] **Solon (c. 630–c. 560 B.C.)** Archon of Athens and one of its most famous lawgivers and reformers.

the power of electing to offices, and of calling the magistrates to account, but they do not allow them to hold office singly. When they meet together their perceptions are quite good enough, and combined with the better class they are useful to the state (just as impure food when mixed with what is pure sometimes makes the entire mass more wholesome than a small quantity of the pure would be), but each individual, left to himself, forms an imperfect judgement. On the other hand, the popular form of government involves certain difficulties. In the first place, it might be objected that he who can judge of the healing of a sick man would be one who could himself heal his disease, and make him whole—that is, in other words, the physician; and so in all professions and arts. As, then, the physician ought to be called to account by physicians, so ought men in general to be called to account by their peers. But physicians are of three kinds: —there is the ordinary practitioner, and there is the physician of the higher class, and thirdly the intelligent man who has studied the art: in all arts there is such a class; and we attribute the power of judging to them quite as much as to professors of the art. Secondly, does not the same principle apply to elections? For a right election can only be made by those who have knowledge; those who know geometry, for example, will choose a geometrician rightly, and those who know how to steer, a pilot; and, even if there be some occupations and arts in which private persons share in the ability to choose, they certainly cannot choose better than those who know. So that, according to this argument, neither the election of magistrates, nor the calling of them to account, should be entrusted to the many. Yet possibly these objections are to a great extent met by our old answer, that if the people are not utterly degraded, although individually they may be worse judges than those who have special knowledge—as a body they are as good or better. Moreover, there are some arts whose products are not judged of solely, or best, by the artists themselves, namely those arts whose products are recognized even by those who do not possess the art; for example, the knowledge of the house is not limited to the builder only; the user, or, in other words, the master, of the house will even be a better judge than the builder, just as the pilot will judge better of a rudder than the carpenter, and the guest will judge better of a feast than the cook.

This difficulty seems now to be sufficiently answered, but there 8 is another akin to it. That inferior persons should have authority in greater matters than the good would appear to be a strange thing, yet the election and calling to account of the magistrates is the greatest of all. And these, as I was saying, are functions which in some states are assigned to the people, for the assembly is supreme in all such matters. Yet persons of any age, and having but a small property qualification, sit in the assembly and deliberate and judge, although for the great officers of state, such as treasurers and generals, a high qualification is required. This difficulty may be solved in the same manner as the preceding, and the present practice of democracies may be really defensible. For the power does not reside in the dicast,[4] or senator, or ecclesiast, but in the court, and the senate, and the assembly, of which individual senators, or ecclesiasts, or dicasts, are only parts or members. And for this reason the many may claim to have a higher authority than the few; for the people, and the senate, and the courts consist of many persons, and their property collectively is greater than the property of one or of a few individuals holding great offices. But enough of this.

The discussion of the first question shows nothing so clearly as 9 that laws, when good, should be supreme; and that the magistrate or magistrates should regulate those matters only on which the laws are unable to speak with precision owing to the difficulty of any general principle embracing all particulars. But what are good laws has not yet been clearly explained; the old difficulty remains. The goodness or badness, justice or injustice, of laws varies of necessity with the constitutions of states. This, however, is clear, that the laws must be adapted to the constitutions. But if so, true forms of government will of necessity have just laws, and perverted forms of government will have unjust laws.

CHAPTER 12

In all sciences and arts the end is a good, and the greatest good 10 and in the highest degree a good in the most authoritative of all— this is the political science of which the good is justice, in other words, the common interest. All men think justice to be a sort of equality; and to a certain extent they agree in the philosophical distinctions which have been laid down by us about Ethics. For they admit that justice is a thing and has a relation to persons, and that equals ought to have equality. But there still remains a question: equality or inequality of what? Here is a difficulty which calls for political speculation. For very likely some persons will say that offices of state ought to be unequally distributed according to superior excellence, in whatever respect, of the citizen, although there is no other difference between him and the rest of the community; for that those who differ in any one respect have different rights and claims. But, surely, if this is true, the complexion or height of a man,

---

[4] **dicast** Athens chose six thousand people each year to act as judge and jury in civil cases. An ecclesiast is a member of the Athenian public assembly known as the ecclesia.

or any other advantage, will be a reason for his obtaining a greater share of political rights. The error here lies upon the surface, and may be illustrated from the other arts and sciences. When a number of flute-players are equal in their art, there is no reason why those of them who are better born should have better flutes given to them; for they will not play any better on the flute, and the superior instrument should be reserved for him who is the superior artist. If what I am saying is still obscure, it will be made clearer as we proceed. For if there were a superior flute-player who was far inferior in birth and beauty, although either of these may be a greater good than the art of flute-playing, and may excel flute-playing in a greater ratio than he excels the others in his art, still he ought to have the best flutes given to him, unless the advantages of wealth and birth contribute to excellence in flute-playing, which they do not. Moreover, upon this principle any good may be compared with any other. For if a given height may be measured against wealth and against freedom, height in general may be so measured. Thus if A excels in height more than B in virtue, even if virtue in general excels height still more, all goods will be commensurable; for if a certain amount is better than some other, it is clear that some other will be equal. But since no such comparison can be made, it is evident that there is good reason why in politics men do not ground their claim to office on every sort of inequality any more than in the arts. For if some be slow, and others swift, that is no reason why the one should have little and the others much; it is in gymnastic contests that such excellence is rewarded. Whereas the rival claims of candidates for office can only be based on the possession of elements which enter into the composition of a state. And therefore the noble, or freeborn, or rich, may with good reason claim office; for holders of offices must be freemen and tax-payers: a state can be no more composed entirely of poor men than entirely of slaves. But if wealth and freedom are necessary elements, justice and valour are equally so; for without the former qualities a state cannot exist at all, without the latter not well.

QUESTIONS FOR CRITICAL READING

1. In paragraph 1, justice is said to be "equality." What does that mean?
2. What is Aristotle's attitude toward "slaves and brute animals"?
3. Why do you think Aristotle believes the "right to intermarry" is "peculiarly characteristic of states" (para. 2)?
4. "The end of the state is the good life" (para. 2). What does Aristotle mean by this? How do you interpret the statement for yourself?
5. What role does friendship play in the creation of a state?

6. Why does Aristotle reject the notion that the most virtuous person should rule the state?

7. Aristotle holds firmly to the view that "the multitude ought to be supreme rather than the few best" (para. 7). Do you agree?

8. In paragraph 10 Aristotle says that the "good" of political science is justice, "in other words, the common interest." What does "the common interest" mean in this context?

SUGGESTIONS FOR WRITING

1. Aristotle says that when people argue about justice they usually are "speaking of a limited and partial justice." What does he mean? What examples do you see in his discussions of justice that back him up? Why is it so difficult to talk about justice in the larger sense of the word rather than to discuss a limited aspect of justice? For example, people talk about taxing the rich very heavily to help the poor as a form of justice. How would Aristotle regard that choice?

2. At the end of paragraph 1, Aristotle refers to a philosopher named Lycophron and reminds us that even though states can create just laws, the laws will not make the "citizens good and just." How true is that of our own time and place? What examples can you think of that illustrate how difficult it is for the nation to use laws to help make its citizens good and just? Is there any relationship between just laws and just citizens?

3. Aristotle tells us that "political society exists for the sake of noble actions, and not of mere companionship" (para. 3). In this sense, he reveals a need for high ideals in a state. How much does our own nation reveal a need for high ideals? Do citizens whom you know imagine the state as being capable of noble actions? How do politicians talk about their vision of the state? How would you talk about your vision and ideals if you were running for office?

4. Explain Aristotle's position on whether the "few and the wealthy" should be the rulers of the state (para. 5). What is your own view on this question? Do you feel that currently the nation is being run by the few and the wealthy, or does such a statement reflect a distortion of reality? What conditions in a modern state might lead to a situation in which the few and the wealthy are the rulers?

5. How do the laws of an oligarchy differ from those of a democracy? When the few and the powerful are the rulers, and the people have no vote and no power, what kinds of laws might be enacted to preserve that situation? Would they be just laws? On what basis would you establish your evaluation? How would you fare in an oligarchic society?

6. What are Aristotle's strongest arguments in favor of a government of the multitude as opposed to a government of the few? Which of these arguments do you feel affected the founders of our nation? Do you think Aristotle is correct in his judgment?

JAMES BALDWIN
Stranger in the Village

From all available evidence no black man had ever set foot in this tiny Swiss village before I came. I was told before arriving that I would probably be a "sight" for the village; I took this to mean that people of my complexion were rarely seen in Switzerland, and also that city people are always something of a "sight" outside of the city. It did not occur to me—possibly because I am an American—that there could be people anywhere who had never seen a Negro.

It is a fact that cannot be explained on the basis of the inaccessibility of the village. The village is very high, but it is only four hours from Milan and three hours from Lausanne. It is true that it is virtually unknown. Few people making plans for a holiday would elect to come here. On the other hand, the villagers are able, presumably, to come and go as they please—which they do: to another town at the foot of the mountain, with a population of approximately five thousand, the nearest place to see a movie or go to the bank. In the village there is no movie house, no bank, no library, no theater; very few radios, one jeep, one station wagon; and, at the moment, one typewriter, mine, an invention which the woman next door to me here had never seen. There are about six hundred people living here, all Catholic—I conclude this from the fact that the Catholic church is open all year round, whereas the Protestant chapel, set off on a hill a little removed from the village, is open only in the summertime when the tourists arrive. There are four or five hotels, all closed now, and four or five *bistros*, of which, however, only two do any business during the winter. These two do not do a great deal, for life in the village seems to end around nine or ten o'clock. There are a few stores, butcher, baker, *épicerie*, a hardware store, and a money-changer—who cannot change travelers' checks, but must send them down to the bank, an operation which takes two or three days. There is something called the *Ballet Haus*, closed in the winter and used for God knows what, certainly not ballet, during the summer. There seems to be only one schoolhouse in the village, and this for the quite young children; I suppose this to mean that their older brothers and sisters at some point descend from these mountains in order to complete their education—possibly, again, to the town just below. The landscape is absolutely forbidding, mountains towering on all four sides, ice and snow as far as the eye can reach. In this white wilderness, men and women and children move all day, carrying washing, wood, buckets of milk or water, sometimes skiing on Sunday afternoons. All week long boys and young men are to be seen shoveling snow off the rooftops, or dragging wood down from the forest in sleds.

The village's only real attraction, which explains the tourist season, is the hot spring water. A disquietingly high proportion of these tourists are cripples, or semi-cripples, who come year after year—from other parts of Switzerland, usually—to take the waters. This lends the village, at the height of the season, a rather terrifying air of sanctity, as though it were a lesser Lourdes. There is often something beautiful, there is always something awful, in the spectacle of a person who has lost one of his faculties, a faculty he never questioned until it was gone, and who struggles to recover it. Yet people remain people, on crutches or indeed on deathbeds; and wherever I passed, the first summer I was here, among the native villagers or among the lame, a wind passed with me—of astonishment, curiosity, amusement, and outrage. That first summer I stayed two weeks and never intended to return. But I did return in the winter, to work; the village offers, obviously, no distractions whatever and has the further advantage of being extremely cheap. Now it is winter again, a year later, and I am here again. Everyone in the village knows my name, though they scarcely ever use it, knows that I come from America—though, this, apparently, they will never really believe: black men come from Africa—and everyone knows that I am the friend of the son of a woman who was born here, and that I am staying in their chalet. But I remain as much a stranger today as I was the first day I arrived, and the children shout *Neger! Neger!* as I walk along the streets.

It must be admitted that in the beginning I was far too shocked to have any real reaction. In so far as I reacted at all, I reacted by trying to be pleasant—it being a great part of the American Negro's education (long before he goes to school) that he must make people "like" him. This smile-and-the-world-smiles-with-you routine worked about as well in this situation as it had in the situation for which it was designed, which is to say that it did not work at all. No one, after all, can be liked whose human weight and complexity cannot be, or has not been, admitted. My smile was simply another unheard-of phenomenon which allowed them to see my teeth—they did not, really, see my smile and I began to think that, should I take to snarling, no one would notice any difference. All of the physical characteristics of the Negro which had caused me, in America, a very different and almost forgotten pain were nothing less than miraculous—or infernal—in the eyes of the village people. Some thought my hair was the color of tar, that it had the texture of wire, or the texture of cotton. It was jocularly suggested that I might let it all grow long and make myself a winter coat. If I sat in the sun for more than five minutes some daring creature was certain to come along and gingerly put his fingers on my hair, as though he were afraid of an electric shock, or put his hand on my hand, astonished that the color did not rub off. In all of this, in which it must be conceded there was the charm of genuine wonder and in which there was certainly no element of intentional unkindness, there was yet no suggestion that I was human: I was simply a living wonder.

I knew that they did not mean to be unkind, and I know it now; it is necessary, nevertheless, for me to repeat this to myself each time that I walk out of the chalet. The children who shout *Neger!* have no way of knowing the echoes this sound raises in me. They are brimming with good humor and the more daring swell with pride when I stop to speak with them. Just the same, there are days when I cannot pause and smile, when I have no heart to play with them; when, indeed, I mutter sourly to myself, exactly as I muttered on the streets of a city these children have never seen, when I was no bigger than these children are now: *Your* mother *was a nigger.* Joyce is right about history being a nightmare—but it may be the nightmare from which no one *can* awaken. People are trapped in history and history is trapped in them.

There is a custom in the village—I am told it is repeated in many villages—of "buying" African natives for the purpose of converting them to Christianity. There stands in the church all year round a small box with a slot for money, decorated with a black figurine, and into this box the villagers drop their francs. During the *carnaval* which precedes Lent, two village children have their faces blackened—out of which bloodless darkness their blue eyes shine like ice—and fantastic horsehair wigs are placed on their blond heads; thus disguised, they solicit among the villagers for money for the missionaries in Africa. Between the box in the church and the blackened children, the village "bought" last year six or eight African natives. This was reported to me with pride by the wife of one of the *bistro* owners and I was careful to express astonishment and pleasure at the solicitude shown by the village for the souls of black folk. The *bistro* owner's wife beamed with a pleasure far more genuine than my own and seemed to feel that I might now breathe more easily concerning the souls of at least six of my kinsmen.

I tried not to think of these so lately baptized kinsmen, of the price paid for them, or the peculiar price they themselves would pay, and said nothing about my father, who having taken his own conversion too literally never, at bottom, forgave the white world (which he described as heathen) for having saddled him with a Christ in whom, to judge at least from their treatment of him, they themselves no longer believed. I thought of white men arriving for the first time in an African village, strangers there, as I am a stranger here, and tried to imagine the astounded populace touching their hair and marveling at the color of their skin. But there is a great difference between being the first white man to be seen by Africans and being the first black man to be seen by whites. The white man takes the astonishment as tribute, for he arrives to conquer and to convert the natives, whose inferiority in relation to himself is not even to be questioned; whereas I, without a thought of conquest, find myself among a people whose culture controls me, has even, in a sense, created me, people who have cost me more in anguish and rage than they will ever know, who yet do not even know of my existence. The astonishment with which I might have greeted them, should they have stumbled into my African village a few hundred years ago, might have rejoiced their hearts. But the astonishment with which they greet me today can only poison mine.

And this is so despite everything I may do to feel differently, despite my friendly conversations with the *bistro* owner's wife, despite their three-year-old son who has at last become my friend, despite the *saluts* and *bonsoirs* which I exchange with people as I walk, despite the fact that I know that no individual can be taken to task for what history is doing, or has done. I say that the culture of these people controls me—but they can scarcely be held responsible for European culture. America comes out of Europe, but these people have never seen America, nor have most of them seen more of Europe than the hamlet at the foot of their mountain. Yet they move with an authority which I shall never have; and they regard me, quite rightly, not only as a stranger in their village but as a suspect latecomer, bearing no credentials, to everything they have—however unconsciously—inherited.

For this village, even were it incomparably more remote and incredibly more primitive, is the West, the West onto which I have been so strangely grafted. These people cannot be, from the point of view of power, strangers anywhere in the world; they have made the modern world, in effect, even if they do not know it. The most illiterate among them is related, in a way that I am not, to Dante, Shakespeare, Michelangelo, Aeschylus, Da Vinci, Rembrandt, and Racine; the cathedral at Chartres says something to them which it cannot say to me, as indeed would New York's Empire State Building, should anyone here ever see it. Out of their hymns and dances come Beethoven and Bach. Go back a few centuries and they are in their full glory—but I am in Africa, watching the conquerors arrive.

The rage of the disesteemed is personally fruitless, but it is also absolutely inevitable; this rage, so generally discounted, so little understood even among the people whose daily bread it is, is one of the things that makes history. Rage can only with difficulty, and never entirely, be brought under the domination of the intelligence and is therefore not susceptible to any arguments whatever. This is a fact which ordinary representatives of the *Herrenvolk*, having never felt this rage and being unable to imagine it, quite fail to understand. Also, rage cannot be hidden, it can only be dissembled. This dissembling deludes the thoughtless, and strengthens rage and adds, to rage, contempt. There are, no doubt, as many ways of coping with the resulting complex of tensions as there are black men in the world, but no black man can hope ever to be entirely liberated from this internal warfare—rage, dissembling, and contempt having inevitably accompanied his first realization of the power of white men. What is crucial here is that, since white men represent in the black man's world so heavy a weight, white men have for black men a reality which is far from being reciprocal; and hence all black men have toward all white men an attitude which is designed, really, either to rob the white man of the jewel of his naïveté, or else to make it cost him dear.

The black man insists, by whatever means he finds at his disposal, that the white man cease to regard him as an exotic rarity and recognize him as a human being. This is a very charged and difficult moment, for there is a great deal of will power involved in the white man's naïveté. Most people are not naturally reflective any more than they are naturally malicious, and the white man prefers to keep the black man at a certain human remove because it is easier for him thus to preserve his simplicity and avoid being called to account for crimes committed by his forefathers, or his neighbors. He is inescapably aware, nevertheless, that he is in a better position in the world than black men are, nor can he quite put to death the suspicion that he is hated by black men therefore. He does not wish to be hated, neither does he wish to change places, and at this point in his uneasiness he can scarcely avoid having recourse to those legends which white men have created about black men, the most usual effect of which is that the white man finds himself enmeshed, so to speak, in his own language which describes hell, as well as the attributes which lead one to hell, as being as black as night.

Every legend, moreover, contains its residuum of truth, and the root function of language is to control the universe by describing it. It is of quite considerable significance that black men remain, in the imagination, and in overwhelming numbers in fact, beyond the disciplines of salvation; and this despite the fact that the West has been "buying" African natives for centuries. There is, I should hazard, an instantaneous necessity to be divorced from this so visibly unsaved stranger, in whose heart, moreover, one cannot guess what dreams of vengeance are being nourished; and, at the same time, there are few things on earth more attractive than the idea of the unspeakable liberty which is allowed the unredeemed. When, beneath the black mask, a human being begins to make himself felt one cannot escape a certain awful wonder as to what kind of human being it is. What one's imagination makes of other people is dictated, of course, by the laws of one's own personality and it is one of the ironies of black-white relations that, by means of what the white man imagines the black man to be, the black man is enabled to know who the white man is.

I have said, for example, that I am as much a stranger in this village today as I was the first summer I arrived, but this is not quite true. The villagers wonder less about the texture of my hair than they did then, and wonder rather more about me. And the fact that their wonder now exists on another level is reflected in their attitudes and in their eyes. There are the children who make those delightful, hilarious, sometimes astonishingly grave overtures of friendship in the unpredictable fashion of children; other children, having been taught that the devil is a black man, scream in genuine anguish as I approach. Some of the older women never pass without a friendly greeting, never pass, indeed, if it seems that they will be able to engage me in conversation; other women look down or look away or rather contemptuously smirk. Some of the men drink with me and suggest that I learn how to ski—partly, I gather, because they cannot imagine what I would look like on skis—and want to know if I am married, and ask questions about my *métier*. But some of the men have accused *le sale negre*—behind my back—of stealing wood and there is already in the eyes of some of them that peculiar, intent, paranoiac malevolence which one sometimes surprises in the eyes of American white men when, out walking with their Sunday girl, they see a Negro male approach.

There is a dreadful abyss between the streets of this village and the streets of the city in which I was born, between the children who shout *Neger!* today and those who shouted *Nigger!* yesterday—the abyss is experience, the American experience. The syllable hurled behind me today expresses, above all, wonder: I am a stranger here. But I am not a stranger in America and the same syllable riding on the American air expresses the war my presence has occasioned in the American soul.

For this village brings home to me this fact: that there was a day, and not really a very distant day, when Americans were scarcely Americans at all but discontented Europeans, facing a great unconquered continent and strolling, say, into a marketplace and seeing black men for the first time. The shock this spectacle afforded is suggested, surely, by the promptness with which they decided that these black men were not really men but cattle. It is true that the necessity on the part of the settlers of the New World of reconciling their moral assumptions with the fact—and the necessity—of slavery enhanced immensely the charm of this idea, and it is also true that this idea expresses, with a truly American bluntness, the attitude which to varying extents all masters have had toward all slaves.

But between all former slaves and slave-owners and the drama which begins for Americans over three hundred years ago at Jamestown, there are at least two differences to be observed. The American Negro slave could not suppose, for one thing, as slaves in past epochs had supposed and often done, that he would ever be able to wrest the power from his master's hands. This was a supposition which the modern era, which was to bring about such vast changes in the aims and dimensions of power, put to death; it only begins, in unprecedented fashion, and with dreadful implications, to be resurrected today. But even had this supposition persisted with undiminished force, the American Negro slave could not have used it to lend his condition dignity, for the reason that this supposition rests on another: that the slave in exile yet remains related to his past, has some means—if only in memory—of revering and sustaining the forms of his former life, is able, in short, to maintain his identity.

This was not the case with the American Negro slave. He is unique among the black men of the world in that his past was taken from him almost literally, at one blow. One wonders what on earth the first slave found to say to the first dark child he bore. I am told that there are Haitians able to trace their ancestry back to African kings, but any American Negro wishing to go back so far will find his journey through time abruptly arrested by the signature on the bill of sale which served as the entrance paper for his ancestor. At the time—to say nothing of the circumstances—of the enslavement of the captive black man who was to become the American Negro, there was not the remotest possibility that he would ever take power from his master's hands. There was no reason to suppose that his situation would ever change, nor was there, shortly, anything to indicate that his situation had ever been different. It was his necessity, in the words of E. Franklin Frazier, to find a "motive for living under American culture or die." The identity of the American Negro comes out of this extreme situation, and the evolution of this identity was a source of the most intolerable anxiety in the minds and the lives of his masters.

For the history of the American Negro is unique also in this: that the question of his humanity, and of his rights therefore as a human being, became a burning one for several generations of Americans, so burning a question that it ultimately became one of those used to divide the nation. It is out of this argument that the venom of the epithet *Nigger!* is derived. It is an argument which Europe has never had, and hence Europe quite sincerely fails to understand how or why the argument arose in the first place, why its effects are so frequently disastrous and always so unpredictable, why it refuses until today to be entirely settled. Europe's black possessions remained—and do remain—in Europe's colonies, at which remove they represented no threat whatever to European identity. If they posed any problem at all for the European conscience, it was a problem which remained comfortingly abstract: in effect, the black man, *as a man,* did not exist for Europe. But in America, even as a slave, he was an inescapable part of the general social fabric and no American could escape having an attitude toward him. Americans attempt until today to make an abstraction of the Negro, but the very nature of these abstractions reveals the tremendous effects the presence of the Negro has had on the American character.

When one considers the history of the Negro in America it is of the greatest importance to recognize that the moral beliefs of a person, or a people, are never really as tenuous as life—which is not moral—very often causes them to appear; these create for them a frame of reference and a necessary hope, the hope being that when life has done its worst they will be enabled to rise above themselves and to triumph over life. Life would scarcely be bearable if this hope did not exist. Again, even when the worst has been said, to betray a belief is not by any means to have put oneself beyond its power; the betrayal of a belief is not the same thing as ceasing to believe. If this were not so there would be no moral standards in the world at all. Yet one must also recognize that morality is based on ideas and that all ideas are dangerous—dangerous because ideas can only lead to action and where the action leads no man can say. And dangerous in this respect: that confronted with the impossibility of remaining faithful to one's beliefs, and the equal impossibility of becoming free of them, one can be driven to the most inhuman excesses. The ideas on which American beliefs are based are not, though Americans often seem to think so, ideas which originated in America. They came out of Europe. And the establishment of democracy on the American continent was scarcely as radical a break with the past as was the necessity, which Americans faced, of broadening this concept to include black men."

This was, literally, a hard necessity. It was impossible, for one thing, for Americans to abandon their beliefs, not only because these beliefs alone seemed able to justify the sacrifices they had endured and the blood that they had spilled, but also because these beliefs afforded them their only bulwark against a moral chaos as absolute as the physical chaos of the continent it was their destiny to conquer. But in the situation in which Americans found themselves, these beliefs threatened an idea which, whether or not one likes to think so, is the very warp and woof of the heritage of the West, the idea of white supremacy.

Americans have made themselves notorious by the shrillness and the brutality with which they have insisted on this idea, but they did not invent it; and it has escaped the world's notice that those very excesses of which Americans have been guilty imply a certain, unprecedented uneasiness over the idea's life and power, if not, indeed, the idea's validity. The idea of white supremacy rests simply on the fact that white men are the creators of civilization (the present civilization, which is the only one that matters; all previous civilizations are simply "contributions" to our own) and are therefore civilization's guardians and defenders. Thus it was impossible for Americans to accept the black man as one of themselves, for to do so was to jeopardize their status as white men. But not so to accept him was to deny his human reality, his human weight and complexity, and the strain of denying the overwhelmingly undeniable forced Americans into rationalizations so fantastic that they approached the pathological.

At the root of the American Negro problem is the necessity of the American white man to find a way of living with the Negro in order to be able to live with himself. And the history of this problem can be reduced to the means used by Americans—lynch law and law, segregation and legal acceptance, terrorization and concession—either to come to terms with this necessity, or to find a way around it, or (most usually) to find a way of doing both these things at once. The resulting spectacle, at once foolish and dreadful, led someone to make the quite accurate observation that "the Negro-in-America is a form of insanity which overtakes white men.

In this long battle, a battle by no means finished, the unforeseeable effects of which will be felt by many future generations, the white man's motive was the protection of his identity; the black man was motivated by the need to establish an identity. And despite the terrorization which the Negro in America endured and endures sporadically until today, despite the cruel and totally inescapable ambivalence of his status in his country, the battle for his identity has long ago been won. He is not a visitor to the West, but a citizen there, an American; as American as the Americans who despise him, the Americans who fear him, the Americans who love him—the Americans who became less than themselves, or rose to be greater than themselves by virtue of the fact that the challenge he represented was inescapable. He is perhaps the only black man in the world whose relationship to white men is more terrible, more subtle, and more meaningful than the relationship of bitter possessed to uncertain possessor. His survival depended, and his development depends, on his ability to turn his peculiar status in the Western world to his own advantage and, it may be, to the very great advantage of that world. It remains for him to fashion out of his experience that which will give him sustenance, and a voice.

The cathedral at Chartres, I have said, says something to the people of this village which it cannot say to me; but it is important to understand that this cathedral says something to me which it cannot say to them. Perhaps they are struck by the power of the spires, the glory of the windows; but they have known God, after all, longer than I have known him, and in a different way; and I am terrified by the slippery bottomless well to be found in the crypt, down which heretics were hurled to death, and by the obscene, inescapable gargoyles jutting out of the stone and seeming to say that God and the devil can never be divorced. I doubt that the villagers think of the devil when they face a cathedral because they have never been identified with the devil. But I must accept the status which myth, if nothing else, gives me in the West before I can hope to change the myth.

Yet, if the American Negro has arrived at his identity by virtue of the absoluteness of his estrangement from his past, American white men still nourish the illusion that there is some means of recovering the European innocence, of returning to a state in which black men do not exist. This is one of the greatest errors Americans can make. The identity they fought so hard to protect has, by virtue of that battle, undergone a change: Americans are as unlike any other white people in the world as it is possible to be. I do not think, for example, that it is too much to suggest that the American vision of the world—which allows so little reality, generally speaking, for any of the darker forces in human life, which tends until today to paint moral issues in glaring black and white—owes a great deal to the battle waged by Americans to maintain between themselves and black men a human separation which could not be bridged. It is only now beginning to be borne in on us—very faintly, it must be admitted, very slowly, and very much against our will—that this vision of the world is dangerously inaccurate, and perfectly useless. For it protects our moral high-mindedness at the terrible expense of weakening our grasp of reality. People who shut their eyes to reality simply invite their own destruction, and anyone who insists on remaining in a state of innocence long after that innocence is dead turns himself into a monster.

The time has come to realize that the interracial drama acted out on the American continent has not only created a new black man, it has created a new white man, too. No road whatever will lead Americans back to the simplicity of this European village where white men still have the luxury of looking on me as a stranger. I am not, really, a stranger any longer for any American alive. One of the things that distinguishes Americans from other people is that no other people has ever been so deeply involved in the lives of black men, and vice versa. This fact faced, with all its implications, it can be seen that the history of the American Negro problem is not merely shameful, it is also something of an achievement. For even when the worst has been said, it must also be added that the perpetual challenge posed by this problem was always, somehow, perpetually met. It is precisely this black-white experience which may prove of indispensable value to us in the world we face today. This world is white no longer, and it will never be white again.

SIMONE DE BEAUVOIR
Woman: Myth and Reality

SIMONE DE BEAUVOIR (1908–1986) was one of the most
important post–World War II French intellectuals. Her work was
primarily philosophical, and she herself taught philosophy and
lived for a time with one of France's preeminent existentialist
philosophers, Jean-Paul Sartre (1905–1980). These two independent and brilliant leftist thinkers represented the ideal couple to
many intellectuals, although recent biographical studies have
demonstrated that in their relationship Beauvoir's ambitions were
subjugated to those of Sartre.

Beauvoir prepared for a career as a teacher at the École Nor-
male Superieure and taught in Marseilles, Rouen, and Paris, all the
while writing novels, memoirs, and essays. Her best-known book is
Le Deuxième Sexe (1949), published in English in 1953 as *The Second Sex*, a book now regarded as a beacon for the modern feminist
movement. When Beauvoir began work on this book, French
women were not permitted to vote (they did not win suffrage until
1945). In *The Second Sex* Beauvoir discusses how women are cast
as the Other, the alienated of society. She explores the implications
of defining women in relation to men — as *what men are not* rather
than as *what women are*, as a category in and of themselves.

According to Beauvoir, a person is not born a woman but
makes herself a woman. This suggestion implies, for Beauvoir, that
the individual is shaped and formed by social convention, especially by conventions associated with gender. Certain conventions
maintain a social fiction that pleases the "ruling caste," which in
Beauvoir's view is exclusively masculine. She compares the myth of
the Eternal Feminine with a Platonic idea. For Plato, the reality of
the world is inferior to the pure ideas that exist in heaven. These

From *The Second Sex*. Translated and edited by H. M. Parshley.

ideas are fixed and unaltered by experience. In that sense, Beauvoir regards the myth of the Eternal Feminine as an idea that does not change, even in the face of human experience that contradicts it.

Part of the idea of the Eternal Feminine involves the myth that women are mysterious and incomprehensible to men; they are completely unlike men and, therefore, the Other. Beauvoir complains that no amount of personal experience seems to shatter the myth of women's mystery. She also states that mysteriousness does not serve women well, nor does it serve men; nevertheless, the concept of mystery lingers. She explains that in the relationship of master to slave, it is always the slave who is mysterious and difficult to understand. The slave is always the Other. Through this logic Beauvoir leads us to understand that as long as the mystery of woman defines her, woman will always be in a subordinate relationship to men.

One important consequence of accepting the myth of woman is that men will fail to understand women as they are—as friends, as equals. Even worse, women who accept the myth will constantly distort their personalities in order to please the "master." Beauvoir asks, which is it that a woman loves: her husband or her marriage? Women who accept the myth will manipulate men for their own purposes by trading on that myth, but in the process they will lose their individual nature, surrendering it to some imagined "immanence." *Immanence* is one of the most frequently repeated words in the essay (see para. 5); by this term, Beauvoir usually means an imagined essential quality, associated here with a myth.

The problem is that the myth of the Eternal Feminine, however it is expressed, contradicts the essential nature of individuals. It is an archetype that cannot be altered even when we see individuals contradicting the archetype. When that happens, Beauvoir says, we assume the individual is aberrant in some way. Beauvoir encourages us to reject the myth of the Eternal Feminine and to accept the reality that presents itself before our eyes. Thus, Beauvoir does not subscribe to the Platonic view; instead she follows the Aristotelian view that prefers examination of a scientific sort, one that accepts perceived facts.

Beauvoir's Rhetoric

This essay makes a plea for equality between men and women on several levels. As society is structured, Beauvoir knows, the concept of equality is impossible. The social order, she tells us, is essentially patriarchal. As a result, women have a subordinate and restricted role that is maintained in part by the persistence of the myth of the Eternal Feminine. Therefore, the general structure of the essay is as an argument decrying the persistence of the myth and revealing the damage that it does to members of society, both men and women.

At the time she wrote this piece, Beauvoir was not known as a feminist. Indeed, in the late 1940s and early 1950s, few modern feminists were known in the United States or in France. Long before Beauvoir aligned herself with certain militant feminists in the 1970s, *The Second Sex* provided a rallying cry because it was a treatise that examined with great authority the representation of women in many different intellectual and cultural arenas. For that reason, the book became a memorable document of great political power. Its rhetoric is not patterned or self-conscious but simple and straightforward. The calm, reasonable, direct style enforces the author's persuasiveness.

Beauvoir's method in this piece is careful analysis of a circumstance that she defines at the outset: the myth of the Eternal Feminine. Once she has described and defined this myth—and in the process established its persistence—she analyzes its character and its implications. Her analysis of the myth's uses in society reveals how it guarantees a woman's subordination. Beauvoir also calls women to task for accepting a myth that ultimately imprisons them. She urges change, suggesting that certain basic transformations may make it possible for men and women to achieve a form of equality that preserves their respective masculinity and femininity without demanding that one become the Other.

Beauvoir has drawn criticism for the tone of her description of women's behavior. Writers such as the poet Stevie Smith have accused Beauvoir of standing aside from the mass of women as if she herself were in a separate category. Some readers and close friends felt that her relationship with Sartre, in which they saw her treated as an absolute equal intellectually, led her to develop a distorted view of the nature of women's subjection and gave her writing a cool, overly reserved, academic quality.

In fact, it is true that this piece is reserved. It is also true, however, that Beauvoir strikes at a given in the social order of mid-century Europe and America. And it is true that she generally talks about women who are in a comfortable social class, women that bell hooks would refer to as bourgeois and privileged. Nonetheless, Beauvoir maintains that as long as women are seen as mysterious and different in a male-dominated world, they will remain subordinate. The myths associated with women may be several, contradictory, and seemingly harmless, but Beauvoir insists they are ultimately damaging to women and to the relationship between the sexes.

One of the most distinctive qualities of *The Second Sex* is its learnedness. Beauvoir avoids giving the impression that she is merely stating opinion by pausing occasionally to make references to important writers such as Auguste Comte, Søren Kierkegaard, André Gide, and Maurice Maeterlinck. Most of the writers she refers to are men, and most are longstanding philosophers and classic authors. By citing such authorities she reveals a capacious mind, one that is not ignorant of the role of male writers and the problems of a society dominated by males.

The power of the piece lies in its clarity and depth of thought. Beauvoir was a consummate intellectual in an environment that nurtured such types of thinkers, and what she has to say demands our attention and respect.

PREREADING QUESTIONS: WHAT TO READ FOR

The following prereading questions may help you anticipate key issues in the discussion on Simone de Beauvoir's "Woman: Myth and Reality." Keeping them in mind during your first reading of the selection should help focus your reactions.

- What is the myth of the Eternal Feminine?
- Why do men prefer the myth of the Eternal Feminine to the reality of women?
- How does men's power benefit from the myth(s) of women?

Woman: Myth and Reality

The myth of woman plays a considerable part in literature; but 1
what is its importance in daily life? To what extent does it affect the customs and conduct of individuals? In replying to this question it will be necessary to state precisely the relations this myth bears to reality.

There are different kinds of myths. This one, the myth of woman, 2
sublimating an immutable aspect of the human condition—namely, the 'division' of humanity into two classes of individuals—is a static

myth. It projects into the realm of Platonic ideas a reality that is directly experienced or is conceptualized on a basis of experience; in place of fact, value, significance, knowledge, empirical law, it substitutes a transcendental Idea, timeless, unchangeable, necessary. This idea is indisputable because it is beyond the given: it is endowed with absolute truth. Thus, as against the dispersed, contingent, and multiple existences of actual women, mythical thought opposes the Eternal Feminine, unique and changeless. If the definition provided for this concept is contradicted by the behavior of flesh-and-blood women, it is the latter who are wrong: we are told not that Femininity is a false entity, but that the women concerned are not feminine. The contrary facts of experience are impotent against the myth. In a way, however, its source is in experience. Thus it is quite true that woman is other than man, and this alterity is directly felt in desire, the embrace, love; but the real relation is one of reciprocity; as such it gives rise to authentic drama. Through eroticism, love, friendship, and their alternatives, deception, hate, rivalry, the relation is a struggle between conscious beings each of whom wishes to be essential, it is the mutual recognition of free beings who confirm one another's freedom, it is the vague transition from aversion to participation. To pose Woman is to pose the absolute Other, without reciprocity, denying against all experience that she is a subject, a fellow human being.

In actuality, of course, women appear under various aspects; ³ but each of the myths built up around the subject of woman is intended to sum her up *in toto;* each aspires to be unique. In consequence, a number of incompatible myths exist, and men tarry musing before the strange incoherencies manifested by the idea of Femininity. As every woman has a share in a majority of these archetypes — each of which lays claim to containing the sole Truth of woman — men of today also are moved again in the presence of their female companions to an astonishment like that of the old sophists who failed to understand how man could be blond and dark at the same time! Transition toward the absolute was indicated long ago in social phenomena: relations are easily congealed in classes, functions in types, just as relations, to the childish mentality, are fixed in things. Patriarchal society, for example, being centered upon the conservation of the patrimony, implies necessarily, along with those who own and transmit wealth, the existence of men and women who take property away from its owners and put it into circulation. The men — adventurers, swindlers, thieves, speculators — are generally repudiated by the group; the women, employing their erotic attraction, can induce young men and even fathers of families to scatter their patrimonies, without ceasing to be within the law. Some of these women appropriate their victims' fortunes or obtain legacies by using undue influence; this role being regarded as evil, those who play it are called 'bad women.' But the fact is that quite to the contrary they are able to appear in some other setting—at home with their fathers, brothers, husbands, or lovers—as guardian angels; and the courtesan who 'plucks' rich financiers is, for painters and writers, a generous patroness. It is easy to understand in actual experience the ambiguous personality of Aspasia or Mme de Pompadour.[1] But if woman is depicted as the Praying Mantis, the Mandrake, the Demon, then it is most confusing to find in woman also the Muse, the Goddess Mother, Beatrice.

As group symbols and social types are generally defined by means of antonyms in pairs, ambivalence will seem to be an intrinsic quality of the Eternal Feminine. The saintly mother has for correlative the cruel stepmother, the angelic young girl has the perverse virgin: thus it will be said sometimes that Mother equals Life, sometimes that Mother equals Death, that every virgin is pure spirit or flesh dedicated to the devil. 4

Evidently it is not reality that dictates to society or to individuals their choice between the two opposed basic categories; in every period, in each case, society and the individual decide in accordance with their needs. Very often they project into the myth adopted the institutions and values to which they adhere. Thus the paternalism that claims woman for hearth and home defines her as sentiment, inwardness, immanence. In fact every existent is at once immanence and transcendence; when one offers the existent no aim, or prevents him from attaining any, or robs him of his victory, then his transcendence falls vainly into the past—that is to say, falls back into immanence. This is the lot assigned to woman in the patriarchate; but it is in no way a vocation, any more than slavery is the vocation of the slave. The development of this mythology is to be clearly seen in Auguste Comte.[2] To identify Woman with Altruism is to guarantee to man absolute rights in her devotion, it is to impose on women a categorical imperative. 5

The myth must not be confused with the recognition of significance; significance is immanent in the object; it is revealed to the mind through a living experience; whereas the myth is a transcendent Idea that escapes the mental grasp entirely. When in *L'Age* 6

---

[1] **Aspasia . . . Mme de Pompadour** Aspasia (5th century B.C.) was mistress to the great Greek statesman, Pericles; Mme. de Pompadour (1721–1764) was mistress to France's Louis XV. Both were powerful women and both were sometimes the object of popular scorn.
[2] **Auguste Comte (1798–1857)** Comte is credited with having founded the study of sociology.

d'homme Michel Leiris[3] describes his vision of the feminine organs, he tells us things of significance and elaborates no myth. Wonder at the feminine body, dislike for menstrual blood, come from perceptions of a concrete reality. There is nothing mythical in the experience that reveals the voluptuous qualities of feminine flesh, and it is not an excursion into myth if one attempts to describe them through comparisons with flowers or pebbles. But to say that Woman is Flesh, to say that the Flesh is Night and Death, or that it is the splendor of the Cosmos, is to abandon terrestrial truth and soar into an empty sky. For man also is flesh for woman; and woman is not merely a carnal object; and the flesh is clothed in special significance for each person and in each experience. And likewise it is quite true that woman—like man—is a being rooted in nature; she is more enslaved to the species than is the male, her animality is more manifest; but in her as in him the given traits are taken on through the fact of existence, she belongs also to the human realm. To assimilate her to Nature is simply to act from prejudice.

Few myths have been more advantageous to the ruling caste   7 than the myth of woman: it justifies all privileges and even authorizes their abuse. Men need not bother themselves with alleviating the pains and the burdens that physiologically are women's lot, since these are 'intended by Nature'; men use them as a pretext for increasing the misery of the feminine lot still further, for instance by refusing to grant to woman any right to sexual pleasure, by making her work like a beast of burden.[4]

Of all these myths, none is more firmly anchored in masculine   8 hearts than that of the feminine 'mystery.' It has numerous advantages. And first of all it permits an easy explanation of all that appears inexplicable; the man who 'does not understand' a woman is happy to substitute an objective resistance for a subjective deficiency of mind; instead of admitting his ignorance, he perceives the presence of a 'mystery' outside himself: an alibi, indeed, that flatters laziness and vanity at once. A heart smitten with love thus avoids many disappointments: if the loved one's behavior is capricious, her remarks stupid, then the mystery serves to excuse it all. And finally, thanks again to the mystery, that negative relation is perpetuated

---

[3] **Michel Leiris (1901–1990)** A popular French writer and art critic.

[4] Cf. Balzac: *Physiology of Marriage:* 'Pay no attention to her murmurs, her cries, her pains; *nature has made her for our use* and for bearing everything: children, sorrows, blows and pains inflicted by man. Do not accuse yourself of hardness. In all the codes of so-called civilized nations, man has written the laws that ranged woman's destiny under this bloody epigraph: *"Vœ victis!* Woe to the weak!" [Beauvoir's note]

which seemed to Kierkegaard[5] infinitely preferable to positive possession; in the company of a living enigma man remains alone — alone with his dreams, his hopes, his fears, his love, his vanity. This subjective game, which can go all the way from vice to mystical ecstasy, is for many a more attractive experience than an authentic relation with a human being. What foundations exist for such a profitable illusion?

Surely woman is, in a sense, mysterious, 'mysterious as is all the world,' according to Maeterlinck.[6] Each is *subject* only for himself; each can grasp in immanence only himself, alone: from this point of view the *other* is always a mystery. To men's eyes the opacity of the self-knowing self, of the *pour-soi*, is denser in the *other* who is feminine; men are unable to penetrate her special experience through any working of sympathy: they are condemned to ignorance of the quality of woman's erotic pleasure, the discomfort of menstruation, and the pains of childbirth. The truth is that there is mystery on both sides: as the *other* who is of masculine sex, every man, also, has within him a presence, an inner self impenetrable to woman; she in turn is in ignorance of the male's erotic feeling. But in accordance with the universal rule I have stated, the categories in which men think of the world are established *from their point of view, as absolute:* they misconceive reciprocity, here as everywhere. A mystery for man, woman is considered to be mysterious in essence.   9

To tell the truth, her situation makes woman very liable to such a view. Her physiological nature is very complex; she herself submits to it as to some rigmarole from outside; her body does not seem to her to be a clear expression of herself; within it she feels herself a stranger. Indeed, the bond that in every individual connects the physiological life and the psychic life — or better the relation existing between the contingence of an individual and the free spirit that assumes it — is the deepest enigma implied in the condition of being human, and this enigma is presented in its most disturbing form in woman.   10

But what is commonly referred to as the mystery is not the subjective solitude of the conscious self, nor the secret organic life. It is on the level of communication that the word has its true meaning: it is not a reduction to pure silence, to darkness, to absence; it implies   11

---

[5] **Søren Kierkegaard (1813 – 1855)** A major Danish philosopher, often credited with having founded the school of philosophy known as existentialism, to which Beauvoir was sympathetic.

[6] **Maurice Maeterlinck (1862 – 1949)** A Belgian playwright whose *Pelleas and Melisande* (1892) was one of the greatest of the symbolist dramas of the late nineteenth century.

a stammering presence that fails to make itself manifest and clear. To say that woman is mystery is to say, not that she is silent, but that her language is not understood; she is there, but hidden behind veils; she exists beyond these uncertain appearances. What is she? Angel, demon, one inspired, an actress? It may be supposed either that there are answers to these questions which are impossible to discover, or, rather, that no answer is adequate because a fundamental ambiguity marks the feminine being; and perhaps in her heart she is even for herself quite indefinable: a sphinx.

The fact is that she would be quite embarrassed to decide *what*   12 she *is;* but this not because the hidden truth is too vague to be discerned: it is because in this domain there is no truth. An existent *is* nothing other than what he does; the possible does not extend beyond the real, essence does not precede existence: in pure subjectivity, the human being *is not anything.* He is to be measured by his acts. Of a peasant woman one can say that she is a good or a bad worker, of an actress that she has or does not have talent; but if one considers a woman in her immanent presence, her inward self, one can say absolutely nothing about her, she falls short of having any qualifications. Now, in amorous or conjugal relations, in all relations where the woman is the vassal, the other, she is being dealt with in her immanence. It is noteworthy that the feminine comrade, colleague, and associate are without mystery; on the other hand, if the vassal is male, if, in the eyes of a man or a woman who is older, or richer, a young fellow, for example, plays the role of the inessential object, then he too becomes shrouded in mystery. And this uncovers for us a substructure under the feminine mystery which is economic in nature.

A sentiment cannot be supposed to *be* anything. 'In the domain   13 of sentiments,' writes Gide,[7] 'the real is not distinguished from the imaginary. And if to imagine one loves is enough to be in love, then also to tell oneself that one imagines oneself to be in love when one is in love is enough to make one forthwith love a little less.' Discrimination between the imaginary and the real can be made only through behavior. Since man occupies a privileged situation in this world, he is in a position to show his love actively; very often he supports the woman or at least helps her; in marrying her he gives her social standing; he makes her presents; his independent economic and social position allows him to take the initiative and think up contrivances: it was M. de Norpois who, when separated from

---

[7] **André Gide (1869–1951)** Gide won the Nobel Prize for Literature in 1947. He was an influential French philosopher, writer, and art critic.

Mme de Villeparisis, made twenty-four-hour trips to visit her. Very often the man is busy, the woman idle: he *gives* her the time he passes with her; she takes it: is it with pleasure, passionately, or only for amusement? Does she accept these benefits through love or through self-interest? Does she love her husband or her marriage? Of course, even the man's evidence is ambiguous: is such and such a gift granted through love or out of pity? But while normally a woman finds numerous advantages in her relations with a man, his relations with a woman are profitable to a man only in so far as he loves her. And so one can almost judge the degree of his affection by the total picture of his attitude.

But a woman hardly has means for sounding her own heart; ac- 14 cording to her moods she will view her own sentiments in different lights, and as she submits to them passively, one interpretation will be no truer than another. In those rare instances in which she holds the position of economic and social privilege, the mystery is reversed, showing that it does not pertain to *one* sex rather than the other, but to the situation. For a great many women the roads to transcendence are blocked: because they *do* nothing, they fail to *make themselves* anything. They wonder indefinitely what they *could have* become, which sets them to asking about what they *are*. It is a vain question. If man fails to discover that secret essence of femininity, it is simply because it does not exist. Kept on the fringe of the world, woman cannot be objectively defined through this world, and her mystery conceals nothing but emptiness.

Furthermore, like all the oppressed, woman deliberately dis- 15 sembles her objective actuality; the slave, the servant, the indigent, all who depend upon the caprices of a master, have learned to turn toward him a changeless smile or an enigmatic impassivity; their real sentiments, their actual behavior, are carefully hidden. And moreover woman is taught from adolescence to lie to men, to scheme, to be wily. In speaking to them she wears an artificial expression on her face; she is cautious, hypocritical, play-acting.

But the Feminine Mystery as recognized in mythical thought is a 16 more profound matter. In fact, it is immediately implied in the mythology of the absolute Other. If it be admitted that the inessential conscious being, too, is a clear subjectivity, capable of performing the *Cogito*,[8] then it is also admitted that this being is in truth sovereign and returns to being essential; in order that all reciprocity may appear quite impossible, it is necessary for the Other to be for

---

[8]***Cogito*** Reference to René Descartes (1596–1650), who "proved" his existence with the Latin phrase, "Cogito, ergo sum"—I think, therefore I am.

itself an other, for its very subjectivity to be affected by its otherness; this consciousness which would be alienated as a consciousness, in its pure immanent presence, would evidently be Mystery. It would be Mystery in itself from the fact that it would be Mystery for itself; it would be absolute Mystery.

In the same way it is true that, beyond the secrecy created by their 17 dissembling, there is mystery in the Black, the Yellow, in so far as they are considered absolutely as the inessential Other. It should be noted that the American citizen, who profoundly baffles the average European, is not, however, considered as being 'mysterious': one states more modestly that one does not understand him. And similarly woman does not always 'understand' man; but there is no such thing as a masculine mystery. The point is that rich America, and the male, are on the Master side and that Mystery belongs to the slave.

To be sure, we can only muse in the twilight byways of bad faith 18 upon the positive reality of the Mystery; like certain marginal hallucinations, it dissolves under the attempt to view it fixedly. Literature always fails in attempting to portray 'mysterious' women; they can appear only at the beginning of a novel as strange, enigmatic figures; but unless the story remains unfinished they give up their secret in the end and they are then simply consistent and transparent persons. The heroes in Peter Cheyney's books, for example, never cease to be astonished at the unpredictable caprices of women: no one can ever guess how they will act, they upset all calculations. The fact is that once the springs of their action are revealed to the reader, they are seen to be very simple mechanisms: this woman was a spy, that one a thief; however clever the plot, there is always a key; and it could not be otherwise, had the author all the talent and imagination in the world. Mystery is never more than a mirage that vanishes as we draw near to look at it.

We can see now that the myth is in large part explained by its 19 usefulness to man. The myth of woman is a luxury. It can appear only if man escapes from the urgent demands of his needs; the more relationships are concretely lived, the less they are idealized. The fellah of ancient Egypt, the Bedouin peasant, the artisan of the Middle Ages, the worker of today has in the requirements of work and poverty relations with his particular woman companion which are too definite for her to be embellished with an aura either auspicious or inauspicious. The epochs and the social classes that have been marked by the leisure to dream have been the ones to set up the images, black and white, of femininity. But along with luxury there was utility; these dreams were irresistibly guided by interests. Surely most of the myths had roots in the spontaneous attitude of man toward his own existence and toward the world around him. But going beyond experience toward the transcendent Idea was deliberately used by patriarchal society for purposes of self-justification; through the myths this society imposed its laws and customs upon individuals in a picturesque, effective manner; it is under a mythical form that the group-imperative is indoctrinated into each conscience. Through such intermediaries as religions, traditions, language, tales, songs, movies, the myths penetrate even into such existences as are most harshly enslaved to material realities. Here everyone can find sublimation of his drab experiences: deceived by the woman he loves, one declares that she is a Crazy Womb; another, obsessed by his impotence, calls her a Praying Mantis; still another enjoys his wife's company: behold, she is Harmony, Rest, the Good Earth! The taste for eternity at a bargain, for a pocket-sized absolute, which is shared by a majority of men, is satisfied by myths. The smallest emotion, a slight annoyance, becomes the reflection of a timeless Idea—an illusion agreeably flattering to the vanity.

The myth is one of those snares of false objectivity into which   20
the man who depends on ready-made valuations rushes headlong. Here again we have to do with the substitution of a set idol for actual experience and the free judgments it requires. For an authentic relation with an autonomous existent, the myth of Woman substitutes the fixed contemplation of a mirage. 'Mirage! Mirage!' cries Laforgue.[9] 'We should kill them since we cannot comprehend them; or better tranquilize them, instruct them, make them give up their taste for jewels, make them our genuinely equal comrades, our intimate friends, real associates here below, dress them differently, cut their hair short, say anything and everything to them.' Man would have nothing to lose, quite the contrary, if he gave up disguising woman as a symbol. When dreams are official community affairs, clichés, they are poor and monotonous indeed beside the living reality; for the true dreamer, for the poet, woman is a more generous fount than is any down-at-heel marvel. The times that have most sincerely treasured women are not the period of feudal chivalry nor yet the gallant nineteenth century. They are the times—like the eighteenth century—when men have regarded women as fellow creatures; then it is that women seem truly romantic, as the reading of *Liaisons dangereuses, Le Rouge et le noir, Farewell to Arms*, is sufficient to show. The heroines of Laclos, Stendhal, Hemingway[10] are

---

[9] **Jules Laforgue (1860–1887)** A French symbolist poet.
[10] **Pierre Choderlos de Laclos (1741–1803), Stendhal (1783–1842), Ernest Hemingway (1899–1961)** Laclos was a French novelist who wrote *Dangerous Liaisons* and *On the Education of Women*; Stendhal was the pen name of Marie-Henri Beyle, a French novelist who wrote *The Red and the Black* and *The Charterhouse of Parma*; Ernest Hemingway an important twentieth-century American novelist, who wrote *The Sun Also Rises* and *Farewell to Arms*.

without mystery, and they are not the less engaging for that. To recognize in woman a human being is not to impoverish man's experience: this would lose none of its diversity, its richness, or its intensity if it were to occur between two subjectivities. To discard the myths is not to destroy all dramatic relation between the sexes, it is not to deny the significance authentically revealed to man through feminine reality; it is not to do away with poetry, love, adventure, happiness, dreaming. It is simply to ask that behavior, sentiment, passion be founded upon the truth.[11]

'Woman is lost. Where are the women? The women of today are   21 not women at all!' We have seen what these mysterious slogans mean. In men's eyes—and for the legion of women who see through men's eyes—it is not enough to have a woman's body nor to assume the female function as mistress or mother in order to be a 'true woman.' In sexuality and maternity woman as subject can claim autonomy; but to be a 'true woman' she must accept herself as the Other. The men of today show a certain duplicity of attitude which is painfully lacerating to women; they are willing on the whole to accept woman as a fellow being, an equal; but they still require her to remain the inessential. For her these two destinies are incompatible; she hesitates between one and the other without being exactly adapted to either, and from this comes her lack of equilibrium. With man there is no break between public and private life: the more he confirms his grasp on the world in action and in work, the more virile he seems to be; human and vital values are combined in him. Whereas woman's independent successes are in contradiction with her femininity, since the 'true woman' is required to make herself object, to be the Other.

It is quite possible that in this matter man's sensibility and sexu-   22 ality are being modified. A new æsthetics has already been born. If the fashion of flat chests and narrow hips—the boyish form—has had its brief season, at least the overopulent ideal of past centuries has not returned. The feminine body is asked to be flesh, but with discretion; it is to be slender and not loaded with fat; muscular, supple, strong, it is bound to suggest transcendence; it must not be pale like a too shaded hothouse plant, but preferably tanned like a workman's torso from being bared to the open sun. Woman's dress in becoming practical need not make her appear sexless: on the contrary, short skirts made the most of legs and thighs as never before.

---

[11] Laforgue goes on to say regarding woman: 'Since she has been left in slavery, idleness, without occupation or weapon other than her sex, she has over-developed this aspect and has become the Feminine. . . . We have permitted this hypertrophy; she is here in the world for our benefit. . . . Well! that is all wrong. . . . Up to now we have played with woman as if she were a doll. This has lasted altogether too long! . . .' [Beauvoir's note]

There is no reason why working should take away woman's sex appeal.[12] It may be disturbing to contemplate woman as at once a social personage and carnal prey: in a recent series of drawings by Peynet (1948), we see a young man break his engagement because he was seduced by the pretty mayoress who was getting ready to officiate at his marriage. For a woman to hold some 'man's position' and be desirable at the same time has long been a subject for more or less ribald joking; but gradually the impropriety and the irony have become blunted, and it would seem that a new form of eroticism is coming into being — perhaps it will give rise to new myths.

What is certain is that today it is very difficult for women to ac-   23
cept at the same time their status as autonomous individuals and their womanly destiny; this is the source of the blundering and restlessness which sometimes cause them to be considered a 'lost sex.' And no doubt it is more comfortable to submit to a blind enslavement than to work for liberation: the dead, for that matter, are better adapted to the earth than are the living. In all respects a return to the past is no more possible than it is desirable. What must be hoped for is that the men for their part will unreservedly accept the situation that is coming into existence; only then will women be able to live in that situation without anguish. Then Laforgue's prayer will be answered: 'Ah, young women, when will you be our brothers, our brothers in intimacy without ulterior thought of exploitation? When shall we clasp hands truly?' Then Breton's 'Mélusine, no longer under the weight of the calamity let loose upon her by man alone, Mélusine set free . . .' will regain 'her place in humanity.' Then she will be a full human being, 'when,' to quote a letter of Rimbaud,[13] the infinite bondage of woman is broken, when she will live in and for herself, man — hitherto detestable — having let her go free.'

QUESTIONS FOR CRITICAL READING

1. What do you understand to be the myth of the Eternal Feminine?
2. In what literary works or films have you seen the myth of woman illustrated?
3. What role does mystery play in the relationship of men to women?
4. Does a myth of the Eternal Masculine exist?
5. What are some of the contradictory aspects of myths about women?
6. What is the patrimony that Beauvoir refers to in paragraph 3, and how does it shape social experience?

---

[12] A point that hardly needs to be made in America, where even cursory acquaintance with any well-staffed business office will afford confirmatory evidence. [Translator's note]

[13] **Arthur Rimbaud (1854–1891)** A French symbolist poet of great imaginative power.

7. Do you think people actually maintain the myth of the Eternal Feminine today?

8. What is Beauvoir's strongest argument for eliminating the myth of the Eternal Feminine?

SUGGESTIONS FOR WRITING

1. Beauvoir points out that whatever the myth of woman might be, it "is intended to sum her up *in toto*" (para. 3). Therefore, she says, there will be necessary contradictions in myths that disagree with each other. Give some examples of what Beauvoir means, and show how they might affect the behavior of those who accept such myths. If possible, draw on experiences of your own to demonstrate how people who accept the myths behave.

2. Explain the very important concept that Beauvoir outlines in paragraph 3 concerning the role of patrimony in "patriarchal society." She refers to moneyed families that pass down their wealth to their sons and expect that those sons will in turn pass it to their own sons. The role of women in this system is obviously restricted. How does Beauvoir treat this issue? How important do you think it is? Why do you think the words *patrimony* and *matrimony* have such distinct meanings for men and women?

3. Beauvoir says, "group symbols and social types are generally defined by means of antonyms in pairs" (para. 4). What symbols can you define that exist in contradictory types? How do they work? What effect are they likely to have on people's behavior? One obvious contradiction is to see woman as either virgin or whore, but nothing in between. Do such contradictions exist in your own social circle? Do such contradictions surprise you? Has your social group made progress in dealing with social symbols of this type?

4. Beauvoir says again and again that reality and experience do not seem to affect the way people think about women. The myths, in other words, stand for reality and seem more powerful than reality. Do you agree with this assertion? Can you see evidence of that behavior at work in your own social experience? Do you know people who seem to ignore reality and prefer the myth?

5. Beauvoir says that woman's "animality is more manifest" than man's (para. 6). Examine this statement, and decide first what she means. Then decide if she is convincing. Take a stand yourself, and treat the issue with some thoroughness. Avoid oversimplifying your position; try to impart an understanding of the complexity of Beauvoir's statement.

6. Why has the "myth of woman" been advantageous for the "ruling caste"? Beauvoir says that no feminine myth "is more firmly anchored in masculine hearts than that of the feminine 'mystery'" (para. 8). How true is this statement? Why is belief in such a myth of advantage for men? How does it "justify all privileges" and authorize their "abuse" (para. 7)?

THOMAS JEFFERSON
The Declaration of Independence

THOMAS JEFFERSON (1743 – 1826) authored one of the most memorable statements in American history: the Declaration of Independence. He composed the work in 1776 under the watchful eyes of Benjamin Franklin, John Adams, and the rest of the Continental Congress, which spent two and a half days going over every word. Although the substance of the document was developed in committee, Jefferson, because of the grace of his writing style, was selected to craft the actual wording.

Jefferson rose to eminence in a time of great political upheaval. By the time he took a seat in the Virginia legislature in 1769, the colony was already on the course toward revolution. His pamphlet "A Summary View of the Rights of British America" (1774) brought him to the attention of those who were agitating for independence and established him as an ardent republican and revolutionary. In 1779 he was elected governor of Virginia. After the Revolutionary War he moved into the national political arena as the first secretary of state (1790 – 1793). He then served as John Adams's vice president (1797 – 1801) and was himself elected president in 1800. Perhaps one of his greatest achievements during his two terms (1801 – 1809) in office was his negotiation of the Louisiana Purchase, in which the United States acquired 828,000 square miles of land west of the Mississippi from France for about $15 million.

One of the fundamental paradoxes of Jefferson's personal and political life has been his attitude toward slavery. Like most wealthy Virginians, Jefferson owned slaves. However, in 1784 he tried to abolish slavery in the western territories that were being added to the United States. His "Report on Government for the Western Territory" failed by one vote. Historians have pointed out that Jefferson had an affair with Sally Hemmings, a mulatto slave who traveled with him abroad, and fathered several of her children.

However unclear his personal convictions, many of Jefferson's accomplishments, which extend from politics to agriculture and mechanical invention, still stand. One of the most versatile Americans of any generation, he wrote a book, *Notes on Virginia* (1782); designed and built Monticello, his famous homestead in Virginia; and in large part founded and designed the University of Virginia (1819).

Despite their revolutionary nature, the ideas Jefferson expressed in the Declaration of Independence were not entirely original. Rousseau's republican philosophies greatly influenced the work. When Jefferson states in the second paragraph that "all men are created equal, that they are endowed by their Creator with certain unalienable rights," he reflects Rousseau's emphasis on the political equality of men and on protecting certain fundamental rights (see Rousseau beginning with paragraph 39, p. 66). Jefferson also wrote that "Governments are instituted among Men, deriving their just powers from the consent of the governed." This is one of Rousseau's primary points, although it was Jefferson who immortalized it in these words.

Jefferson's Rhetoric

Jefferson's techniques include the use of the periodic sentence, which was especially typical of the age. The first sentence of the Declaration of Independence is periodic—that is, it is long and carefully balanced, and the main point comes at the end. Such sentences are not popular today, although an occasional periodic sentence can still be powerful in contemporary prose. Jefferson's first sentence says (in paraphrase): When one nation must sever its relations with a parent nation...and stand as an independent nation itself...the causes ought to be explained. Moreover, the main body of the Declaration of Independence lists the "causes" that lead to the final and most important element of the sentence. Causal analysis was a method associated with legal thought and reflects his training in eighteenth-century legal analysis. One understood things best when one understood their causes.

The periodic sentence demands certain qualities of balance and parallelism that all good writers should heed. The first sentence in paragraph 2 demonstrates both qualities. The balance is achieved by making each part of the sentence roughly the same length. The parallelism is achieved by linking words in deliberate repetition for effect (they are in italicized type in the following analysis). Note how the "truths" mentioned in the first clause are enumerated in the succession of noun clauses beginning with "that"; "Rights" are enumerated in the final clause:

> We hold these truths to be self evident,
>   *that* all men are created equal,
>   *that* they are endowed by their Creator with certain unalienable Rights,
>   *that* among these are Life, Liberty and the pursuit of Happiness.

Parallelism is one of the greatest stylistic techniques available to a writer sensitive to rhetoric. It is a natural technique: many untrained writers and speakers develop it on their own. The periodicity of the sentences and the balance of their parallelism suggest thoughtfulness, wisdom, and control.

Parallelism creates a natural link to the useful device of enumeration, or listing. Many writers using this technique establish their purpose from the outset— "I wish to address three important issues..."—and then number them: "First, I want to say...Second...," and so on. Jefferson devotes paragraphs 3 through 29 to enumerating the "causes" he mentions in paragraph 1. Each one constitutes a separate paragraph; thus, each has separate weight and importance. Each begins with "He" or "For" and is therefore in parallel structure. The technique of repetition of the same words at the beginning of successive lines is called *anaphora*. Jefferson's use of anaphora here is one of the best known and most effective in all literature. The "He" referred to is Britain's King George III (1738 – 1820), who is never mentioned by name. Congress is opposed not to a personality but to the sovereign of a nation that is oppressing the United States and a tyrant who is not dignified by being named. The "For" introduces grievous acts the king has given his assent to; these are offenses against the colonies.

However, Jefferson does not develop the causes in detail. We do not have specific information about what trade was cut off by the British, what taxes were imposed without consent, or how King George waged war or abdicated government in the colonies. Presumably, Jefferson's audience knew the details and was led by the twenty-seven paragraphs to observe how numerous the causes were. And all are serious; any one alone was enough cause for revolution. The effect of Jefferson's enumeration is to illustrate the patience of the colonies up to this point and to tell the world that the colonies have finally lost patience on account of the reasons listed. The Declaration of Independence projects the careful meditations and decisions of exceptionally calm, patient, and reasonable people.

PREREADING QUESTIONS:
WHAT TO READ FOR

The following prereading questions may help you anticipate key issues in the discussion on Thomas Jefferson's Declaration of Independence. Keeping them in mind during your first reading of the selection should help focus your reactions.

- Under what conditions may a people alter or abolish their government?
- Why does Jefferson consider King George a tyrant?

The Declaration of Independence

In Congress, July 4, 1776

The Unanimous Declaration of the Thirteen United States of America

When in the Course of human events, it becomes necessary for 1 one people to dissolve the political bands which have connected them with another, and to assume among the Powers of the earth, the separate and equal station to which the Laws of Nature and of Nature's God entitle them, a decent respect to the opinions of mankind requires that they should declare the causes which impel them to the separation.

We hold these truths to be self-evident, that all men are created 2 equal, that they are endowed by their Creator with certain inalienable Rights, that among these are Life, Liberty and the pursuit of Happiness. That to secure these rights, Governments are instituted among Men, deriving their just powers from the consent of the governed. That whenever any Form of Government becomes destructive of these ends, it is the Right of the People to alter or to abolish it, and to institute new Government, laying its foundation on such principles and organizing its powers in such form, as to them shall seem most likely to effect their Safety and Happiness. Prudence, indeed, will dictate that Governments long established should not be changed for light and transient causes; and accordingly all experience hath shown, that mankind are more disposed to suffer, while evils are sufferable, than to right themselves by abolishing the forms to which they are accustomed. But when a long train of abuses and usurpations, pursuing invariably the same Object evinces a design to reduce them under absolute Despotism, it is their right, it is their duty, to throw off such Government, and to provide new Guards for their future security. — Such has been the patient sufferance of these Colonies; and such is now the necessity which constrains them to alter their former Systems of Government. The history of the present King of Great Britain is a history of repeated injuries and usurpations, all having in direct object the establishment of an absolute Tyranny over these States. To prove this, let Facts be submitted to a candid world.

He has refused his Assent to Laws, the most wholesome and necessary for the public good. 3

He has forbidden his Governors to pass Laws of immediate and pressing importance, unless suspended in their operation till his Assent should be obtained; and when so suspended, he has utterly neglected to attend to them. 4

He has refused to pass other laws for the accommodation of large districts of people, unless those people would relinquish the right of Representation in the Legislature, a right inestimable to them and formidable to tyrants only. 5

He has called together legislative bodies at places unusual, uncomfortable, and distant from the depository of their Public Records, for the sole purpose of fatiguing them into compliance with his measures. 6

He has dissolved Representative Houses repeatedly, for opposing with manly firmness his invasions on the rights of the people. 7

He has refused for a long time, after such dissolutions, to cause others to be elected; whereby the Legislative Powers, incapable of Annihilation, have returned to the People at large for their exercise; the State remaining in the mean time exposed to all the dangers of invasion from without, and convulsions within. 8

He has endeavoured to prevent the population of these States;[1] for that purpose obstructing the Laws for Naturalization of Foreigners; refusing to pass others to encourage their migration hither, and raising the conditions of new Appropriations of Lands. 9

He has obstructed the Administration of Justice, by refusing his Assent to Laws for establishing Judiciary Powers. 10

He has made Judges dependent on his Will alone, for the tenure of their offices, and the amount and payment of their salaries. 11

He has erected a multitude of New Offices, and sent hither swarms of Officers to harass our People, and eat out their substance. 12

---

[1] **prevent the population of these States** This meant limiting emigration to the Colonies, thus controlling their growth.

He has kept among us, in times of peace, Standing Armies with- 13
out the Consent of our legislature.

He has affected to render the Military independent of and supe- 14
rior to the Civil Power.

He has combined with others to subject us to a jurisdiction for- 15
eign to our constitution, and unacknowledged by our laws; giving
his Assent to their acts of pretended Legislation:

For quartering large bodies of armed troops among us: 16

For protecting them, by a mock Trial, from Punishment for any 17
Murders which they should commit on the Inhabitants of these
States:

For cutting off our Trade with all parts of the world: 18

For imposing taxes on us without our Consent: 19

For depriving us in many cases, of the benefits of Trial by Jury: 20

For transporting us beyond Seas to be tried for pretended of- 21
fences:

For abolishing the free System of English Laws in a neighbour- 22
ing Province, establishing therein an Arbitrary government, and enlarging its Boundaries so as to render it at once an example and fit
instrument for introducing the same absolute rule into these
Colonies:

For taking away our Charters, abolishing our most valuable 23
Laws, and altering fundamentally the Forms of our Governments:

For suspending our own Legislatures, and declaring themselves 24
invested with Power to legislate for us in all cases whatsoever.

He has abdicated Government here, by declaring us out of his 25
Protection and waging War against us.

He has plundered our seas, ravaged our Coasts, burnt our 26
towns, and destroyed the lives of our people.

He is at this time transporting large armies of foreign mercenar- 27
ies to compleat the works of death, desolation and tyranny, already
begun with circumstances of Cruelty & perfidy scarcely paralleled in
the most barbarous ages, and totally unworthy the Head of a civilized nation.

He has constrained our fellow Citizens taken Captive on the 28
high Seas to bear Arms against their Country, to become the execu-
tioners of their friends and Brethren, or to fall themselves by their
Hands.

He has excited domestic insurrections amongst us, and has en- 29
deavoured to bring on the inhabitants of our frontiers, the merciless
Indian Savages, whose known rule of warfare, is an undistinguished
destruction of all ages, sexes and conditions.

In every stage of these Oppressions We have Petitioned for Re- 30
dress in the most humble terms: Our repeated Petitions have been

answered only by repeated injury. A Prince, whose character is thus marked by every act which may define a Tyrant, is unfit to be the ruler of a free People.

Nor have We been wanting in attention to our British brethren. We have warned them from time to time of attempts by their legislature to extend an unwarrantable jurisdiction over us. We have reminded them of the circumstances of our emigration and settlement here. We have appealed to their native justice and magnanimity, and we have conjured them by the ties of our common kindred to disavow these usurpations, which, would inevitably interrupt our connections and correspondence. They too have been deaf to the voice of justice and of consanguinity. We must, therefore, acquiesce in the necessity, which denounces our Separation, and hold them, as we hold the rest of mankind, Enemies in War, in Peace Friends.   31

We, therefore, the Representatives of the United States of America, in General Congress, Assembled, appealing to the Supreme Judge of the world for the rectitude of our intentions, do, in the Name, and by Authority of the good People of these Colonies, solemnly publish and declare, That these United Colonies are, and of Right ought to be Free and Independent States, that they are Absolved from all Allegiance to the British Crown, and that all political connection between them and the State of Great Britain, is and ought to be totally dissolved; and that as Free and Independent States, they have full Power to levy War, conclude Peace, contract Alliances, establish Commerce, and to do all other Acts and Things which Independent States may of right do. And for the support of this Declaration, with a firm reliance on the Protection of Divine Providence, we mutually pledge to each other our Lives, our Fortunes and our sacred Honor.   32

QUESTIONS FOR CRITICAL READING

1. What laws of nature does Jefferson refer to in paragraph 1?
2. What do you think Jefferson feels is the function of government (para. 2)?
3. What does Jefferson say about women? Is there any way you can determine his views from reading this document? Does he appear to favor a patriarchal system?
4. Find at least one use of parallel structure in the Declaration (see p. 76 in the section on Jefferson's Rhetoric for a description of parallelism). What key terms are repeated in identical or equivalent constructions, and to what effect?

5. Which causes listed in paragraphs 3 through 29 are the most serious? Are any trivial? Which ones are serious enough to cause a revolution?
6. What do you consider to be the most graceful sentence in the entire Declaration? Where is it placed in the Declaration? What purpose does it serve there?
7. In what ways does the king's desire for stable government interfere with Jefferson's sense of his own independence?

SUGGESTIONS FOR WRITING

1. Jefferson defines the inalienable rights of a citizen as "Life, Liberty and the pursuit of Happiness." Do you think these are indeed unalienable rights? Answer this question by including some sentences that use parallel structure and repeat key terms in similar constructions. Be certain that you define each of these rights both for yourself and for our time.
2. Write an essay discussing what you feel the function of government should be. Include at least three periodic sentences (underline them). You may first want to establish Jefferson's view of government and then compare or contrast it with your own.
3. Jefferson envisioned a government that allowed its citizens to exercise their rights to life, liberty, and the pursuit of happiness. Has Jefferson's revolutionary vision been achieved in America? Begin with a definition of these three key terms: "life," "liberty," and "the pursuit of happiness." Then, for each term use examples—drawn from current events, your own experience, American history—to take a clear and well-argued stand on whether the nation has achieved Jefferson's goal.
4. Slavery was legal in America in 1776, and Jefferson reluctantly owned slaves. He never presented his plan for gradual emancipation of the slaves to Congress because he realized that Congress would never approve it. But Jefferson and Franklin did finance a plan to buy slaves and return them to Africa, where in 1821 returning slaves founded the nation of Liberia. Agree or disagree with the following statement and defend your position: the ownership of slaves by the people who wrote the Declaration of Independence invalidates it. You may wish to read the relevant chapters on Jefferson and slavery in Merrill D. Peterson's *Thomas Jefferson and the New Nation* (1970).
5. What kind of government does Jefferson seem to prefer? In what ways would his government differ from that of the king he is reacting against? Is he talking about an entirely different system or about the same system but with a different kind of "prince" at the head? How would Jefferson protect the individual against the whim of the state, while also protecting the state against the whim of the individual?

MARTIN LUTHER KING JR.
Letter from Birmingham Jail

MARTIN LUTHER KING JR. (1929–1968) was the most influential civil rights leader in America for a period of more than fifteen years. He was an ordained minister with a doctorate in theology from Boston University. He worked primarily in the South, where he labored steadily to overthrow laws that promoted segregation and to increase the number of black voters registered in southern communities.

From 1958 to 1968 demonstrations and actions opened up opportunities for African Americans who in the South hitherto had been prohibited from sitting in certain sections of buses, using facilities such as water fountains in bus stations, and sitting at luncheon counters with whites. Such laws—unjust and insulting, not to mention unconstitutional—were not challenged by local authorities. Martin Luther King Jr., who became famous for supporting a program to integrate buses in Montgomery, Alabama, was asked by the Southern Christian Leadership Conference (SCLC) to assist in the fight for civil rights in Birmingham, Alabama, where an SCLC meeting was to be held.

King was arrested as the result of a program of sit-ins at luncheon counters and wrote the letter printed here to a group of clergymen who had criticized his position. King had been arrested before and would be arrested again—resembling Thoreau somewhat in his attitude toward laws that did not conform to moral justice.

King, like Thoreau, was willing to suffer for his views, especially when he found himself faced with punitive laws denying civil rights to all citizens. His is a classic case in which the officers of the government pled that they were dedicated to maintaining a stable civil society, even as they restricted King's individual rights. In 1963, many of the good people to whom King addressed this letter firmly believed that peace and order might be threatened by granting African Americans the true independence and freedom that King insisted were their rights and indeed were guaranteed under the constitution. This is why King's letter objects to an injustice that was rampant in Frederick Douglass's time but inexcusable in the time of John F. Kennedy.

Eventually the causes King promoted were victorious. His efforts helped change attitudes in the South and spur legislation that has benefited all Americans. His views concerning nonviolence spread throughout the world, and by the early 1960s he had become famous as a man who stood for human rights and human dignity virtually everywhere. He won the Nobel Peace Prize in 1964.

Although King himself was nonviolent, his program left both him and his followers open to the threat of violence. The sit-ins and voter registration programs spurred countless bombings, threats, and murders by members of the white community. King's life was often threatened, his home bombed, his followers harassed. He was assassinated at the Lorraine Motel in Memphis, Tennessee, on April 4, 1968. But before he died he saw—largely through his own efforts, influence, and example—the face of America change.

King's Rhetoric

The most obvious rhetorical tradition King assumes in this important work is that of the books of the Bible that were originally letters, such as Paul's Epistle to the Ephesians and his several letters to the Corinthians. Many of Paul's letters were written while he was in prison in Rome, and he established a moral position that could inspire the citizens who received the letters. At the same time Paul carried out the most important work of the early Christian church—spreading the word of Jesus to those who wished to be Christians but who needed clarification and encouragement.

It is not clear that the clergymen who received King's letter fully appreciated the rhetorical tradition he drew upon—but they were men who preached from the Bible and certainly should have understood it. The text itself alludes to the mission of Paul and to his communications to his people. King works with this rhetorical tradition not only because it is effective but because it resonates with the deepest aspect of his calling—spreading the gospel of Christ. Brotherhood and justice were his message.

King's tone is one of utmost patience with his critics. He seems bent on winning them over to his point of view, just as he seems confident that—because they are, like him, clergymen—their goodwill should help them see the justice of his views.

His method is that of careful reasoning, focusing on the substance of their criticism, particularly on their complaints that his actions were "unwise and untimely" (para. 1). King takes each of those charges in turn, carefully analyzes it against his position, and then follows with the clearest possible statement of his own views and why he feels they are worth adhering to. The "Letter from Birmingham Jail" is a model of close and reasonable analysis of a very complex situation. It succeeds largely because it remains concrete, treating one issue after another carefully, refusing to be caught up in passion or posturing. Above all, King remains grounded in logic, convinced that his arguments will in turn convince his audience.

PREREADING QUESTIONS: WHAT TO READ FOR

The following prereading questions may help you anticipate key issues in the discussion on Martin Luther King's "Letter from Birmingham Jail." Keeping them in mind during your first reading of the selection should help focus your reactions.

- What kind of injustice did Martin Luther King find in Birmingham?
- Why was Martin Luther King disappointed in the white churches?

Letter from Birmingham Jail

April 16, 1963

MY DEAR FELLOW CLERGYMEN:[1]

While confined here in the Birmingham city jail, I came across   1
your recent statement calling my present activities "unwise and untimely." Seldom do I pause to answer criticism of my work and

---

[1] This response to a published statement by eight fellow clergymen from Alabama (Bishop C. C. J. Carpenter, Bishop Joseph A. Durick, Rabbi Hilton L. Grafman, Bishop Paul Hardin, Bishop Holan B. Harmon, the Reverend George M. Murray, the Reverend Edward V. Ramage, and the Reverend Earl Stallings) was composed under somewhat constricting circumstances. Begun on the margins of the newspaper in which the statement appeared while I was in jail, the letter was continued on scraps of writing paper supplied by a friendly Negro trusty, and concluded on a pad my attorneys were eventually permitted to leave me. Although the text remains in substance unaltered, I have indulged in the author's prerogative of polishing it for publication. [King's note]

ideas. If I sought to answer all the criticisms that cross my desk, my secretaries would have little time for anything other than such correspondence in the course of the day, and I would have no time for constructive work. But since I feel that you are men of genuine good will and that your criticisms are sincerely set forth, I want to try to answer your statement in what I hope will be patient and reasonable terms.

I think I should indicate why I am here in Birmingham, since 2 you have been influenced by the view which argues against "outsiders coming in." I have the honor of serving as president of the Southern Christian Leadership Conference, an organization operating in every southern state, with headquarters in Atlanta, Georgia. We have some eighty-five affiliated organizations across the South, and one of them is the Alabama Christian Movement for Human Rights. Frequently we share staff, educational, and financial resources with our affiliates. Several months ago the affiliate here in Birmingham asked us to be on call to engage in a nonviolent direct-action program if such were deemed necessary. We readily consented, and when the hour came we lived up to our promise. So I, along with several members of my staff, am here because I was invited here. I am here because I have organizational ties here.

But more basically, I am in Birmingham because injustice is 3 here. Just as the prophets of the eighth century B.C. left their villages and carried their "thus saith the Lord" far beyond the boundaries of their home towns, and just as the Apostle Paul left his village of Tarsus[2] and carried the gospel of Jesus Christ to the far corners of the Greco-Roman world, so am I compelled to carry the gospel of freedom beyond my own home town. Like Paul, I must constantly respond to the Macedonian call for aid.[3]

Moreover, I am cognizant of the interrelatedness of all commu- 4 nities and states. I cannot sit idly by in Atlanta and not be concerned about what happens in Birmingham. Injustice anywhere is a threat to justice everywhere. We are caught in an inescapable network of mutuality, tied in a single garment of destiny. Whatever affects one directly, affects all indirectly. Never again can we afford to live with the narrow, provincial, "outside agitator" idea. Anyone who lives

---

[2] **village of Tarsus** Birthplace of St. Paul (? – A.D. 67), in Asia Minor, present-day Turkey, close to Syria.

[3] **the Macedonian call for aid** The citizens of Philippi, in Macedonia (northern Greece), were among the staunchest Christians. Paul went to their aid frequently; he also had to resolve occasional bitter disputes within the Christian community there (see Philippians 2:2 – 14).

inside the United States can never be considered an outsider anywhere within its bounds.

You deplore the demonstrations taking place in Birmingham. 5
But your statement, I am sorry to say, fails to express a similar concern for the conditions that brought about the demonstrations. I am
sure that none of you would want to rest content with the superficial
kind of social analysis that deals merely with effects and does not
grapple with underlying causes. It is unfortunate that demonstrations are taking place in Birmingham, but it is even more unfortunate that the city's white power structure left the Negro community
with no alternative.

In any nonviolent campaign there are four basic steps: collec- 6
tion of the facts to determine whether injustices exist; negotiation;
self-purification; and direct action. We have gone through all these
steps in Birmingham. There can be no gainsaying the fact that racial
injustice engulfs this community. Birmingham is probably the most
thoroughly segregated city in the United States. Its ugly record of
brutality is widely known. Negroes have experienced grossly unjust
treatment in the courts. There have been more unsolved bombings
of Negro homes and churches in Birmingham than in any other city
in the nation. These are the hard brutal facts of the case. On the
basis of these conditions, Negro leaders sought to negotiate with the
city fathers. But the latter consistently refused to engage in good-
faith negotiation.

Then, last September, came the opportunity to talk with leaders 7
of Birmingham's economic community. In the course of the negotia-
tions, certain promises were made by the merchants — for example,
to remove the stores' humiliating racial signs. On the basis of these
promises, the Reverend Fred Shuttlesworth and the leaders of the
Alabama Christian Movement for Human Rights agreed to a morato-
rium on all demonstrations. As the weeks and months went by, we
realized that we were the victims of a broken promise. A few signs,
briefly removed, returned; the others remained.

As in so many past experiences, our hopes had been blasted, 8
and the shadow of deep disappointment settled upon us. We had no
alternative except to prepare for direct action, whereby we would
present our very bodies as a means of laying our case before the conscience of the local and the national community. Mindful of the
difficulties involved, we decided to undertake a process of self-
purification. We began a series of workshops on nonviolence, and
we repeatedly asked ourselves: "Are you able to accept blows without retaliating?" "Are you able to endure the ordeal of jail?" We decided to schedule our direct-action program for the Easter season,
realizing that except for Christmas, this is the main shopping period

of the year. Knowing that a strong economic-withdrawal program would be the by-product of direct action, we felt that this would be the best time to bring pressure to bear on the merchants for the needed change.

Then it occurred to us that Birmingham's mayoral election was 9 coming up in March, and we speedily decided to postpone action until after election day. When we discovered that the Commissioner of Public Safety, Eugene "Bull" Connor, had piled up enough votes to be in the run-off, we decided again to postpone action until the day after the run-off so that the demonstrations could not be used to cloud the issues. Like many others, we waited to see Mr. Connor defeated, and to this end we endured postponement after postponement. Having aided in this community need, we felt that our direct-action program could be delayed no longer.

You may well ask, "Why direct action? Why sit-ins, marches, 10 and so forth? Isn't negotiation a better path?" You are quite right in calling for negotiation. Indeed, this is the very purpose of direct action. Nonviolent direct action seeks to create such a crisis and foster such a tension that a community which has constantly refused to negotiate is forced to confront the issue. It seeks so to dramatize the issue that it can no longer be ignored. My citing the creation of tension as part of the work of the nonviolent resister may sound rather shocking. But I must confess that I am not afraid of the word "tension." I have earnestly opposed violent tension, but there is a type of constructive, nonviolent tension which is necessary for growth. Just as Socrates[4] felt that it was necessary to create a tension in the mind so that individuals could rise from the bondage of myths and half truths to the unfettered realm of creative analysis and objective appraisal, so must we see the need for nonviolent gadflies to create the kind of tension in society that will help men rise from the dark depths of prejudice and racism to the majestic heights of understanding and brotherhood.

The purpose of our direct-action program is to create a situation 11 so crisis-packed that it will inevitably open the door to negotiation. I therefore concur with you in your call for negotiation. Too long has our beloved Southland been bogged down in a tragic effort to live in monologue rather than dialogue.

---

[4] **Socrates (470?–399 B.C.)** The "tension in the mind" King refers to is created by the question-answer technique known as the Socratic method. By posing questions in the beginning of the paragraph, King shows his willingness to share Socrates' rhetorical techniques. Socrates was imprisoned and killed for his civil disobedience (see para. 21). He was the greatest of the Greek philosophers.

One of the basic points in your statement is that the action that I   12
and my associates have taken in Birmingham is untimely. Some have
asked: "Why didn't you give the new city administration time to
act?" The only answer that I can give to this query is that the new
Birmingham administration must be prodded about as much as the
outgoing one, before it will act. We are sadly mistaken if we feel that
the election of Albert Boutwell as mayor will bring the millennium[5]
to Birmingham. While Mr. Boutwell is a much more gentle person
than Mr. Connor, they are both segregationists, dedicated to maintenance of the status quo. I have hoped that Mr. Boutwell will be reasonable enough to see the futility of massive resistance to desegregation. But he will not see this without pressure from devotees of civil
rights. My friends, I must say to you that we have not made a single
gain in civil rights without determined legal and nonviolent pressure. Lamentably, it is an historical fact that privileged groups seldom give up their privileges voluntarily. Individuals may see the
moral light and voluntarily give up their unjust posture; but, as
Reinhold Niebuhr[6] has reminded us, groups tend to be more immoral than individuals.

We know through painful experience that freedom is never vol-   13
untarily given by the oppressor; it must be demanded by the oppressed. Frankly, I have yet to engage in a direct-action campaign
that was "well timed" in the view of those who have not suffered unduly from the disease of segregation. For years now I have heard the
word "Wait!" It rings in the ear of every Negro with piercing famil-
iarity. This "Wait" has almost always meant "Never." We must come
to see, with one of our distinguished jurists, that "justice too long
delayed is justice denied."[7]

We have waited for more than 340 years for our constitutional and   14
God-given rights. The nations of Asia and Africa are moving with jet-
like speed toward gaining political independence, but we still creep at
horse-and-buggy pace toward gaining a cup of coffee at a lunch

---

[5] **the millennium** A reference to Revelation 20, according to which the second
coming of Christ will be followed by one thousand years of peace, when the devil
will be incapacitated. After this will come a final battle between good and evil, followed by the Last Judgment.

[6] **Reinhold Niebuhr (1892–1971)** Protestant American philosopher who
urged church members to put their beliefs into action against social injustice. He
urged Protestantism to develop and practice a code of social ethics and wrote in
Moral Man and Immoral Society (1932) of the point King mentions here.

[7] **"justice too long delayed is justice denied"** Chief Justice Earl Warren's
expression in 1954 was adapted from English writer Walter Savage Landor's phrase
"Justice delayed is justice denied."

counter. Perhaps it is easy for those who have never felt the stinging darts of segregation to say, "Wait." But when you have seen vicious mobs lynch your mothers and fathers at will and drown your sisters and brothers at whim; when you have seen hate-filled policemen curse, kick, and even kill your black brothers and sisters; when you see the vast majority of your twenty million Negro brothers smothering in an airtight cage of poverty in the midst of an affluent society; when you suddenly find your tongue twisted and your speech stammering as you seek to explain to your six-year-old daughter why she can't go to the public amusement park that has just been advertised on television, and see tears welling up in her eyes when she is told that Funtown is closed to colored children, and see ominous clouds of inferiority beginning to form in her little mental sky, and see her beginning to distort her personality by developing an unconscious bitterness toward white people; when you have to concoct an answer for a five-year-old son who is asking, "Daddy, why do white people treat colored people so mean?"; when you take a cross-country drive and find it necessary to sleep night after night in the uncomfortable corners of your automobile because no motel will accept you; when you are humiliated day in and day out by nagging signs reading "white" and "colored"; when your first name becomes "nigger," your middle name becomes "boy" (however old you are) and your last name becomes "John," and your wife and mother are never given the respected title "Mrs."; when you are harried by day and haunted by night by the fact that you are a Negro, living constantly at tiptoe stance, never quite knowing what to expect next, and are plagued with inner fears and outer resentments; when you are forever fighting a degenerating sense of "nobodiness"—then you will understand why we find it difficult to wait. There comes a time when the cup of endurance runs over, and men are no longer willing to be plunged into the abyss of despair. I hope, sirs, you can understand our legitimate and unavoidable impatience.

You express a great deal of anxiety over our willingness to break 15 laws. This is certainly a legitimate concern. Since we so diligently urge people to obey the Supreme Court's decision of 1954 outlawing segregation in the public schools, at first glance it may seem rather paradoxical for us consciously to break laws. One may well ask: "How can you advocate breaking some laws and obeying others?" The answer lies in the fact that there are two types of laws: just and unjust. I would be the first to advocate obeying just laws. One has not only a legal but a moral responsibility to obey just laws. Conversely, one has a moral responsibility to disobey unjust laws. I would agree with St. Augustine[8] that "an unjust law is no law at all."

---

[8] **St. Augustine (354–430)** Early bishop of the Christian Church who deeply influenced the spirit of Christianity for many centuries.

Now, what is the difference between the two? How does one de-   16
termine whether a law is just or unjust? A just law is a manmade
code that squares with the moral law or the law of God. An unjust
law is a code that is out of harmony with the moral law. To put it in
the terms of St. Thomas Aquinas:[9] An unjust law is a human law
that is not rooted in eternal law and natural law. Any law that uplifts
human personality is just. Any law that degrades human personality
is unjust. All segregation statutes are unjust because segregation distorts the soul and damages the personality. It gives the segregator a
false sense of superiority and the segregated a false sense of inferiority. Segregation, to use the terminology of the Jewish philosopher
Martin Buber,[10] substitutes an "I-it" relationship for an "I-thou" relationship and ends up relegating persons to the status of things.
Hence segregation is not only politically, economically, and socio-
logically unsound, it is morally wrong and sinful. Paul Tillich[11] has
said that sin is separation. Is not segregation an existential expression of man's tragic separation, his awful estrangement, his terrible
sinfulness? Thus it is that I can urge men to obey the 1954 decision
of the Supreme Court, for it is morally right; and I can urge them to
disobey segregation ordinances, for they are morally wrong.

Let us consider a more concrete example of just and unjust   17
laws. An unjust law is a code that a numerical or power majority
group compels a minority group to obey but does not make binding
on itself. This is *difference* made legal. By the same token, a just law
is a code that a majority compels a minority to follow and that it is
willing to follow itself. This is *sameness* made legal.

Let me give another explanation. A law is unjust if it is inflicted   18
on a minority that, as a result of being denied the right to vote, had
no part in enacting or devising the law. Who can say that the legislature of Alabama which set up that state's segregation laws was democratically elected? Throughout Alabama all sorts of devious methods are used to prevent Negroes from becoming registered voters,
and there are some counties in which, even though Negroes constitute a majority of the population, not a single Negro is registered.

---

[9] **St. Thomas Aquinas (1225–1274)** The greatest of the medieval Christian
philosophers and one of the greatest church authorities.

[10] **Martin Buber (1878–1965)** Jewish theologian. *I and Thou* (1923) is his
most famous book.

[11] **Paul Tillich (1886–1965)** An important twentieth-century Protestant theologian who held that Christianity was reasonable and effective in modern life.
Tillich saw sin as an expression of man's separation from God, from himself, and
from his fellow man. King sees the separation of the races as a further manifestation
of man's sinfulness. Tillich, who was driven out of Germany by the Nazis, stresses
the need for activism and the importance of action in determining moral vitality, just
as King does.

Can any law enacted under such circumstances be considered democratically structured?

Sometimes a law is just on its face and unjust in its application. 19 For instance, I have been arrested on a charge of parading without a permit. Now, there is nothing wrong in having an ordinance which requires a permit for a parade. But such an ordinance becomes unjust when it is used to maintain segregation and to deny citizens the First Amendment privilege of peaceful assembly and protest.

I hope you are able to see the distinction I am trying to point 20 out. In no sense do I advocate evading or defying the law, as would the rabid segregationist. That would lead to anarchy. One who breaks an unjust law must do so openly, lovingly, and with a willingness to accept the penalty. I submit that an individual who breaks a law that conscience tells him is unjust, and who willingly accepts the penalty of imprisonment in order to arouse the conscience of the community over its injustice, is in reality expressing the highest respect for law.

Of course, there is nothing new about this kind of civil disobe- 21 dience. It was evidenced subliminally in the refusal of Shadrach, Meshach, and Abednego to obey the laws of Nebuchadnezzar,[12] on the ground that a higher moral law was at stake. It was practiced superbly by the early Christians, who were willing to face hungry lions and the excruciating pain of chopping blocks rather than submit to certain unjust laws of the Roman Empire. To a degree, academic freedom is a reality today because Socrates practiced civil disobedience. In our own nation, the Boston Tea Party represented a massive act of civil disobedience.

We should never forget that everything Adolf Hitler did in Ger- 22 many was "legal" and everything the Hungarian freedom fighters[13] did in Hungary was "illegal." It was "illegal" to aid and comfort a Jew in Hitler's Germany. Even so, I am sure that, had I lived in Germany at the time, I would have aided and comforted my Jewish brothers. If today I lived in a Communist country where certain principles dear to the Christian faith are suppressed, I would openly advocate disobeying that country's antireligious laws.

---

[12] **Nebuchadnezzar (c. 630–562 B.C.)** Chaldean king who twice attacked Jerusalem. He ordered Shadrach, Meshach, and Abednego to worship a golden image. They refused, were cast into a roaring furnace, and were saved by God (see Daniel 1:7–3:30).

[13] **Hungarian freedom fighters** The Hungarians rose in revolt against Soviet rule in 1956. Russian tanks put down the uprising with great force that shocked the world. Many freedom fighters died, and many others escaped to the West.

I must make two honest confessions to you, my Christian and   23
Jewish brothers. First, I must confess that over the past few years I
have been gravely disappointed with the white moderate. I have almost reached the regrettable conclusion that the Negro's great stum-
bling block in his stride toward freedom is not the White Citizen's
Counciler[14] or the Ku Klux Klanner, but the white moderate, who is
more devoted to "order" than to justice; who prefers a negative
peace which is the absence of tension to a positive peace which is
the presence of justice; who constantly says, "I agree with you in the
goal you seek, but I cannot agree with your methods of direct action"; who paternalistically believes he can set the timetable for another man's freedom; who lives by a mythical concept of time and
who constantly advises the Negro to wait for a "more convenient
season." Shallow understanding from people of good will is more
frustrating than absolute misunderstanding from people of ill will.
Lukewarm acceptance is much more bewildering than outright
rejection.

I had hoped that the white moderate would understand that law   24
and order exist for the purpose of establishing justice and that when
they fail in this purpose they become the dangerously structured
dams that block the flow of social progress. I had hoped that the
white moderate would understand that the present tension in the
South is a necessary phase of the transition from an obnoxious negative peace, in which the Negro passively accepted his unjust plight,
to a substantive and positive peace, in which all men will respect the
dignity and worth of human personality. Actually, we who engage in
nonviolent direct action are not the creators of tension. We merely
bring to the surface the hidden tension that is already alive. We
bring it out in the open, where it can be seen and dealt with. Like a
boil that can never be cured so long as it is covered up but must be
opened with all its ugliness to the natural medicines of air and light,
injustice must be exposed, with all the tension its exposure creates,
to the light of human conscience and the air of national opinion, before it can be cured.

In your statement you assert that our actions, even though   25
peaceful, must be condemned because they precipitate violence. But
is this a logical assertion? Isn't this like condemning a robbed man
because his possession of money precipitated the evil act of robbery?

---

[14] **White Citizen's Counciler** White Citizen's Councils organized in southern
states in 1954 to fight school desegregation as ordered by the Supreme Court in May
1954. The councils were not as secret or violent as the Klan; they were also ineffec-
tive.

Isn't this like condemning Socrates because his unswerving commitment to truth and his philosophical inquiries precipitated the act by the misguided populace in which they made him drink hemlock? Isn't this like condemning Jesus because his unique God-consciousness and never-ceasing devotion to God's will precipitated the evil act of crucifixion? We must come to see that, as the federal courts have consistently affirmed, it is wrong to urge an individual to cease his efforts to gain his basic constitutional rights because the quest may precipitate violence. Society must protect the robbed and punish the robber.

I had also hoped that the white moderate would reject the myth 26
concerning time in relation to the struggle for freedom. I have just received a letter from a white brother in Texas. He writes: "All Christians know that the colored people will receive equal rights eventually, but it is possible that you are in too great a religious hurry. It has taken Christianity almost two thousand years to accomplish what it has. The teachings of Christ take time to come to earth." Such an attitude stems from a tragic misconception of time, from the strangely irrational notion that there is something in the very flow of time that will inevitably cure all ills. Actually, time itself is neutral; it can be used either destructively or constructively. More and more I feel that the people of ill will have used time much more effectively than have the people of good will. We will have to repent in this generation not merely for the hateful words and actions of the bad people, but for the appalling silence of the good people. Human progress never rolls in on wheels of inevitability; it comes through the tireless efforts of men willing to be co-workers with God, and without this hard work, time itself becomes an ally of the forces of social stagnation. We must use time creatively, in the knowledge that the time is always ripe to do right. Now is the time to make real the promise of democracy and transform our pending national elegy into a creative psalm of brotherhood. Now is the time to lift our national policy from the quicksand of racial injustice to the solid rock of human dignity.

You speak of our activity in Birmingham as extreme. At first I 27
was rather disappointed that fellow clergymen would see my nonviolent efforts as those of an extremist. I began thinking about the fact that I stand in the middle of two opposing forces in the Negro community. One is a force of complacency, made up in part of Negroes who, as a result of long years of oppression, are so drained of self-respect and a sense of "somebodiness" that they have adjusted to segregation; and in part of a few middle-class Negroes who, because of a degree of academic and economic security and because in some ways they profit by segregation, have become insensitive to the

problems of the masses. The other force is one of bitterness and hatred, and it comes perilously close to advocating violence. It is expressed in the various black nationalist groups that are springing up across the nation, the largest and best known being Elijah Muhammad's Muslim movement.[15] Nourished by the Negro's frustration over the continued existence of racial discrimination, this movement is made up of people who have lost faith in America, who have absolutely repudiated Christianity, and who have concluded that the white man is an incorrigible "devil."

I have tried to stand between these two forces, saying that we need emulate neither the "do-nothingism" of the complacent nor the hatred and despair of the black nationalist. For there is the more excellent way of love and nonviolent protest. I am grateful to God that, through the influence of the Negro church, the way of nonviolence became an integral part of our struggle.   28

If this philosophy had not emerged, by now many streets of the South would, I am convinced, be flowing with blood. And I am further convinced that if our white brothers dismiss as "rabble-rousers" and "outside agitators" those of us who employ nonviolent direct action, and if they refuse to support our nonviolent efforts, millions of Negroes will, out of frustration and despair, seek solace and security in black nationalist ideologies—a development that would inevitably lead to a frightening racial nightmare.[16]   29

Oppressed people cannot remain oppressed forever. The yearning for freedom eventually manifests itself, and that is what has happened to the American Negro. Something within has reminded him of his birthright of freedom, and something without has reminded him that it can be gained. Consciously or unconsciously, he has been caught up by the *Zeitgeist*,[17] and with his black brothers of Africa and his brown and yellow brothers of Asia, South America, and the Caribbean, the United States Negro is moving with a sense of great urgency toward the promised land of racial justice. If one   30

----

[15] **Elijah Muhammad's Muslim movement** The Black Muslim movement, which began in the 1920s but flourished in the 1960s under its leader, Elijah Muhammad (1897–1975). Among notable figures who became Black Muslims were the poet Imamu Amiri Baraka (b. 1934), the world championship prizefighter Muhammad Ali (b. 1942), and the controversial reformer and religious leader Malcolm X (1925–1965). King saw their rejection of white society (and consequently brotherhood) as a threat.

[16] **a frightening racial nightmare** The black uprisings of the 1960s in all major American cities, and the conditions that led to them, were indeed a racial nightmare. King's prophecy was quick to come true.

[17] *Zeitgeist* German word for the intellectual, moral, and cultural spirit of the times.

recognizes this vital urge that has engulfed the Negro community, one should readily understand why public demonstrations are taking place. The Negro has many pent-up resentments and latent frustrations, and he must release them. So let him march; let him make prayer pilgrimages to the city hall; let him go on freedom rides[18]— and try to understand why he must do so. If his repressed emotions are not released in nonviolent ways, they will seek expression through violence; this is not a threat but a fact of history. So I have not said to my people, "Get rid of your discontent." Rather, I have tried to say that this normal and healthy discontent can be channeled into the creative outlet of nonviolent direct action. And now this approach is being termed extremist.

But though I was initially disappointed at being categorized as 31 an extremist, as I continued to think about the matter I gradually gained a measure of satisfaction from the label. Was not Jesus an extremist for love: "Love your enemies, bless them that curse you, do good to them that hate you, and pray for them which despitefully use you, and persecute you." Was not Amos an extremist for justice: "Let justice roll down like waters and righteousness like an everflowing stream." Was not Paul an extremist for the Christian gospel: "I bear in my body the marks of the Lord Jesus." Was not Martin Luther an extremist: "Here I stand; I cannot do otherwise, so help me God." And John Bunyan: "I will stay in jail to the end of my days before I make a butchery of my conscience." And Abraham Lincoln: "This nation cannot survive half slave and half free." And Thomas Jefferson: "We hold these truths to be self-evident, that all men are created equal..."[19] So the question is not whether we will be extremists, but what kind of extremists we will be. Will we be extremists for hate or for love? Will we be extremists for the preservation of injustice or for the extension of justice? In that dramatic scene on Calvary's hill three men were crucified. We must never forget that all three were crucified for the same crime—the crime of extrem-

---

[18] **freedom rides** In 1961 the Congress of Racial Equality (CORE) organized rides of whites and blacks to test segregation in southern buses and bus terminals with interstate passengers. More than 600 federal marshals were needed to protect the riders, most of whom were arrested.

[19] **Amos, Old Testament prophet (eighth century B.C.); Paul (?–A.D. 67); Martin Luther (1483–1546); John Bunyan (1628–1688); Abraham Lincoln (1809–1865); and Thomas Jefferson (1743–1826)** These figures are all noted for religious, moral, or political innovations that changed the world. Amos was a prophet who favored social justice; Paul argued against Roman law; Luther began the Reformation of the Christian Church; Bunyan was imprisoned for preaching the gospel according to his own understanding; Lincoln freed America's slaves; Jefferson drafted the Declaration of Independence.

ism. Two were extremists for immorality, and thus fell below their environment. The other, Jesus Christ, was an extremist for love, truth, and goodness, and thereby rose above his environment. Perhaps the South, the nation, and the world are in dire need of creative extremists.

I had hoped that the white moderate would see this need. Perhaps   32
I was too optimistic; perhaps I expected too much. I suppose I should have realized that few members of the oppressor race can understand the deep groans and passionate yearnings of the oppressed race, and still fewer have the vision to see that injustice must be rooted out by strong, persistent, and determined action. I am thankful, however, that some of our white brothers in the South have grasped the meaning of this social revolution and committed themselves to it. They are still all too few in quantity, but they are big in quality. Some—such as Ralph McGill, Lillian Smith, Harry Golden, James McBride Dabbs, Ann Braden, and Sarah Patton Boyle—have written about our struggle[20] in eloquent and prophetic terms. Others have marched with us down nameless streets of the South. They have languished in filthy, roach-infested jails, suffering the abuse and brutality of policemen who view them as "dirty nigger-lovers." Unlike so many of their moderate brothers and sisters, they have recognized the urgency of the moment and sensed the need for powerful "action" antidotes to combat the disease of segregation.

Let me take note of my other major disappointment. I have been   33
so greatly disappointed with the white church and its leadership. Of course, there are some notable exceptions. I am not unmindful of the fact that each of you has taken some significant stands on this issue. I commend you, Reverend Stallings, for your Christian stand on this past Sunday, in welcoming Negroes to your worship service on a nonsegregated basis. I commend the Catholic leaders of this state for integrating Spring Hill College several years ago.

But despite these notable exceptions, I must honestly reiterate   34
that I have been disappointed with the church. I do not say this as one of those negative critics who can always find something wrong with the church. I say this as a minister of the gospel, who loves the church; who was nurtured in its bosom; who has been sustained by its spiritual blessings and who will remain true to it as long as the cord of life shall lengthen.

---

[20]**written about our struggle** These are all prominent southern writers who expressed their feelings regarding segregation in the South. Some of them, like Smith and Golden, wrote very popular books with a wide influence. Some, like McGill and Smith, were severely rebuked by white southerners.

When I was suddenly catapulted into the leadership of the bus 35
protest in Montgomery, Alabama, a few years ago, I felt we would be
supported by the white church. I felt that the white ministers,
priests, and rabbis of the South would be among our strongest allies.
Instead, some have been outright opponents, refusing to understand
the freedom movement and misrepresenting its leaders; all too many
others have been more cautious than courageous and have remained
silent behind the anesthetizing security of stained-glass windows.

In spite of my shattered dreams, I came to Birmingham with the 36
hope that the white religious leadership of this community would
see the justice of our cause and, with deep moral concern, would
serve as the channel through which our just grievances could reach
the power structure. I had hoped that each of you would understand. But again I have been disappointed. . . .

There was a time when the church was very powerful—in the 37
time when the early Christians rejoiced at being deemed worthy to
suffer for what they believed. In those days the church was not
merely a thermometer that recorded the ideas and principles of popular opinion; it was a thermostat that transformed the mores of society. Whenever the early Christians entered a town, the people in
power became disturbed and immediately sought to convict the
Christians for being "disturbers of the peace" and "outside agitators."
But the Christians pressed on, in the conviction that they were
"a colony of heaven," called to obey God rather than man. Small
in number, they were big in commitment. They were too God-
intoxicated to be "astronomically intimidated." By their effort and
example they brought an end to such ancient evils as infanticide and
gladiatorial contests.

Things are different now. So often the contemporary church is a 38
weak, ineffectual voice with an uncertain sound. So often it is an
archdefender of the status quo. Far from being disturbed by the
presence of the church, the powerful structure of the average community is consoled by the church's silent—and often even vocal—
sanction of things as they are.

But the judgment of God is upon the church as never before. If 39
today's church does not recapture the sacrificial spirit of the early
church, it will lose its authenticity, forfeit the loyalty of millions, and
be dismissed as an irrelevant social club with no meaning for the
twentieth century. Every day I meet young people whose disappointment with the church has turned into outright disgust.

Perhaps I have once again been too optimistic. Is organized reli- 40
gion too inextricably bound to the status quo to save our nation and
the world? Perhaps I must turn my faith to the inner spiritual

church, the church within the church, as the true *ekklesia*[21] and the hope of the world. But again I am thankful to God that some noble souls from the ranks of organized religion have broken loose from the paralyzing chains of conformity and joined us as active partners in the struggle for freedom. They have left their secure congregations and walked the streets of Albany, Georgia, with us. They have gone down the highways of the South on torturous rides for freedom. Yes, they have gone to jail with us. Some have been dismissed from their churches, have lost the support of their bishops and fellow ministers. But they have acted in the faith that right defeated is stronger than evil triumphant. Their witness has been the spiritual salt that has preserved the true meaning of the gospel in these troubled times. They have carved a tunnel of hope through the dark mountain of disappointment.

41   I hope the church as a whole will meet the challenge of this decisive hour. But even if the church does not come to the aid of justice, I have no despair about the future. I have no fear about the outcome of our struggle in Birmingham, even if our motives are at present misunderstood. We will reach the goal of freedom in Birmingham and all over the nation, because the goal of America is freedom. Abused and scorned though we may be, our destiny is tied up with America's destiny. Before the pilgrims landed at Plymouth, we were here. Before the pen of Jefferson etched the majestic words of the Declaration of Independence across the pages of history, we were here. For more than two centuries our forebears labored in this country without wages; they made cotton king; they built the homes of their masters while suffering gross injustice and shameful humiliation—and yet out of a bottomless vitality they continued to thrive and develop. If the inexpressible cruelties of slavery could not stop us, the opposition we now face will surely fail. We will win our freedom because the sacred heritage of our nation and the eternal will of God are embodied in our echoing demands.

42   Before closing I feel impelled to mention one other point in your statement that has troubled me profoundly. You warmly commended the Birmingham police force for keeping "order" and "preventing violence." I doubt that you would have so warmly commended the police force if you had seen its dogs sinking their teeth into unarmed, nonviolent Negroes. I doubt that you would so quickly commend the policemen if you were to observe their ugly

---

[21] ***ekklesia*** Greek word for "church" meaning not just the institution but the spirit of the church.

and inhumane treatment of Negroes here in the city jail; if you were to watch them push and curse old Negro women and young Negro girls; if you were to see them slap and kick old Negro men and young boys; if you were to observe them, as they did on two occasions, refuse to give us food because we wanted to sing our grace together. I cannot join you in your praise of the Birmingham police department.

It is true that the police have exercised a degree of discipline in handling the demonstrators. In this sense they have conducted themselves rather "nonviolently" in public. But for what purpose? To preserve the evil system of segregation. Over the past few years I have consistently preached that nonviolence demands that the means we use must be as pure as the ends we seek. I have tried to make clear that it is wrong to use immoral means to attain moral ends. But now I must affirm that it is just as wrong, or perhaps even more so, to use moral means to preserve immoral ends. Perhaps Mr. Connor and his policemen have been rather nonviolent in public, as was Chief Pritchett in Albany, Georgia, but they have used the moral means of nonviolence to maintain the immoral end of racial injustice. As T. S. Eliot[22] has said, "The last temptation is the greatest treason: To do the right deed for the wrong reason." 43

I wish you had commended the Negro sit-inners and demonstrators of Birmingham for their sublime courage, their willingness to suffer, and their amazing discipline in the midst of great provocation. One day the South will recognize its real heroes. They will be the James Merediths,[23] with the noble sense of purpose that enables them to face jeering and hostile mobs, and with the agonizing loneliness that characterizes the life of the pioneer. They will be old, oppressed, battered Negro women, symbolized in a seventy-two-year-old woman in Montgomery, Alabama, who rose up with a sense of dignity and with her people decided not to ride segregated buses, and who responded with ungrammatical profundity to one who inquired about her weariness: "My feets is tired, but my soul is at rest." 44

---

[22]**Thomas Stearns Eliot (1888–1965)** Renowned as one of the twentieth century's major poets, Eliot was born in the United States but in 1927 became a British subject and a member of the Church of England. Many of his poems focused on religious and moral themes. These lines are from Eliot's play *Murder in the Cathedral*, about Saint Thomas à Becket (1118–1170), the archbishop of Canterbury, who was martyred for his opposition to King Henry II.

[23]**the James Merediths** James Meredith (b. 1933) was the first black to become a student at the University of Mississippi. His attempt to register for classes in 1962 created the first important confrontation between federal and state authorities, when Governor Ross Barnett personally blocked Meredith's entry to the university. Meredith graduated in 1963 and went on to study law at Columbia University.

They will be the young high school and college students, the young ministers of the gospel and a host of their elders, courageously and nonviolently sitting in at lunch counters and willingly going to jail for conscience' sake. One day the South will know that when these disinherited children of God sat down at lunch counters, they were in reality standing up for what is best in the American dream and for the most sacred values in our Judaeo-Christian heritage, thereby bringing our nation back to those great wells of democracy which were dug deep by the founding fathers in their formulation of the Constitution and the Declaration of Independence.

Never before have I written so long a letter. I'm afraid it is much 45 too long to take your precious time. I can assure you that it would have been much shorter if I had been writing from a comfortable desk, but what else can one do when he is alone in a narrow jail cell, other than write long letters, think long thoughts, and pray long prayers?

If I have said anything in this letter that overstates the truth and 46 indicates an unreasonable impatience, I beg you to forgive me. If I have said anything that understates the truth and indicates my having a patience that allows me to settle for anything less than brotherhood, I beg God to forgive me.

I hope this letter finds you strong in the faith. I also hope that 47 circumstances will soon make it possible for me to meet each of you, not as an integrationist or a civil rights leader but as a fellow clergyman and a Christian brother. Let us all hope that the dark clouds of racial prejudice will soon pass away and the deep fog of misunderstanding will be lifted from our fear-drenched communities, and in some not too distant tomorrow the radiant stars of love and brotherhood will shine over our great nation with all their scintillating beauty.

Yours in the cause of
Peace and Brotherhood,
MARTIN LUTHER KING, JR.

QUESTIONS FOR CRITICAL READING

1. Define "nonviolent direct action" (para. 2). In what areas of human experience is it best implemented? Is politics its best area of application? What are the four steps in a nonviolent campaign?
2. Do you agree that "law and order exist for the purpose of establishing justice" (para. 24)? Why? Describe how law and order either do or do not establish justice in your community. Compare notes with your peers.

3. King describes an unjust law as "a code that a numerical or power majority group compels a minority group to obey but does not make binding on itself" (para. 17). Devise one or two other definitions of an unjust law. What unjust laws currently on the books do you disagree with?
4. What do you think is the best-written paragraph in the essay? Why?
5. King cites "tension" in paragraph 10 and elsewhere as a beneficial force. Do you agree? What kind of tension does he mean?
6. In what ways was King an extremist (paras. 30–31)?
7. In his letter, to what extent does King consider the needs of women? Would he feel that issues of women's rights are unrelated to issues of racial equality?
8. According to King, how should a government function in relation to the needs of the individual? Does he feel, like Thoreau's "Chinese philosopher," that the empire is built on the individual?

SUGGESTIONS FOR WRITING

1. Write a brief letter protesting an injustice that you feel may not be entirely understood by people you respect. Clarify the nature of the injustice, the reasons that people hold an unjust view, and the reasons your views should be accepted. Consult King's letter, and use his techniques.
2. In paragraph 43, King says, "I have consistently preached that nonviolence demands that the means we use must be as pure as the ends we seek." What does he mean by this? Define the ends he seeks and the means he approves. Do you agree with him on this point?
3. The first part of the letter defends King's journey to Birmingham as a Christian to help his fellows gain justice. He challenges the view that he is an outsider, using such expressions as "network of mutuality" and "garment of destiny" (para. 4). How effective is his argument? Examine the letter for other expressions that justify King's intervention on behalf of his brothers and sisters. Using his logic, describe other social areas where you might be justified in acting on your own views on behalf of humanity. Do you expect your endeavors would be welcomed? Are there any areas where you think it would be wrong to intervene?
4. In paragraphs 15–22, King discusses two kinds of laws—those that are morally right and those that are morally wrong. Which laws did King regard as morally right? Which laws did he consider morally wrong? Analyze one or two current laws that you feel are morally wrong. Be sure to be fair in describing the laws and establishing their nature. Then explain why you feel they are morally wrong. Would you feel justified in breaking these laws? Would you feel prepared, as King was, to pay the penalties demanded of one who breaks the law?

5. Compare King's letter with sections of Paul's letters to the faithful in the New Testament. Either choose a single letter, such as the Epistle to the Romans, or select passages from Romans, the two letters to the Corinthians, the Galatians, the Ephesians, the Thessalonians, or the Philippians. How did Paul and King agree and disagree about brotherly love, the mission of Christ, the mission of the church, concern for the law, and the duties of the faithful? Inventory the New Testament letters and King's letter carefully for concrete evidence of similar or contrary positions.

KARL MARX
The Communist Manifesto

KARL MARX (1818–1883) was born in Germany to Jewish parents who converted to Lutheranism. A scholarly man, Marx studied literature and philosophy, ultimately earning a doctorate in philosophy at the University of Jena. After being denied a university position, however, he turned to make a living from journalism.

Soon after beginning his journalistic career, Marx came into conflict with Prussian authorities because of his radical social views, and after a period of exile in Paris he moved to Brussels. After several more moves, Marx found his way to London, where he finally settled in absolute poverty; his friend Friedrich Engels (1820–1895) contributed money to prevent Marx and his family from starving. During this time in London, Marx wrote the books for which he is famous while also writing for and editing newspapers. His contributions to the *New York Daily Tribune* number over 300 items between the years 1851 and 1862.

Marx is best known for his theories of socialism, as expressed in *The Communist Manifesto* (1848) — which, like much of his important work, was written with Engels's help — and in the three-volume *Das Kapital (Capital)*, the first volume of which was published in 1867. In his own lifetime he was not well known, nor were his ideas widely debated. Yet he was part of an ongoing movement composed mainly of intellectuals. Vladimir Lenin (1870–1924) was a disciple whose triumph in the Russian Revolution of 1917 catapulted Marx to the forefront of world thought. Since 1917 Marx's thinking has been scrupulously analyzed, debated, and argued. Capitalist thinkers have found him unconvincing, whereas Communist thinkers have found him a prophet and keen analyst of social structures.

Translated by Samuel Moore. Part III of *The Communist Manifesto*, "Socialist and Communist Literature," is omitted here.

In England, Marx's studies centered on the concept of an ongoing class struggle between those who owned property — the bourgeoisie — and those who owned nothing but whose work produced wealth — the proletariat. Marx was concerned with the forces of history, and his view of history was that it is progressive and, to an extent, inevitable. This view is prominent in *The Communist Manifesto,* particularly in Marx's review of the overthrow of feudal forms of government by the bourgeoisie. He thought it inevitable that the bourgeoisie and the proletariat would engage in a class struggle, from which the proletariat would emerge victorious. In essence, Marx took a materialist position. He denied the providence of God in the affairs of humans and defended the view that economic institutions evolve naturally and that, in their evolution, they control the social order. Thus, communism was an inevitable part of the process, and in the *Manifesto* he worked to clarify the reasons for its inevitability.

One of Marx's primary contentions was that capital is "not a personal, it is a social power" (para. 78). Thus, according to Marx, the "past dominates the present" (para. 83), because the accumulation of past capital determines how people will live in the present society. Capitalist economists, however, see capital as a personal power, but a power that, as John Kenneth Galbraith might say, should be used in a socially responsible way.

Marx's Rhetoric

The selection included here omits one section, the least important for the modern reader. The first section has a relatively simple rhetorical structure that depends on comparison. The title, "Bourgeois and Proletarians," tells us that the section will clarify the nature of each class and then go on to make some comparisons and contrasts. These concepts were by no means as widely discussed or thought about in 1848 as they are today, so Marx is careful to define his terms. At the same time, he establishes his theories regarding history by making further comparisons with class struggles in earlier ages.

Marx's style is simple and direct. He moves steadily from point to point, establishing his views on the nature of classes, on the nature of bourgeois society, and on the questions of industrialism and its effects on modern society. He considers wealth, worth, nationality, production, agriculture, and machinery. Each point is addressed in turn, usually in its own paragraph.

The organization of the next section, "Proletarians and Communists" (paras. 60–133), is not, despite its title, comparative in nature. Rather, with the proletariat defined as the class of the future, Marx tries to show that the Communist cause is the proletarian cause. In the process, Marx uses a clever rhetorical strategy. He assumes that he is addressed by an antagonist—presumably a bourgeois or a proletarian who is in sympathy with the bourgeoisie. He then proceeds to answer each popular complaint against communism. He shows that it is not a party separate from other workers' parties (para. 61). He clarifies the question of abolishing existing property relations (paras. 68–93). He emphasizes the antagonism between capital and wage labor (para. 76); he discusses the disappearance of culture (para. 94); he clarifies the questions of the family (paras. 98–100) and of the exploitation of children (para. 101). He brings up the new system of public education (paras. 102–4). He raises the touchy issue of the "community of women" (paras. 105–10), as well as the charge that Communists want to abolish nations (paras. 111–15). He brushes aside religion (para. 116). When he is done with the complaints, he gives us a rhetorical signal: "But let us have done with the bourgeois objections to Communism" (para. 126).

The rest of the second section contains a brief summary, and then Marx presents his ten-point program (para. 131). The structure is simple, direct, and effective. In the process of answering the charges against communism, Marx is able to clarify exactly what it is and what it promises. In contrast to his earlier arguments, the ten points of his Communist program seem clear, easy, and (again by contrast) almost acceptable. Although the style is not dashing (despite a few memorable lines), the rhetorical structure is extraordinarily effective for the purposes at hand.

In the last section (paras. 135 – 45), in which Marx compares the Communists with other reform groups such as those agitating for redistribution of land and other agrarian reforms, he indicates that the Communists are everywhere fighting alongside existing groups for the rights of people who are oppressed by their societies. As Marx says, "In short, the Communists everywhere support every revolutionary movement against the existing social and political order of things" (para. 141). Nothing could be a more plain and direct declaration of sympathies.

PREREADING QUESTIONS:
WHAT TO READ FOR

The following prereading questions may help you anticipate key issues in the discussion on Karl Marx's *Communist Manifesto*. Keeping them in mind during your first reading of the selection should help focus your reactions.

- What is the economic condition of the bourgeoisie? What is the economic condition of the proletariat?
- How does the expanding world market for goods affect national identity?
- What benefits does Marx expect communism to provide the proletariat?

The Communist Manifesto

A specter is haunting Europe—the specter of Communism. All 1
the Powers of old Europe have entered into a holy alliance to exorcise this specter; Pope and Czar, Metternich[1] and Guizot,[2] French Radicals[3] and German police-spies.

Where is the party in opposition that has not been decried as 2
communistic by its opponents in power? Where the Opposition that has not hurled back the branding reproach of Communism against the more advanced opposition parties, as well as against its reactionary adversaries?

Two things result from this fact.   3

I. Communism is already acknowledged by all European Pow- 4
ers to be itself a Power.

II. It is high time that Communists should openly, in the face of 5
the whole world, publish their views, their aims, their tendencies, and meet this nursery tale of the specter of Communism with a Manifesto of the party itself.

To this end, Communists of various nationalities have assem- 6
bled in London and sketched the following Manifesto, to be published in the English, French, German, Italian, Flemish and Danish languages.

---

[1] **Prince Klemens von Metternich (1773–1859)** Foreign minister of Austria (1809–1848) who had a hand in establishing the peace after the final defeat in 1815 of Napoleon (1769–1821); Metternich was highly influential in the crucial Congress of Vienna (1814–1815).
[2] **François Pierre Guizot (1787–1874)** Conservative French statesman, author, and philosopher. Like Metternich, he was opposed to communism.
[3] **French Radicals** Actually middle-class liberals who wanted a return to a republic in 1848 after the eighteen-year reign of Louis-Philippe (1773–1850), the "citizen king."

Bourgeois and Proletarians[4]

The history of all hitherto existing society is the history of class 7
struggles.

Freeman and slave, patrician and plebeian, lord and serf, guild- 8
master and journeyman, in a word, oppressor and oppressed, stood
in constant opposition to one another, carried on uninterrupted,
now hidden, now open fight, a fight that each time ended, either in
a revolutionary re-constitution of society at large, or in the common
ruin of the contending classes.

In the earlier epochs of history we find almost everywhere a 9
complicated arrangement of society into various orders, a manifold
gradation of social rank. In ancient Rome we have patricians,
knights, plebeians, slaves; in the Middle Ages, feudal lords, vassals,
guild-masters, journeymen, apprentices, serfs; in almost all of these
classes, again, subordinate gradations.

The modern bourgeois society that has sprouted from the ruins 10
of feudal society, has not done away with class antagonisms. It has
but established new classes, new conditions of oppression, new
forms of struggle in place of the old ones.

Our epoch, the epoch of the bourgeoisie, possesses, however, 11
this distinctive feature; it has simplified the class antagonisms. Society as a whole is more and more splitting up into two great hostile
camps, into two great classes directly facing each other: Bourgeoisie
and Proletariat.

From the serfs of the Middle Ages sprang the chartered burghers 12
of the earliest towns. From these burgesses the first elements of the
bourgeoisie were developed.

The discovery of America, the rounding of the Cape,[5] opened 13
up fresh ground for the rising bourgeoisie. The East Indian and Chinese markets, the colonization of America, trade with the colonies,
the increase in the means of exchange and in commodities generally,
gave to commerce, to navigation, to industry, an impulse never before known, and thereby, to the revolutionary element in the tottering feudal society, a rapid development.

---

[4] By bourgeois is meant the class of modern Capitalists, owners of the means of
social production and employers of wage labor. By proletarians, the class of modern
wage laborers who, having no means of production of their own, are reduced to selling their labor-power in order to live. [Engels's note]

[5] **the Cape** The Cape of Good Hope, at the southern tip of Africa. This was a
main sea route for trade with India and the Orient. Europe profited immensely from
the opening up of these new markets in the sixteenth century.

The feudal system of industry, under which industrial produc-   14
tion was monopolized by closed guilds, now no longer sufficed for
the growing wants of the new market. The manufacturing system
took its place. The guild-masters were pushed on one side by the
manufacturing middle-class: division of labor between the different
corporate guilds vanished in the face of division of labor in each
single workshop.

Meantime the markets kept ever growing, the demand ever ris-   15
ing. Even manufacture no longer sufficed. Thereupon, steam and
machinery revolutionized industrial production. The place of manufacture was taken by the giant, Modern Industry, the place of the industrial middle-class, by industrial millionaires, the leaders of whole
industrial armies, the modern bourgeois.

Modern industry has established the world-market, for which   16
the discovery of America paved the way. This market has given an
immense development to commerce, to navigation, to communication by land. This development has, in its turn, reacted on the extension of industry; and in proportion as industry, commerce, navigation, railways extended, in the same proportion the bourgeoisie
developed, increased its capital, and pushed into the background
every class handed down from the Middle Ages.

We see, therefore, how the modern bourgeoisie is itself the   17
product of a long course of development, of a series of revolutions in
the modes of production and of exchange.

Each step in the development of the bourgeoisie was accompa-   18
nied by a corresponding political advance of that class. An oppressed class under the sway of the feudal nobility, an armed and
self-governing association in the medieval commune,[6] here independent urban republic (as in Italy and Germany), there taxable "third
estate"[7] of the monarchy (as in France), afterwards, in the period of
manufacture proper, serving either the semi-feudal or the absolute
monarchy as a counterpoise against nobility, and, in fact, corner
stone of the great monarchies in general, the bourgeoisie has at last,
since the establishment of Modern Industry and of the world-
market, conquered for itself, in the modern representative State, exclusive political sway. The executive of the modern State is but a committee for managing the common affairs of the whole bourgeoisie.

The bourgeoisie, historically, has played a most revolutionary   19
part.

---

[6] **the medieval commune** Refers to the growth in the eleventh century of
towns whose economy was highly regulated by mutual interest and agreement.

[7] **"third estate"** The clergy was the first estate, the aristocracy the second estate, and the bourgeoisie the third estate.

The bourgeoisie, wherever it has got the upper hand, has put an 20 end to all feudal, patriarchal, idyllic relations. It has pitilessly torn asunder the motley feudal ties that bound man to his "natural superiors," and has left no other nexus between man and man than naked self-interest, than callous "cash payment." It has drowned the most heavenly ecstasies of religious fervor,[8] of chivalrous enthusiasm, of Philistine sentimentalism, in the icy water of egotistical calculation. It has resolved personal worth into exchange value, and in place of the numberless indefeasible chartered freedoms, has set up that single, unconscionable freedom—Free Trade. In one word, for exploitation, veiled by religious and political illusions, it has substituted naked, shameless, direct, brutal exploitation.

The bourgeoisie has stripped of its halo every occupation hith- 21 erto honored and looked up to with reverent awe. It has converted the physician, the lawyer, the priest, the poet, the man of science, into its paid wage laborers.

The bourgeoisie has torn away from the family its sentimental 22 veil, and has reduced the family relation to a mere money relation.

The bourgeoisie has disclosed how it came to pass that the bru- 23 tal display of vigor in the Middle Ages, which reactionists so much admire, found its fitting complement in the most slothful indolence. It has been the first to show what man's activity can bring about. It has accomplished wonders far surpassing Egyptian pyramids, Roman aqueducts and Gothic cathedrals; it has conducted expeditions that put in the shade all former Exoduses of nations and crusades.

The bourgeoisie cannot exist without constantly revolutionizing 24 the instruments of production, and thereby the relations of production, and with them the whole relations of society. Conservation of the old modes of production in unaltered form was, on the contrary, the first condition of existence for all earlier industrial classes. Constant revolutionizing of production, uninterrupted disturbance of all social conditions, everlasting uncertainty and agitation distinguish the bourgeois epoch from all earlier ones. All fixed, fast frozen relations, with their train of ancient and venerable prejudices and

---

[8] **religious fervor** This and other terms in this sentence contain a compressed historical observation. "Religious fervor" refers to the Middle Ages; "chivalrous enthusiasm" refers to the rise of the secular state and to the military power of knights; "Philistine sentimentalism" refers to the development of popular arts and literature in the sixteenth, seventeenth, and eighteenth centuries. "Philistine" refers to those who were generally uncultured, that is, the general public. "Sentimentalism" is a code word for the encouragement of emotional response rather than rational thought.

opinions, are swept away, all new formed ones become antiquated before they can ossify. All that is solid melts into the air, all that is holy is profaned, and man is at last compelled to face with sober senses, his real conditions of life, and his relations with his kind.

The need of a constantly expanding market for its prod- 25 ucts chases the bourgeoisie over the whole surface of the globe. It must nestle everywhere, settle everywhere, establish connections everywhere.

The bourgeoisie has through its exploitation of the world- 26 market given a cosmopolitan character to production and consumption in every country. To the great chagrin of reactionists, it has drawn from under the feet of industry the national ground on which it stood. All old-established national industries have been destroyed or are daily being destroyed. They are dislodged by new industries, whose introduction becomes a life and death question for all civilized nations, by industries that no longer work up indigenous raw material, but raw material drawn from the remotest zones; industries whose products are consumed, not only at home, but in every quarter of the globe. In place of the old wants, satisfied by the productions of the country, we find new wants, requiring for their satisfaction the products of distant lands and climes. In place of the old local and national seclusion and self-sufficiency, we have intercourse in every direction, universal interdependence of nations. And as in material, so also in intellectual production. The intellectual creations of individual nations become common property. National onesidedness and narrowmindedness become more and more impossible, and from the numerous national and local literatures there arises a world-literature.

The bourgeoisie, by the rapid improvement of all instruments of 27 production, by the immensely facilitated means of communication, draws all, even the most barbarian nations into civilization. The cheap prices of its commodities are the heavy artillery with which it batters down all Chinese walls, with which it forces the barbarians' intensely obstinate hatred of foreigners to capitulate. It compels all nations, on pain of extinction, to adopt the bourgeois mode of production; it compels them to introduce what it calls civilization into their midst, i.e., to become bourgeois themselves. In a word, it creates a world after its own image.

The bourgeoisie has subjected the country to the rule of the 28 towns. It has created enormous cities, has greatly increased the urban population as compared with the rural and has thus rescued a considerable part of the population from the idiocy of rural life. Just as it has made the country dependent on the towns, so it has made barbarian and semi-barbarian countries dependent on civilized ones, nations of peasants on nations of bourgeois, the East on the West.

The bourgeoisie keeps more and more doing away with the scattered state of the population, of the means of production, and of property. It has agglomerated population, centralized means of production, and has concentrated property in a few hands. The necessary consequence of this was political centralization. Independent, or but loosely connected provinces, with separate interests, laws, governments and systems of taxation, became lumped together in one nation, with one government, one code of laws, one national class interest, one frontier and one customs tariff. 29

The bourgeoisie, during its rule of scarce one hundred years, has created more massive and more colossal productive forces than have all preceding generations together. Subjection of Nature's forces to man, machinery, application of chemistry to industry and agriculture, steam-navigation, railways, electric telegraphs, clearing of whole continents for cultivation, canalization of rivers, whole populations conjured out of the ground—what earlier century had even a presentiment that such productive forces slumbered in the lap of social labor? 30

We see then: the means of production and of exchange on whose foundation the bourgeoisie built itself up, were generated in feudal society. At a certain stage in the development of these means of production and of exchange, the conditions under which feudal society produced and exchanged, the feudal organization of agriculture and manufacturing industry, in one word, the feudal relations of property became no longer compatible with the already developed productive forces; they became so many fetters. They had to burst asunder; they were burst asunder. 31

Into their place stepped free competition, accompanied by a social and political constitution adapted to it, and by the economical and political sway of the bourgeois class. 32

A similar movement is going on before our own eyes. Modern bourgeois society with its relations of production, of exchange and of property, a society that has conjured up such gigantic means of production and of exchange, is like the sorcerer, who is no longer able to control the powers of the nether world whom he has called up by his spells. For many a decade past, the history of industry and commerce is but the history of the revolt of modern productive forces against modern conditions of production, against the property relations that are the conditions for the existence of the bourgeoisie and of its rule. It is enough to mention the commercial crises that by their periodical return put on its trial, each time more threateningly, the existence of the entire bourgeois society. In these 33 crises a great part not only of the existing products, but also of the previously created productive forces, are periodically destroyed. In these crises there breaks out an epidemic that, in all earlier epochs, would have seemed an absurdity—the epidemic of overproduction. Society suddenly finds itself put back into a state of momentary barbarism; it appears as if a famine, a universal war of devastation, had cut off the supply of every means of subsistence; industry and commerce seem to be destroyed; and why? Because there is too much civilization, too much means of subsistence, too much industry, too much commerce. The productive forces at the disposal of society no longer tend to further the development of the conditions of the bourgeois property; on the contrary, they have become too powerful for these conditions by which they are fettered, and as soon as they overcome these fetters they bring disorder into the whole of bourgeois society, endanger the existence of bourgeois property. The conditions of bourgeois society are too narrow to comprise the wealth created by them. And how does the bourgeoisie get over these crises? On the one hand by enforced destruction of a mass of productive forces; on the other, by the conquest of new markets, and by the more thorough exploitation of the old ones. That is to say, by paving the way for more extensive and more destructive crises, and by diminishing the means whereby crises are prevented.

The weapons with which the bourgeoisie felled feudalism to the ground are now turned against the bourgeoisie itself. 34

But not only has the bourgeoisie forged the weapons that bring death to itself; it has also called into existence the men who are to wield those weapons—the modern working class—the proletarians. 35

In proportion as the bourgeoisie, i.e., capital, is developed, in the same proportion is the proletariat, the modern working class, developed, a class of laborers who live only so long as they find work, and who find work only so long as their labor increases capital. These laborers, who must sell themselves piecemeal, are a commodity, like every other article of commerce, and are consequently exposed to all the vicissitudes of competition, to all the fluctuations of the market. 36

Owing to the extensive use of machinery and to division of labor, the work of the proletarians has lost all individual character, and, consequently, all charm for the workman. He becomes an appendage of the machine, and it is only the most simple, most monotonous and most easily acquired knack that is required of him. Hence, the cost of production of a workman is restricted almost entirely to the means of subsistence that he requires for his 37 maintenance, and for the propagation of his race. But the price of a commodity, and also of labor, is equal to its cost of production. In proportion, therefore, as the repulsiveness of the work increases the wage decreases. Nay more, in proportion as the use of machinery and division of labor increases, in the same proportion the burden of toil increases, whether by prolongation of the working hours, by increase of the work enacted in a given time, or by increased speed of the machinery, etc.

Modern industry has converted the little workshop of the patri- 38 archal master into the great factory of the industrial capitalist. Masses of laborers, crowded into factories, are organized like sol- diers. As privates of the industrial army they are placed under the command of a perfect hierarchy of officers and sergeants. Not only are they the slaves of the bourgeois class and of the bourgeois state, they are daily and hourly enslaved by the machine, by the over- looker, and, above all, by the individual bourgeois manufacturer himself. The more openly this despotism proclaims gain to be its end and aim, the more petty, the more hateful and the more embit- tering it is.

The less the skill and exertion or strength implied in manual 39 labor, in other words, the more modern industry becomes devel- oped, the more is the labor of men superseded by that of women. Differences of age and sex have no longer any distinctive social va- lidity for the working class. All are instruments of labor, more or less expensive to use, according to their age and sex.

No sooner is the exploitation of the laborer by the manufac- 40 turer, so far at an end, that he receives his wages in cash, than he is set upon by the other portions of the bourgeoisie, the landlord, the shopkeeper, the pawnbroker, etc.

The lower strata of the middle class—the small trades-people, 41 shopkeepers and retired tradesmen generally, the handicraftsmen and peasants—all these sink gradually into the proletariat, partly because their diminutive capital does not suffice for the scale on which Modern Industry is carried on, and is swamped in the com- petition with the large capitalists, partly because their specialized skill is rendered worthless by new methods of production. Thus the proletariat is recruited from all classes of the population.

The proletariat goes through various stages of development. 42 With its birth begins its struggle with the bourgeoisie. At first the contest is carried on by individual laborers, then by the workpeople of a factory, then by the operatives of one trade, in one locality, against the individual bourgeois who directly exploits them. They direct their attacks not against the bourgeois conditions of produc- tion, but against the instruments of production themselves; they destroy imported wares that compete with their labor, they smash to pieces machinery, they set factories ablaze, they seek to restore by force the vanished status of the workman of the Middle Ages.

At this stage the laborers still form an incoherent mass scattered 43 over the whole country, and broken up by their mutual competition. If anywhere they unite to form more compact bodies, this is not yet the consequence of their own active union, but of the union of the bourgeoisie, which class, in order to attain its own political ends, is compelled to set the whole proletariat in motion, and is moreover yet, for a time, able to do so. At this stage, therefore, the proletarians do not fight their enemies, but the enemies of their enemies, the remnants of absolute monarchy, the landowners, the non-industrial bourgeois, the petty bourgeoisie. Thus the whole historical movement is concentrated in the hands of the bourgeoisie, every victory so obtained is a victory for the bourgeoisie.

But with the development of industry the proletariat not only 44 increases in number; it becomes concentrated in greater masses, its strength grows and it feels that strength more. The various interests and conditions of life within the ranks of the proletariat are more and more equalized, in proportion as machinery obliterates all distinctions of labor, and nearly everywhere reduces wages to the same low level. The growing competition among the bourgeois, and the resulting commercial crisis, make the wages of the workers even more fluctuating. The unceasing improvement of machinery, ever more rapidly developing, makes their livelihood more and more precarious; the collisions between individual workmen and individual bourgeois take more and more the character of collisions between two classes. Thereupon the workers begin to form combinations (Trades' Unions)[9] against the bourgeois; they club together in order to keep up the rate of wages; they found permanent associations in order to make provision beforehand for these occasional revolts. Here and there the contest breaks out into riots.

Now and then the workers are victorious, but only for a time. 45 The real fruit of their battle lies not in the immediate result but in the ever-expanding union of workers. This union is helped on by the improved means of communication that are created by modern industry, and that places the workers of different localities in contact with one another. It was just this contact that was needed to centralize the numerous local struggles, all of the same character, into one

---

[9] **combinations (Trades' Unions)** The labor movement was only beginning in 1848. It consisted of trades' unions that started as social clubs but soon began agitating for labor reform. They represented an important step in the growth of socialism in Europe.

national struggle between classes. But every class struggle is a political struggle. And that union, to attain which the burghers of the Middle Ages with their miserable highways, required centuries, the modern proletarians, thanks to railways, achieve in a few years.

This organization of the proletarians into a class, and conse- 46 quently into a political party, is continually being upset again by the competition between the workers themselves. But it ever rises up again, stronger, firmer, mightier. It compels legislative recognition of particular interests of the workers by taking advantage of the divisions among the bourgeoisie itself. Thus the ten hours' bill in England[10] was carried.

Altogether collisions between the classes of the old society fur- 47 ther, in many ways, the course of development of the proletariat. The bourgeoisie finds itself involved in a constant battle. At first with the aristocracy; later on, with those portions of the bourgeoisie itself whose interests have become antagonistic to the progress of industry; at all times, with the bourgeoisie of foreign countries. In all these battles it sees itself compelled to appeal to the proletariat, to ask for its help, and thus, to drag it into the political arena. The bourgeoisie itself, therefore, supplies the proletariat with its own elements of political and general education; in other words, it furnishes the proletariat with weapons for fighting the bourgeoisie.

Further, as we have already seen, entire sections of the ruling 48 classes are, by the advance of industry, precipitated into the proletariat, or are at least threatened in their conditions of existence. These also supply the proletariat with fresh elements of enlightenment and progress.

Finally, in times when the class struggle nears the decisive hour, 49 the process of dissolution going on within the ruling class — in fact, within the whole range of an old society — assumes such a violent, glaring character that a small section of the ruling class cuts itself adrift and joins the revolutionary class, the class that holds the future in its hands. Just as, therefore, at an earlier period, a section of the nobility went over to the bourgeoisie, so now a portion of the bourgeoisie goes over to the proletariat, and in particular, a portion of the bourgeois ideologists, who have raised themselves to the level of comprehending theoretically the historical movements as a whole.

---

[10] **the ten hours' bill in England** This bill (1847) was an important labor reform. It limited the working day for women and children in factories to only ten hours, at a time when it was common for some people to work sixteen hours a day. The bill's passage was a result of political division, not of benevolence on the managers' part.

Of all the classes that stand face to face with the bourgeoisie 50
today the proletariat alone is a really revolutionary class. The other
classes decay and finally disappear in the face of Modern Industry;
the proletariat is its special and essential product.

The lower middle class, the small manufacturer, the shop- 51
keeper, the artisan, the peasant, all these fight against the bourgeoisie, to save from extinction their existence as fractions of the
middle class. They are therefore not revolutionary, but conservative.
Nay, more; they are reactionary, for they try to roll back the wheel
of history. If by chance they are revolutionary, they are so only in
view of their impending transfer into the proletariat; they thus defend not their present, but their future interests; they desert their
own standpoint to place themselves at that of the proletariat.

The "dangerous class," the social scum, that passively rotting 52
mass thrown off by the lowest layers of old society, may, here and
there, be swept into the movement by a proletarian revolution; its
conditions of life, however, prepare it far more for the part of a
bribed tool of reactionary intrigue.

In the conditions of the proletariat, those of the old society at large 53
are already virtually swamped. The proletarian is without property; his
relation to his wife and children has no longer anything in common
with the bourgeois family relations; modern industrial labor, modern
subjection to capital, the same in England as in France, in America as in
Germany, has stripped him of every trace of national character. Law,
morality, religion, are to him so many bourgeois prejudices, behind
which lurk in ambush just as many bourgeois interests.

All the preceding classes that got the upper hand sought to for- 54
tify their already acquired status by subjecting society at large to
their conditions of appropriation. The proletarians cannot become
masters of the productive forces of society, except by abolishing
their own previous mode of appropriation, and thereby also every
other previous mode of appropriation. They have nothing of their
own to secure and to fortify; their mission is to destroy all previous
securities for and insurances of individual property.

All previous historical movements were movements of minori- 55
ties, or in the interest of minorities. The proletarian movement is the
self-conscious, independent movement of the immense majority.
The proletariat, the lowest stratum of our present society, cannot
stir, cannot raise itself up without the whole superincumbent strata
of official society being sprung into the air.

Though not in substance, yet in form, the struggle of the pro- 56
letariat with the bourgeoisie is at first a national struggle. The
proletariat of each country must, of course, first of all settle matters
with its own bourgeoisie.

In depicting the most general phases of the development of the 57 proletariat, we traced the more or less veiled civil war, raging within existing society, up to the point where that war breaks out into open revolution, and where the violent overthrow of the bourgeoisie, lays the foundations for the sway of the proletariat.

Hitherto every form of society has been based, as we have al- 58 ready seen, on the antagonism of oppressing and oppressed classes. But in order to oppress a class, certain conditions must be assured to it under which it can, at least, continue its slavish existence. The serf, in the period of serfdom, raised himself to membership in the commune, just as the petty bourgeois, under the yoke of feudal absolutism, managed to develop into a bourgeois. The modern laborer, on the contrary, instead of rising with the progress of industry, sinks deeper and deeper below the conditions of existence of his own class. He becomes a pauper, and pauperism develops more rapidly than population and wealth. And here it becomes evident that the bourgeoisie is unfit any longer to be the ruling class in society, and to impose its conditions of existence upon society as an over-riding law. It is unfit to rule, because it is incompetent to assure an existence to its slave within his slavery, because it cannot help letting him sink into such a state that it has to feed him, instead of being fed by him. Society can no longer live under this bourgeoisie; in other words, its existence is no longer compatible with society.

The essential condition for the existence, and for the sway of the 59 bourgeois class, is the formation and augmentation of capital; the condition for capital is wage labor. Wage labor rests exclusively on competition between the laborers. The advance of industry, whose involuntary promoter is the bourgeoisie, replaces the isolation of the laborers, due to competition, by their involuntary combination, due to association. The development of Modern Industry, therefore, cuts from under its feet the very foundation on which the bourgeoisie produces and appropriates products. What the bourgeoisie therefore produces, above all, are its own grave diggers. Its fall and the victory of the proletariat are equally inevitable.

Proletarians and Communists

In what relation do the Communists stand to the proletarians as 60 a whole?

The Communists do not form a separate party opposed to other 61 working class parties.

They have no interests separate and apart from those of the pro- 62 letariat as a whole.

They do not set up any sectarian principles of their own, by 63 which to shape and mold the proletarian movement.

The Communists are distinguished from the other working class 64 parties by this only: 1. In the national struggles of the proletarians of the different countries, they point out and bring to the front the common interests of the entire proletariat, independently of all nationality. 2. In the various stages of development which the struggle of the working class against the bourgeoisie has to pass through, they always and everywhere represent the interests of the movement as a whole.

The Communists, therefore, are on the one hand practically the 65 most advanced and resolute section of the working class parties of every country, that section which pushes forward all others; on the other hand, theoretically, they have over the great mass of the proletariat the advantage of clearly understanding the line of march, the conditions, and the ultimate general results of the proletarian movement.

The immediate aim of the Communists is the same as that of all 66 the other proletarian parties: formation of the proletariat into a class, overthrow of the bourgeois of supremacy, conquest of political power by the proletariat.

The theoretical conclusions of the Communists are in no way 67 based on ideas or principles that have been invented or discovered by this or that would-be universal reformer.

They merely express, in general terms, actual relations springing 68 from an existing class struggle, from a historical movement going on under our very eyes. The abolition of existing property relations is not at all a distinctive feature of Communism.

All property relations in the past have continually been sub- 69 ject to historical change consequent upon the change in historical conditions.

The French Revolution, for example, abolished feudal property 70 in favor of bourgeois property.

The distinguishing feature of Communism is not the abolition 71 of property generally, but the abolition of bourgeois property. But modern bourgeois private property is the final and most complete expression of the system of producing and appropriating products, that is based on class antagonism, on the exploitation of the many by the few.

In this sense, the theory of the Communists may be summed up 72 in the single sentence: Abolition of private property.

We Communists have been reproached with the desire of abol- 73 ishing the right of personally acquiring property as the fruit of a man's own labor, which property is alleged to be the groundwork of all personal freedom, activity and independence.

Hard won, self-acquired, self-earned property! Do you mean the   74
property of the petty artisan and of the small peasant, a form of
property that preceded the bourgeois form? There is no need to
abolish that; the development of industry has to a great extent already destroyed it, and is still destroying it daily.

Or do you mean modern bourgeois private property?   75

But does wage labor create any property for the laborer? Not a   76
bit. It creates capital, i.e., that kind of property which exploits wage
labor, and which cannot increase except upon condition of getting a
new supply of wage labor for fresh exploitation. Property, in its
present form, is based on the antagonism of capital and wage labor.
Let us examine both sides of this antagonism.

To be a capitalist is to have not only a purely personal, but a so-   77
cial status in production. Capital is a collective product, and only by
the united action of many members, nay, in the last resort, only by
the united action of all members of society, can it be set in motion.

Capital is therefore not a personal, it is a social power.   78

When, therefore, capital is converted into common property,   79
into the property of all members of society, personal property is not
thereby transformed into social property. It is only the social character of the property that is changed. It loses its class character.

Let us now take wage labor.   80

The average price of wage labor is the minimum wage, i.e., that   81
quantum of the means of subsistence which is absolutely requisite to
keep the laborer in bare existence as a laborer. What, therefore, the
wage laborer appropriates by means of his labor, merely suffices to
prolong and reproduce a bare existence. We by no means intend to
abolish this personal appropriation of the products of labor, an appropriation that is made for the maintenance and reproduction of
human life, and that leaves no surplus wherewith to command the
labor of others. All that we want to do away with is the miserable
character of this appropriation, under which the laborer lives merely
to increase capital and is allowed to live only in so far as the interests
of the ruling class require it.

In bourgeois society, living labor is but a means to increase ac-   82
cumulated labor. In Communist society accumulated labor is but a
means to widen, to enrich, to promote the existence of the laborer.

In bourgeois society, therefore, the past dominates the present;   83
in Communist society the present dominates the past. In bourgeois
society, capital is independent and has individuality, while the living
person is dependent and has no individuality.

And the abolition of this state of things is called by the bour-   84
geois abolition of individuality and freedom! And rightly so. The
abolition of bourgeois individuality, bourgeois independence and
bourgeois freedom is undoubtedly aimed at.

By freedom is meant, under the present bourgeois conditions of 85
production, free trade, free selling and buying.

But if selling and buying disappears, free selling and buying dis- 86
appears also. This talk about free selling and buying, and all the other
"brave words" of our bourgeoisie about freedom in general have a
meaning, if any, only in contrast with restricted selling and buying,
with the fettered traders of the Middle Ages, but have no meaning
when opposed to the Communistic abolition of buying and selling, of
the bourgeois conditions of production, and of the bourgeoisie itself.

You are horrified at our intending to do away with private prop- 87
erty. But in your existing society private property is already done
away with for nine-tenths of the population; its existence for the few
is solely due to its non-existence in the hands of those nine-tenths.
You reproach us, therefore, with intending to do away with a form
of property, the necessary condition for whose existence is the non-
existence of any property for the immense majority of society.

In one word, you reproach us with intending to do away with 88
your property. Precisely so: that is just what we intend.

From the moment when labor can no longer be converted into 89
capital, money, or rent, into a social power capable of being monopolized, i.e., from the moment when individual property can no
longer be transformed into bourgeois property, into capital, from
that moment, you say, individuality vanishes.

You must, therefore, confess that by "individual" you mean no 90
other person than the bourgeois, than the middle-class owner of
property. This person must, indeed, be swept out of the way and
made impossible.

Communism deprives no man of the power to appropriate the 91
products of society: all that it does is to deprive him of the power to
subjugate the labor of others by means of such appropriation.

It has been objected that upon the abolition of private property 92
all work will cease and universal laziness will overtake us.

According to this, bourgeois society ought long ago to have 93
gone to the dogs through sheer idleness; for those of its members
who work acquire nothing, and those who acquire anything do not
work. The whole of this objection is but another expression of the
tautology:[11] that there can no longer be any wage labor when there
is no longer any capital.

All objections urged against the Communistic mode of produc- 94
ing and appropriating material products have, in the same way, been

---

[11] **tautology** A statement whose two parts say essentially the same thing. The
second half of the previous sentence is a tautology.

urged against the Communistic modes of producing and appropriating intellectual products. Just as, to the bourgeois, the disappearance of class property is the disappearance of production itself, so
the disappearance of class culture is to him identical with the disappearance of all culture.

That culture, the loss of which he laments, is, for the enormous   95
majority, a mere training to act as a machine.

But don't wrangle with us so long as you apply, to our intended   96
abolition of bourgeois property, the standard of your bourgeois notions of freedom, culture, law, etc. Your very ideas are but the out-
growth of the conditions of your bourgeois production and bourgeois
property, just as your jurisprudence is but the will of your class made
into a law for all, a will whose essential character and direction are determined by the economical conditions of existence of your class.

The selfish misconception that induces you to transform into   97
eternal laws of nature and of reason the social forms springing from
your present mode of production and form of property—historical
relations that rise and disappear in the progress of production—this
misconception you share with every ruling class that has preceded
you. What you see clearly in the case of ancient property, what you
admit in the case of feudal property, you are of course forbidden to
admit in the case of your own bourgeois form of property.

Abolition of the family! Even the most radical flare up at this in-   98
famous proposal of the Communists.

On what foundation is the present family, the bourgeois family,   99
based? On capital, on private gain. In its completely developed form
this family exists only among the bourgeoisie. But this state of things
finds its complement in the practical absence of the family among
the proletarians, and in public prostitution.

The bourgeois family will vanish as a matter of course when its   100
complement vanishes, and both will vanish with the vanishing of
capital.

Do you charge us with wanting to stop the exploitation of chil-   101
dren by their parents? To this crime we plead guilty.

But, you will say, we destroy the most hallowed of relations   102
when we replace home education by social.

And your education! Is not that also social, and determined by   103
the social conditions under which you educate; by the intervention,
direct or indirect, of society by means of schools, etc.? The Communists have not invented the intervention of society in education; they
do but seek to alter the character of that intervention, and to rescue
education from the influence of the ruling class.

The bourgeois clap-trap about the family and education, about   104
the hallowed correlation of parent and child, become all the more

disgusting, the more, by the action of Modern Industry, all family ties among the proletarians are torn asunder and their children transformed into simple articles of commerce and instruments of labor.

But you Communists would introduce community of women, 105 screams the whole bourgeoisie chorus.

The bourgeois sees in his wife a mere instrument of production. 106 He hears that the instruments of production are to be exploited in common, and, naturally, can come to no other conclusion, than that the lot of being common to all will likewise fall to the women.

He has not even a suspicion that the real point aimed at is to do 107 away with the status of women as mere instruments of production.

For the rest, nothing is more ridiculous than the virtuous indig- 108 nation of our bourgeois at the community of women which, they pretend, is to be openly and officially established by the Communists. The Communists have no need to introduce community of women, it has existed almost from time immemorial.

Our bourgeois, not content with having the wives and daugh- 109 ters of their proletarians at their disposal, not to speak of common prostitutes, take the greatest pleasure in seducing each others' wives.

Bourgeois marriage is in reality a system of wives in common, 110 and thus, at the most, what the Communists might possibly be reproached with, is that they desire to introduce, in substitution for a hypocritically concealed, an openly legalized community of women. For the rest, it is self-evident that the abolition of the present system of production must bring with it the abolition of the community of women springing from that system, i.e., of prostitution both public and private.

The Communists are further reproached with desiring to abol- 111 ish countries and nationalities.

The working men have no country. We cannot take from them 112 what they don't possess. Since the proletariat must first of all acquire political supremacy, must rise to be the leading class of the nation, must constitute itself the nation, it is, so far, itself national, though not in the bourgeois sense of the word.

National differences and antagonisms between peoples are daily 113 more and more vanishing, owing to the development of the bourgeoisie, to freedom of commerce, to the world-market, to uniformity in the mode of production and in the conditions of life corresponding thereto.

The supremacy of the proletariat will cause them to vanish still 114 faster. United action, of the leading civilized countries at least, is one of the first conditions for the emancipation of the proletariat.

In proportion as the exploitation of one individual by another is 115 put an end to, the exploitation of one nation by another will also be put an end to. In proportion as the antagonism between classes within the nation vanishes, the hostility of one nation to another will come to an end.

The charges against Communism made from a religious, a 116 philosophical, and generally, from an ideological standpoint, are not deserving of serious examination.

Does it require deep intuition to comprehend that man's ideas, 117 views and conceptions, in one word, man's consciousness, changes with every change in the conditions of his material existence, in his social relations and in his social life?

What else does the history of ideas prove than that intellectual 118 production changes in character in proportion as material production is changed? The ruling ideas of each age have ever been the ideas of its ruling class.

When people speak of ideas that revolutionize society they do 119 but express the fact that within the old society the elements of a new one have been created, and that the dissolution of the old ideas keeps even pace with the dissolution of the old conditions of existence.

When the ancient world was in its last throes the ancient reli- 120 gions were overcome by Christianity. When Christian ideas succumbed in the 18th century to rationalist ideas, feudal society fought its death battle with the then revolutionary bourgeoisie. The ideas of religious liberty and freedom of conscience merely gave expression to the sway of free competition within the domain of knowledge.

"Undoubtedly," it will be said, "religious, moral, philosophical 121 and judicial ideas have been modified in the course of historical development. But religion, morality, philosophy, political science, and law, constantly survived this change.

"There are, besides, eternal truths such as Freedom, Justice, etc., 122 that are common to all states of society. But Communism abolishes eternal truths, it abolishes all religion and all morality, instead of constituting them on a new basis; it therefore acts in contradiction to all past historical experience."

What does this accusation reduce itself to? The history of all 123 past society has consisted in the development of class antagonisms, antagonisms that assumed different forms at different epochs.

But whatever form they may have taken, one fact is common to 124 all past ages, viz., the exploitation of one part of society by the other. No wonder, then, that the social consciousness of past ages, despite all the multiplicity and variety it displays, moves within certain common forms, or general ideas, which cannot completely vanish except with the total disappearance of class antagonisms.

The Communist revolution is the most radical rupture with tra- 125
ditional property relations; no wonder that its development involves
the most radical rupture with traditional ideas.

But let us have done with the bourgeois objections to Com- 126
munism.

We have seen above that the first step in the revolution by the 127
working class is to raise the proletariat to the position of ruling class,
to win the battle of democracy.

The proletariat will use its political supremacy to wrest, by de- 128
grees, all capital from the bourgeoisie, to centralize all instruments
of production in the hands of the State, i.e., of the proletariat organized as a ruling class; and to increase the total productive forces as
rapidly as possible.

Of course, in the beginning, this cannot be effected except by 129
means of despotic inroads on the rights of property, and on the conditions of bourgeois production; by means of measures, therefore,
which appear economically insufficient and untenable, but which in
the course of the movement outstrip themselves, necessitate further
inroads upon the old social order, and are unavoidable as a means of
entirely revolutionizing the mode of production.

These measures will of course be different in different countries. 130

Nevertheless in the most advanced countries the following will 131
be pretty generally applicable:

1. Abolition of property in land and application of all rents of land
   to public purposes.
2. A heavy progressive or graduated income tax.
3. Abolition of all right of inheritance.
4. Confiscation of the property of all emigrants and rebels.
5. Centralization of credit in the hands of the State, by means of a
   national bank with State capital and an exclusive monopoly.
6. Centralization of the means of communication and transport in
   the hands of the State.
7. Extension of factories and instruments of production owned by
   the State; the bringing into cultivation of waste lands, and the
   improvement of the soil generally in accordance with a common
   plan.
8. Equal liability of all to labor. Establishment of industrial armies,
   especially for agriculture.
9. Combination of agriculture with manufacturing industries; gradual abolition of the distinction between town and country by a
   more equable distribution of the population over the country.
10. Free education for all children in public schools. Abolition of
    children's factory labor in its present form. Combination of edu-
    cation with industrial production, etc., etc.

When, in the course of development, class distinctions have dis- 132 appeared, and all production has been concentrated in the hands of a vast association of the whole nation, the public power will lose its political character. Political power, properly so called, is merely the organized power of one class for oppressing another. If the proletariat during its contest with the bourgeoisie is compelled, by the force of circumstances, to organize itself as a class, if, by means of a revolution, it makes itself the ruling class, and, as such, sweeps away by force the old conditions of production, then it will, along with these conditions, have swept away the conditions for the existence of class antagonism, and of classes generally, and will thereby have abolished its own supremacy as a class.

In place of the old bourgeois society, with its classes and class 133 antagonisms, we shall have an association in which the free development of each is the condition for the free development of all....

Position of the Communists in Relation to the Various Existing Opposition Parties

[The preceding section] has made clear the relations of the 134 Communists to the existing working class parties, such as the Chartists in England and the Agrarian Reforms[12] in America.

The Communists fight for the attainment of the immediate 135 aims, for the enforcement of the momentary interests of the working class; but in the movement of the present they also represent and take care of the future of that movement. In France the Communists ally themselves with the Social-Democrats[13] against the conservative and radical bourgeoisie, reserving, however, the right to take up a critical position in regard to phrases and illusions traditionally handed down from the great Revolution.

In Switzerland they support the Radicals,[14] without losing sight 136 of the fact that this party consists of antagonistic elements, partly

---

[12] **Agrarian Reforms** Agrarian reform was a very important issue in America after the Revolution. The Chartists were a radical English group established in 1838; they demanded political and social reforms. They were among the more violent revolutionaries of the day. Agrarian reform, or redistribution of the land, was slow to come, and the issue often sparked violence between social classes.

[13] **Social-Democrats** In France in the 1840s, a group that proposed the ideal of labor reform through the establishment of workshops supplied with government capital.

[14] **Radicals** By 1848, European Radicals, taking their name from the violent revolutionaries of the French Revolution (1789–1799), were a nonviolent group content to wait for change.

of Democratic Socialists, in the French sense, partly of radical bourgeois.

In Poland they support the party that insists on an agrarian rev- 137 olution, as the prime condition for national emancipation, that party which fomented the insurrection of Cracow in 1846.[15]

In Germany they fight with the bourgeoisie whenever it acts in a 138 revolutionary way, against the absolute monarchy, the feudal squirearchy, and the petty bourgeoisie.

But they never cease for a single instant to instill into the work- 139 ing class the clearest possible recognition of the hostile antagonism between bourgeoisie and proletariat, in order that the German workers may straightway use, as so many weapons against the bourgeoisie, the social and political conditions that the bourgeoisie must necessarily introduce along with its supremacy, and in order that, after the fall of the reactionary classes in Germany, the fight against the bourgeoisie itself may immediately begin.

The Communists turn their attention chiefly to Germany, be- 140 cause that country is on the eve of a bourgeois revolution,[16] that is bound to be carried out under more advanced conditions of European civilization, and with a more developed proletariat, than that of England was in the seventeenth and of France in the eighteenth century, and because the bourgeois revolution in Germany will be but the prelude to an immediately following proletarian revolution.

In short, the Communists everywhere support every revolution- 141 ary movement against the existing social and political order of things.

In all these movements they bring to the front, as the leading 142 question in each, the property question, no matter what its degree of development at the time.

Finally, they labor everywhere for the union and agreement of 143 the democratic parties of all countries.

The Communists disdain to conceal their views and aims. They 144 openly declare that their ends can be attained only by the forcible overthrow of all existing social conditions. Let the ruling classes tremble at a Communistic revolution. The proletarians have nothing to lose but their chains. They have a world to win.

Working men of all countries, unite!   145

---

[15] **the insurrection of Cracow in 1846** Cracow was an independent city in 1846. The insurrection was designed to join Cracow with Poland and to further large-scale social reforms.

[16] **on the eve of a bourgeois revolution** Ferdinand Lassalle (1825–1864) developed the German labor movement and was in basic agreement with Marx, who was nevertheless convinced that Lassalle's approach was wrong. The environment in Germany seemed appropriate for revolution, in part because of its fragmented political structure and in part because no major revolution had yet occurred there.

QUESTIONS FOR CRITICAL READING

1. Begin by establishing your understanding of the terms *bourgeois* and *proletarian*. Does Marx make a clear distinction between the terms? Are such terms applicable to American society today? Which of these groups, if any, do you feel that you belong to?
2. Marx makes the concept of social class fundamental to his theories. Can "social class" be easily defined? Are social classes evident in our society? Are they engaged in a struggle of the sort Marx assumes to be inevitable?
3. What are Marx's views about the value of work in the society he describes? What is his attitude toward wealth?
4. Marx says that every class struggle is a political struggle. Do you agree?
5. Examine the first part. Which class gets more paragraphs — the bourgeoisie or the proletariat? Why?
6. Is the modern proletariat a revolutionary class?
7. Is Marx's analysis of history clear? Try to summarize his views on the progress of history.
8. Is capital a social force, or is it a personal force? Do you think of your savings (either now or in the future) as belonging to you alone or as in some way belonging to your society?
9. What, in Marx's view, is the responsibility of wealthy citizens?

SUGGESTIONS FOR WRITING

1. Defend or attack Marx's statement: "The executive of the modern State is but a committee for managing the common affairs of the whole bourgeoisie" (para. 18). Is this generally true? Take three "affairs of the whole bourgeoisie" and test each one in turn.
2. Examine Marx's statements regarding women. Refer especially to paragraphs 39, 98, 105, and 110. Does he imply that his views are in conflict with those of his general society? After you have a list of his statements, see if you can establish exactly what he is recommending. Do you approve of his recommendations?
3. Marx's program of ten points is listed in paragraph 131. Using the technique that Marx himself uses — taking each point in its turn, clarifying the problems with the point, and finally deciding for or against the point — evaluate his program. Which points do you feel are most beneficial to society? Which are detrimental to society? What is your overall view of the general worth of the program? Do you think it would be possible to put such a program into effect?
4. All Marx's views are predicated on the present nature of property ownership and the changes that communism will institute. He claims, for example, that a rupture with property relations "involves the most radical rupture with traditional ideas" (para. 125). And he discusses in depth his proposal for the rupture of property relations (paras. 68–93). Clarify traditional property relations — what can be owned and by

whom—and then contrast with these the proposals Marx makes. Establish your own views as you go along. Include your reasons for taking issue or expressing agreement with Marx. What kinds of property relations do you see around you? What kinds are most desirable for a healthy society?

5. What is the responsibility of the state toward the individual in the kind of economic circumstances that Marx describes? How can the independence of individuals who have amassed great wealth and wish to operate freely be balanced against the independence of those who are poor and have no wealth to manipulate? What kinds of abuse are possible in such circumstances, and what remedies can a state achieve through altering the economic system? What specific remedies does Marx suggest? Are they workable?

6. Do you feel that Marx's suggestions are desirable? Or that they are likely to produce the effects he desires? Critics sometimes complain about Marx's misunderstanding of human nature. Do you feel he has an adequate understanding of human nature? What do you see as impediments to the full success of his program?

7. How accurate is Marx's view of the bourgeoisie? He identifies the bourgeoisie with capital and capitalists. He also complains that the bourgeoisie has established a world market for goods and by doing so has destroyed national and regional identities. Examine his analysis in paragraphs 22–36 in terms of what you see happening in the economic world today and decide whether or not his ideas about how the bourgeoisie functions still apply and ring true. Has Marx foreseen the problems of globalization that incited protests and riots such as those aimed at the World Bank, the World Trade Organization, and the International Monetary Fund during the last years of the twentieth century into the early part of the twenty-first century?

PLATO
Crito

CHARACTERS
SOCRATES
CRITO
Scene—The Prison of Socrates

SOCRATES. Why have you come at this hour, Crito? Is it not still 1 early?

CRITO. Yes, very early.

SOCR. About what time is it?

CRITO. It is just daybreak.

SOCR. I wonder that the jailer was willing to let you in.

CRITO. He knows me now, Socrates; I come here so often, and besides, I have given him a tip.

SOCR. Have you been here long?

CRITO. Yes, some time.

SOCR. Then why did you sit down without speaking? Why did you not wake me at once?

CRITO. Indeed, Socrates, I wish that I myself were not so sleepless and sorrowful. But I have been wondering to see how soundly you sleep. And I purposely did not wake you, for I was anxious not to disturb your repose. Often before, all through your life, I have thought that your temperament was a happy one; and I think so more than ever now when I see how easily and calmly you bear the calamity that has come to you.

SOCR. Nay, Crito, it would be absurd if at my age I were disturbed at having to die.

Translated by F. J. Church

CRITO. Other men as old are overtaken by similar calamities, Socrates; but their age does not save them from being disturbed by their fate.

SOCR. That is so; but tell me why are you here so early?

CRITO. I am the bearer of sad news, Socrates; not sad, it seems, for you, but for me and for all your friends, both sad and hard to bear; and for none of them, I think, is it as hard to bear as it is for me.

SOCR. What is it? Has the ship come from Delos, at the arrival of which I am to die?

CRITO. No, it has not actually arrived, but I think that it will be here today, from the news which certain persons have brought from Sunium, who left it there. It is clear from their report that it will be here today; and so, Socrates, tomorrow your life will have to end.

SOCR. Well, Crito, may it end well. Be it so, if so the gods will. But II I do not think that the ship will be here today.

CRITO. Why do you suppose not?

SOCR. I will tell you. I am to die on the day after the ship arrives, am I not?[1]

CRITO. That is what the authorities say.

SOCR. Then I do not think that it will come today, but tomorrow. I am counting on a dream I had a little while ago in the night, so it seems to be fortunate that you did not wake me.

CRITO. And what was this dream?

SOCR. A fair and beautiful woman, clad in white, seemed to come to me, and call me and say, "O Socrates—

On the third day shall you fertile Phthia reach." [2]

CRITO. What a strange dream, Socrates!

SOCR. But its meaning is clear, at least to me, Crito.

CRITO. Yes, too clear, it seems. But, O my good Socrates, I beg you III for the last time to listen to me and save yourself. For to me your death will be more than a single disaster; not only shall I lose a friend the like of whom I shall never find again, but many persons who do not know you and me well will think that I might have saved you if I had been willing to spend money, but that I neglected to do so. And what reputation could be more disgraceful than the reputation of

---

[1] Criminals could not be put to death while the sacred ship was away on its voyage.—Ed.

[2] Homer, *Iliad*, ix, 363.

caring more for money than for one's friends? The public will never believe that we were anxious to save you, but that you yourself refused to escape.

SOCR. But, my dear Crito, why should we care so much about public opinion? Reasonable men, of whose opinion it is worth our while to think, will believe that we acted as we really did.

CRITO. But you see, Socrates, that it is necessary to care about public opinion, too. This very thing that has happened to you proves that the multitude can do a man not the least, but almost the greatest harm, if he is falsely accused to them.

SOCR. I wish that the multitude were able to do a man the greatest harm, Crito, for then they would be able to do him the greatest good, too. That would have been fine. But, as it is, they can do neither. They cannot make a man either wise or foolish: they act wholly at random.

CRITO. Well, as you wish. But tell me this, Socrates. You surely are IV not anxious about me and your other friends, and afraid lest, if you escape, the informers would say that we stole you away, and get us into trouble, and involve us in a great deal of expense, or perhaps in the loss of all our property, and, it may be, bring some other punishment upon us besides? If you have any fear of that kind, dismiss it. For of course we are bound to run these risks, and still greater risks than these, if necessary, in saving you. So do not, I beg you, refuse to listen to me.

SOCR. I am anxious about that, Crito, and about much besides.

CRITO. Then have no fear on that score. There are men who, for no very large sum, are ready to bring you out of prison into safety. And then, you know, these informers are cheaply bought, and there would be no need to spend much upon them. My fortune is at your service, and I think that it is adequate; and if you have any feeling about making use of my money, there are strangers in Athens whom you know, ready to use theirs; and one of them, Simmias of Thebes, has actually brought enough for this very purpose. And Cebes and many others are ready, too. And therefore, I repeat, do not shrink from saving yourself on that ground. And do not let what you said in the court—that if you went into exile you would not know what to do with yourself—stand in your way; for there are many places for you to go to, where you will be welcomed. If you choose to go to Thessaly, I have friends there who will make much of you and protect you from any annoyance from the people of Thessaly.

And besides, Socrates, I think that you will be doing V what is unjust if you abandon your life when you might preserve it. You are simply playing into your enemies' hands; it is exactly what they wanted—to destroy you. And what is more, to me you seem to be abandoning your children, too. You will leave them to take their chance in life, as far as you are concerned, when you might bring them up and educate them. Most likely their fate will be the usual fate of children who are left orphans. But you ought not to bring children into the world unless you mean to take the trouble of bringing them up and educating them. It seems to me that you are choosing the easy way, and not the way of a good and brave man, as you ought, when you have been talking all your life long of the value that you set upon human excellence. For my part, I feel ashamed both for you and for us who are your friends. Men will think that the whole thing which has happened to you—your appearance in court to face trial, when you need not have appeared at all; the very way in which the trial was conducted; and then last of all this, the crowning absurdity of the whole affair— is due to our cowardice. It will look as if we had shirked the danger out of miserable cowardice; for we did not save you, and you did not save yourself, when it was quite possible to do so if we had been good for anything at all. Take care, Socrates, lest these things be not evil only, but also dishonorable to you and to us. Reflect, then, or rather the time for reflection is past; we must make up our minds. And there is only one plan possible. Everything must be done tonight. If we delay any longer, we are lost. Socrates, I implore you not to refuse to listen to me.

SOCR. My dear Crito, if your anxiety to save me be right, it is most VI valuable; but if not, the greater it is the harder it will be to cope with. We must reflect, then, whether we are to do as you say or not; for I am still what I always have been—a man who will accept no argument but that which on reflection I find to be truest. I cannot cast aside my former arguments because this misfortune has come to me. They seem to me to be as true as ever they were, and I respect and honor the same ones as I used to. And if we have no better argument to substitute for them, I certainly shall not agree to your proposal, not even though the power of the multitude should scare us with fresh terrors, as children are scared with hobgoblins, and inflict upon us new fines and imprisonments, and deaths. What is the most appropriate way of examining the question? Shall we go back first to what you say about opinions, and ask if we used to be right in thinking that we ought to pay attention to some opinions, and not to others? Were we right in saying so before I was condemned to die, and has it now become apparent that we were talking at random and arguing for the sake of argument, and that it was really nothing but playful nonsense? I am anxious, Crito, to examine our former argument with your help, and to see whether my present circumstance will appear to me to have affected its truth in any way or not; and whether we are to set it aside, or to yield assent to it. Those of us who thought at all seriously always used to say, I think, exactly what I said just now, namely, that we ought to respect some of the opinions which men form, and not others. Tell me, Crito, I beg you, do you not think that they were right? For you in all probability will not have to die tomorrow, and your judgment will not be biased by that circumstance. Reflect, then, do you not think it reasonable to say that we should not respect all the opinions of men but only some, nor the opinions of all men but only of some men? What do you think? Is not this true?

CRITO. It is.

SOCR. And we should respect the good opinions, and not the worthless ones?

CRITO. Yes.

SOCR. But the good opinions are those of the wise, and the worthless ones those of the foolish?

CRITO. Of course.

SOCR. And what did we say about this? Does a man who is in VII training, and who is serious about it, pay attention to the praise and blame and opinion of all men, or only of the one man who is a doctor or a trainer?

CRITO. He pays attention only to the opinion of the one man.

SOCR. Then he ought to fear the blame and welcome the praise of this one man, not of the multitude?

CRITO. Clearly.

SOCR. Then he must act and exercise, and eat and drink in whatever way the one man who is his director, and who understands the matter, tells him; not as others tell him?

CRITO. That is so.

SOCR. Good. But if he disobeys this one man, and disregards his opinion and his praise, and respects instead what the many say, who understand nothing of the matter, will he not suffer for it?

CRITO.	Of course he will.	IX
SOCR.	And how will he suffer? In what way and in what part of himself?	
CRITO.	Of course in his body. That is disabled.	
SOCR.	You are right. And, Crito, to be brief, is it not the same in everything? And, therefore, in questions of justice and injustice, and of the base and the honorable, and of good and evil, which we are now examining, ought we to follow the opinion of the many and fear that, or the opinion of the one man who understands these matters (if we can find him), and feel more shame and fear before him than before all other men? For if we do not follow him, we shall corrupt and maim that part of us which, we used to say, is improved by justice and disabled by injustice. Or is this not so?	
CRITO.	No, Socrates, I agree with you.	VIII
SOCR.	Now, if, by listening to the opinions of those who do not understand, we disable that part of us which is improved by health and corrupted by disease, is our life worth living when it is corrupt? It is the body, is it not?	
CRITO.	Yes.	
SOCR.	Is life worth living with the body corrupted and crippled?	
CRITO.	No, certainly not.	
SOCR.	Then is life worth living when that part of us which is maimed by injustice and benefited by justice is corrupt? Or do we consider that part of us, whatever it is, which has to do with justice and injustice to be of less consequence than our body?	
CRITO.	No, certainly not.	
SOCR.	But more valuable?	
CRITO.	Yes, much more so.	
SOCR.	Then, my good friend, we must not think so much of what the many will say of us; we must think of what the one man who understands justice and injustice, and of what truth herself will say of us. And so you are mistaken, to begin with, when you invite us to regard the opinion of the multitude concerning the just and the honorable and the good, and their opposites. But, it may be said, the multitude can put us to death?	
CRITO.	Yes, that is evident. That may be said, Socrates.	
SOCR.	True. But, my good friend, to me it appears that the conclusion which we have just reached is the same as our conclusion of former times. Now consider whether we still hold to the belief that we should set the highest value, not on living, but on living well?	

CRITO. Yes, we do.

SOCR. And living well and honorably and justly mean the same thing: do we hold to that or not?

CRITO. We do.

SOCR. Then, starting from these premises, we have to consider IX whether it is just or not for me to try to escape from prison, without the consent of the Athenians. If we find that it is just, we will try; if not, we will give up the idea. I am afraid that considerations of expense, and of reputation, and of bringing up my children, of which you talk, Crito, are only the opinions of the many, who casually put men to death, and who would, if they could, as casually bring them to life again, without a thought. But reason, which is our guide, shows us that we can have nothing to consider but the question which I asked just now—namely, shall we be acting justly if we give money and thanks to the men who are to aid me in escaping, and if we ourselves take our respective parts in my escape? Or shall we in truth be acting unjustly if we do all this? And if we find that we should be acting unjustly, then we must not take any account either of death, or of any other evil that may be the consequence of remaining here, where we are, but only of acting unjustly.

CRITO. I think that you are right, Socrates. But what are we to do?

SOCR. Let us examine this question together, my friend, and if you can contradict anything that I say, do so, and I shall be persuaded. But if you cannot, do not go on repeating to me any longer, my dear friend, that I should escape without the consent of the Athenians. I am very anxious to act with your approval and consent. I do not want you to think me mistaken. But now tell me if you agree with the premise from which I start, and try to answer my questions as you think best.

CRITO. I will try.

SOCR. Ought we never to act unjustly voluntarily? Or may we act X unjustly in some ways, and not in others? Is it the case, as we have often agreed in former times, that it is never either good or honorable to act unjustly? Or have all our former conclusions been overturned in these few days; and did we at our age fail to recognize all along, when we were seriously conversing with each other, that we were no better than children? Is not what we used to say most certainly the truth, whether the multitude agrees with us or not? Is not acting unjustly evil and shameful in every case, whether we incur a heavier or a lighter punishment as the consequence? Do we believe that?

CRITO. We do.

SOCR. Then we ought never to act unjustly?

CRITO. Certainly not.

SOCR. If we ought never to act unjustly at all, ought we to repay injustice with injustice, as the multitude thinks we may?

CRITO. Clearly not.

SOCR. Well, then, Crito, ought we to do evil to anyone?

CRITO. Certainly I think not, Socrates.

SOCR. And is it just to repay evil with evil, as the multitude thinks, or unjust?

CRITO. Certainly it is unjust.

SOCR. For there is no difference, is there, between doing evil to a man and acting unjustly?

CRITO. True.

SOCR. Then we ought not to repay injustice with injustice or to do harm to any man, no matter what we may have suffered from him. And in conceding this, Crito, be careful that you do not concede more than you mean. For I know that only a few men hold, or ever will hold, this opinion. And so those who hold it and those who do not have no common ground of argument; they can of necessity only look with contempt on each other's belief. Do you therefore consider very carefully whether or not you agree with me and share my opinion. Are we to start in our inquiry from the premise that it is never right either to act unjustly, or to repay injustice with injustice, or to avenge ourselves on any man who harms us, by harming him in return? Or do you disagree with me and dissent from my premise? I myself have believed in it for a long time, and I believe in it still. But if you differ in any way, explain to me how. If you still hold to our former opinion, listen to my next point.

CRITO. Yes, I hold to it, and I agree with you. Go on.

SOCR. Then, my next point, or rather my next question, is this: Ought a man to carry out his just agreements, or may he shuffle out of them?

CRITO. He ought to carry them out.

SOCR. Then consider. If I escape without the state's consent, shall I XI be injuring those whom I ought least to injure, or not? Shall I be abiding by my just agreements or not?

CRITO. I cannot answer your question, Socrates. I do not understand it.

SOCR. Consider it in this way. Suppose the laws and the commonwealth were to come and appear to me as I was preparing to run away (if that is the right phrase to describe my escape) and were to ask, "Tell us, Socrates, what have you in your mind to do? What do you mean by trying to escape but to destroy us, the laws and the whole state, so far as you are able? Do you think that a state can exist and not be over-thrown, in which the decisions of law are of no force, and are disregarded and undermined by private individuals?" How shall we answer questions like that, Crito? Much might be said, especially by an orator, in defense of the law which makes judicial decisions supreme. Shall I reply, "But the state has injured me by judging my case unjustly?" Shall we say that?

CRITO.   Certainly we will, Socrates.

SOCR.   And suppose the laws were to reply, "Was that our agree-   XII ment? Or was it that you would abide by whatever judg-ments the state should pronounce?" And if we were sur-prised by their words, perhaps they would say, "Socrates, don't be surprised by our words, but answer us; you your-self are accustomed to ask questions and to answer them. What complaint have you against us and the state, that you are trying to destroy us? Are we not, first of all, your par-ents? Through us your father took your mother and brought you into the world. Tell us, have you any fault to find with those of us that are the laws of marriage?" "I have none, I should reply. "Or have you any fault to find with those of us that regulate the raising of the child and the ed-ucation which you, like others, received? Did we not do well in telling your father to educate you in music and ath-letics?" "You did," I should say. "Well, then, since you were brought into the world and raised and educated by us, how, in the first place, can you deny that you are our child and our slave, as your fathers were before you? And if this be so, do you think that your rights are on a level with ours? Do you think that you have a right to retaliate if we should try to do anything to you? You had not the same rights that your father had, or that your master would have had if you had been a slave. You had no right to retaliate if they ill-treated you, or to answer them if they scolded you, or to strike them back if they struck you, or to repay them evil with evil in any way. And do you think that you may retali-ate in the case of your country and its laws? If we try to de-stroy you, because we think it just, will you in return do all that you can to destroy us, the laws, and your country, and say that in so doing you are acting justly—you, the man who really thinks so much of excellence? Or are you too wise to see that your country is worthier, more to be revered, more sacred, and held in higher honor both by the gods and by all men of understanding, than your father and your mother and all your other ancestors; and that you ought to reverence it, and to submit to it, and to approach it more humbly when it is angry with you than you would approach your father; and either to do whatever it tells you to do or to persuade it to excuse you; and to obey in silence if it orders you to endure flogging or imprisonment, or if it sends you to battle to be wounded or to die? That is just. You must not give way, nor retreat, nor desert your station. In war, and in the court of justice, and everywhere, you must do whatever your state and your country tell you to do, or you must persuade them that their commands are unjust. But it is impious to use violence against your father or your mother; and much more impious to use violence against your country." What answer shall we make, Crito? Shall we say that the laws speak the truth, or not?

CRITO. I think that they do.

SOCR. "Then consider, Socrates," perhaps they would say, "if we XIII are right in saying that by attempting to escape you are attempting an injustice. We brought you into the world, we raised you, we educated you, we gave you and every other citizen a share of all the good things we could. Yet we proclaim that if any man of the Athenians is dissatisfied with us, he may take his goods and go away wherever he pleases; we give that privilege to every man who chooses to avail himself of it, so soon as he has reached manhood, and sees us, the laws, and the administration of our state. No one of us stands in his way or forbids him to take his goods and go wherever he likes, whether it be to an Athenian colony or to any foreign country, if he is dissatisfied with us and with the state. But we say that every man of you who remains here, seeing how we administer justice, and how we govern the state in other matters, has agreed, by the very fact of remaining here, to do whatsoever we tell him. And, we say, he who disobeys us acts unjustly on three counts: he disobeys us who are his parents, and he disobeys us who reared him, and he disobeys us after he has agreed to obey us, without persuading us that we are wrong. Yet we did not tell him sternly to do whatever we told him. We offered him an alternative; we gave him his choice either to obey us or to convince us that we were wrong; but he does neither.

"These are the charges, Socrates, to which we say that you XIV will expose yourself if you do what you intend; and you are more exposed to these charges than other Athenians." And if I were to ask, "Why?" they might retort with justice that I have bound myself by the agreement with them more than other Athenians. They would say, "Socrates, we have very strong evidence that you were satisfied with us and with the state. You would not have been content to stay at home in it more than other Athenians unless you had been satisfied with it more than they. You never went away from Athens to the festivals, nor elsewhere except on military service; you never made other journeys like other men; you had no desire to see other states or other laws; you were contented with us and our state; so strongly did you prefer us, and agree to be governed by us. And what is more, you had children in this city, you found it so satisfactory. Besides, if you had wished, you might at your trial have offered to go into exile. At that time you could have done with the state's consent what you are trying now to do without it. But then you gloried in being willing to die. You said that you preferred death to exile. And now you do not honor those words: you do not respect us, the laws, for you are trying to destroy us; and you are acting just as a miserable slave would act, trying to run away, and breaking the contracts and agreement which you made to live as our citizen. First, therefore, answer this question. Are we right, or are we wrong, in saying that you have agreed not in mere words, but in your actions, to live under our government?" What are we to say, Crito? Must we not admit that it is true?

CRITO. We must, Socrates.

SOCR. Then they would say, "Are you not breaking your contracts and agreements with us? And you were not led to make them by force or by fraud. You did not have to make up your mind in a hurry. You had seventy years in which you might have gone away if you had been dissatisfied with us, or if the agreement had seemed to you unjust. But you preferred neither Sparta nor Crete, though you are fond of saying that they are well governed, nor any other state, either of the Greeks or the Barbarians. You went away from Athens less than the lame and the blind and the crippled. Clearly you, far more than other Athenians, were satisfied with the state, and also with us who are its laws; for who would be satisfied with a state which had no laws? And now will you not abide by your agreement? If you take our advice, you will, Socrates; then you will not make yourself ridiculous by going away from Athens.

"Reflect now. What good will you do yourself or your xv friends by thus transgressing and breaking your agreement? It is tolerably certain that they, on their part, will at least run the risk of exile, and of losing their civil rights, or of forfeiting their property. You yourself might go to one of the neighboring states, to Thebes or to Megara, for instance—for both of them are well governed—but, Socrates, you will come as an enemy to these governments, and all who care for their city will look askance at you, and think that you are a subverter of law. You will confirm the judges in their opinion, and make it seem that their verdict was a just one. For a man who is a subverter of law may well be supposed to be a corrupter of the young and thoughtless. Then will you avoid well-governed states and civilized men? Will life be worth having, if you do? Will you associate with such men, and converse without shame—about what, Socrates? About the things which you talk of here? Will you tell them that excellence and justice and institutions and law are the most valuable things that men can have? And do you not think that that will be a disgraceful thing for Socrates? You ought to think so. But you will leave these places; you will go to the friends of Crito in Thessaly. For there is found the greatest disorder and license, and very likely they will be delighted to hear of the ludicrous way in which you escaped from prison, dressed up in peasant's clothes, or in some other disguise which people put on when they are running away, and with your appearance altered. But will no one say how you, an old man, with probably only a few more years to live, clung so greedily to life that you dared to break the highest laws? Perhaps not, if you do not annoy them. But if you do, Socrates, you will hear much that will make you blush. You will pass your life as the flatterer and the slave of all men; and what will you be doing but feasting in Thessaly?[3] It will be as if you had made a journey to Thessaly for a banquet. And where will be all our old arguments about justice and excellence then? But you wish to live for the sake of your children? You want to bring them up and educate them? What? Will you take them with you to Thessaly, and bring them up and educate them there? Will you make them strangers to their own country, that you may bestow this benefit of exile on them too? Or supposing that you leave them in Athens, will they be brought up and educated better if you are alive, though you are not with them? Yes, your friends will take care of them. Will your friends take care of them if you make a journey to Thessaly, and not if you make a journey to

---

3 The Athenians disdained the Thessalians as heavy eaters and drinkers.—Ed.

Hades? You ought not to think that, at least if those who call themselves your friends are worth anything at all.

"No, Socrates, be persuaded by us who have reared XVI you. Think neither of children nor of life, nor of any other thing before justice, so that when you come to the other world you may be able to make your defense before the rulers who sit in judgment there. It is clear that neither you nor any of your friends will be happier, or juster, or more pious in this life, if you do this thing, nor will you be happier after you are dead. Now you will go away a victim of the injustice, not of the laws, but of men. But if you repay evil with evil, and injustice with injustice in this shameful way, and break your agreements and covenants with us, and injure those whom you should least injure, yourself and your friends and your country and us, and so escape, then we shall be angry with you while you live, and when you die our brothers, the laws in Hades, will not receive you kindly; for they will know that on earth you did all that you could to destroy us. Listen then to us, and let not Crito persuade you to do as he says."

Be sure, my dear friend Crito, that this is what I seem to hear, as the worshippers of Cybele seem, in their passion, to hear the music of flutes; and the sound of these arguments rings so loudly in my ears, that I cannot hear any other arguments. And I feel sure that if you try to change my mind you will speak in vain. Nevertheless, if you think that you will succeed, speak.

CRITO. I have nothing more to say, Socrates.

SOCR. Then let it be, Crito, and let us do as I say, since the god is our guide.

PLATO
The Apology

Socrates/Meletus
THE SPEECH OF DEFENSE

INTRODUCTION

SOCR. To what degree, Gentlemen of Athens, you have been affected by my accusers, I do not know. I, at any rate, was almost led to forget who I am—so convincingly did they
speak. Yet hardly anything they have said is true. Among
their many falsehoods, I was especially surprised by one:
they said you must be on guard lest I deceive you, since I am
a clever speaker. To have no shame at being directly refuted
by facts when I show myself in no way clever with words—
that, I think, is the very height of shamelessness. Unless, of
course, they call a man a clever speaker if he speaks the
truth. If that is what they mean, why, I would even admit to
being an orator—though not after their fashion.

These men, I claim, have said little or nothing true. But
from me, Gentlemen, you will hear the whole truth. To be
sure, it will not be prettily tricked out in elegant speeches
like theirs, words and phrases all nicely arranged. On the
contrary, you will hear me speak naturally in the words
which happen to occur to me. For I believe what I say to be
just, and let no one of you expect otherwise. Besides, it
would hardly be appropriate in a man of my age, Gentlemen, to come before you making up speeches like a boy.[1]

Translated by R. E. Allen

1. Meletus was quite young when he lodged his prosecution. See *Euthyphro 2b*.

So I must specifically ask one thing of you, Gentlemen. If you hear me make my defense in the same words I customarily use at the tables in the Agora, and other places where many of you have heard me, please do not be surprised or make a disturbance because of it. For things stand thus: I am now come into court for the first time; I am seventy years old; and I am an utter stranger to this place. If I were a foreigner, you would unquestionably make allowances if I spoke in the dialect and manner in which I was raised. In just the same way, I specifically ask you now, and justly so, I think, to pay no attention to my manner of speech—it may perhaps be poor, but perhaps an improvement—and look strictly to this one thing, whether or not I speak justly. For that is the virtue of a judge, and the virtue of an orator is to speak the truth.

STATEMENT

SOCR.　First of all, Gentlemen, it is right for me to defend myself against the first false accusations lodged against me, and my first accusers; and next, against later accusations and later accusers. For the fact is that many accusers have risen before you against me; at this point they have been making accusations for many years, and they have told no truth. Yet I fear them more than I fear Anytus and those around him—though they too are clever. Still, the others are more dangerous. They took hold of most of you in childhood, persuading you of the truth of accusations which were in fact quite false: "There is a certain Socrates . . . wise man . . . thinker on things in the Heavens . . . inquirer into things beneath Earth . . . making the weaker argument stronger." Those men, Gentlemen of Athens, the ones who spread that report, are my dangerous accusers; for their hearers believe that those who inquire into such things acknowledge no gods.

Again, there have been many such accusers, and they have now been at work for a long time; they spoke to you at a time when you were especially credulous—some of you children, some only a little older—and they lodged their accusations quite by default, no one appearing in defense. But the most absurd thing is that one cannot even know or tell their names—unless perhaps in the case of a comic poet.[2] But those who use malicious slander to persuade you, and those who, themselves persuaded, persuade others—

---

2. A reference to Aristophanes, whose description of Socrates in the *Clouds* has in effect just been quoted, and who will later be mentioned by name.

all these are most difficult to deal with. For it is impossible to bring any one of them forward as a witness and cross-examine him. I must rather, as it were, fight with shadows in making my defense, and question where no one answers.

Please grant, then, as I say, that two sets of accusers have risen against me: those who now lodge their accusations, and those who lodged accusations long since. And please accept the fact that I must defend myself against the latter first. For in fact you heard their accusations earlier, and with far greater effect than those which came later.

Very well then. A defense is to be made, Gentlemen of Athens. I am to attempt to remove from you in this short time that prejudice which you have been so long in acquiring. I might wish that this should come to pass, if it were in some way better for you and for me—wish that I might succeed in my defense. But I think that difficult, and its nature hardly escapes me. Still, let that go as pleases the God; the law must be obeyed, and a defense conducted.

REFUTATION OF THE OLD ACCUSERS

SOCR. Let us then take up from the beginning the charges which have given rise to the prejudice—the charges on which Meletus in fact relied in lodging his indictment. Very well, what do those who slander me say? It is necessary to read, as it were, their sworn indictment: "Socrates is guilty of needless curiosity and meddling interference, inquiring into things beneath Earth and in the Sky; making the weaker argument stronger, and teaching others to do the same." The charge is something like that. Indeed, you have seen it for yourselves in a comedy by Aristophanes—a certain Socrates being carried around on the stage, talking about walking on air and babbling a great deal of other nonsense, of which I understand neither much nor little. Mark you, I do not mean to disparage such knowledge, if anyone in fact has it— let me not be brought to trial by Meletus on such a charge as that! But Gentlemen, I have no share in it. Once again, I offer the majority of you as witnesses, and ask those of you who have heard me in conversation—there are many among you—inform each other, please, whether any of you ever heard anything of that sort. From that you will recognize the nature of the other things the multitude says about me.

The fact is that there is nothing in these accusations. And if you have heard from anyone that I undertake to educate men, and make money doing it, that is false too. Once again, I think it would be a fine thing to be able to educate men, as Gorgias of Leontini does, or Prodicus of Ceos, or Hippias of Elis. For each of them, Gentlemen, can enter any given city and convince the youth—who might freely associate with any of their fellow citizens they please—to drop those associations and associate rather with them, to pay money for it, and give thanks in the bargain. As a matter of fact, there is a man here right now, a Parian, and a wise one, who, as I learn, has just come to town. For I happened to meet a person who has spent more money on Sophists than everyone else put together: Callias, son of Hipponicus. So I asked him—for he has two sons—"Callias," I said, "if your two sons were colts or calves, we could get an overseer for them and hire him, and his business would be to make them excellent in their appropriate virtue. He would be either a horse-trainer or a farmer. But as it is, since the two of them are men, whom do you intend to get as an overseer? Who has knowledge of that virtue which belongs to a man and a citizen? Since you have sons, I'm sure you have considered this. Is there such a person." I said, "or not?"

"To be sure." he said.

"Who is he?" I said. "Where is he from, and how much does he charge to teach?"

"Evenus. Socrates," he said. "A Parian. Five minae."[3]

And I counted Evenus fortunate indeed, if he really possesses that art and teaches it so modestly. For my own part, at any rate. I would be puffed up with vanity and pride if I had such knowledge. But I do not, Gentlemen.

Perhaps one of you will ask, "But Socrates, what is this all about? Whence have these slanders against you arisen? You must surely have been busying yourself with something out of the ordinary; so grave a report and rumor would not have arisen had you not been doing something rather different from most folk. Tell us what it is, so that we may not take action in your case unadvisedly." That, I think, is a fair request, and I shall try to indicate what it is that has given me the name I have. Hear me, then. Perhaps some of you will think I joke; be well assured that I shall tell you the whole truth.

Gentlemen of Athens, I got this name through nothing but a kind of wisdom. What kind? The kind which is per-

---

3. Callias's answer is in the "short-answer" style of the Sophists. Cf. *Gorgias* 449b*ff*. *Protagoras* 334e–335c.

haps peculiarly human, for it may be I am really wise in that. And perhaps the men I just mentioned are wise with a wisdom greater than human—either that, or I cannot say what. In any case, I have no knowledge of it, and whoever says I do is lying and speaks to my slander.

Please, Gentlemen of Athens. Do not make a disturbance, even if I seem to you to boast. For it will not be my own words I utter; I shall refer you to the speaker, as one worthy of credit. For as witness to you of my own wisdom—whether it is wisdom of a kind, and what kind of wisdom is—I shall call the God at Delphi.

You surely knew Chaerephon. He was my friend from youth, and a friend of your democratic majority. He went into exile with you,[4] and with you he returned. And you know what kind of a man he was, how eager and impetuous in whatever he rushed into. Well, he once went to Delphi and boldly asked the oracle—as I say, Gentlemen, please do not make a disturbance—he asked whether anyone is wiser than I. Now, the Pythiae[5] replied that no one is wiser. And to this his brother here will testify, since Chaerephon is dead.

Why do I mention this? I mention it because I intend to inform you whence the slander against me has arisen. For when I heard it, I reflected: "What does the God mean? What is the sense of this riddling utterance? I know that I am not wise at all; what then does the God mean by saying I am wisest? Surely he does not speak falsehood; it is not permitted to him." So I puzzled for a long time over what he meant, and then. with great reluctance, I turned to inquire into the matter in some such way as this.

I went to someone with a reputation for wisdom, in the belief that there if anywhere I might test the meaning of the utterance and declare to the oracle that "this man is wiser than I am, and you said I was wisest." So I examined him—there is no need to mention a name, but it was someone in political life who produced this effect on me in discussion, Gentlemen of Athens—and I concluded that though he seemed wise to many other men, and most especially to himself, he was not. I tried to show him this; and thence I became hated, by him and by many who were present. But I left thinking to myself. "I am wiser than that man. Probably

---

4. The leading democrats in Athens were forced into exile when the Thirty Tyrants came to power in 404 B.C.
5. The Priestess of Apollo. Whose major shrine was Delphi.

neither of us knows anything worthwhile; but he thinks he does and does not, and I do not and do not think I do. So it seems at any rate that I am wiser in this one small respect: I do not think I know what I do not." I then went to another man who was reputed to be even wiser, and the same thing seemed true again; there too I became hated, by him and by many others.

Nevertheless, I went on, perceiving with grief and fear that I was becoming hated, but still, it seemed necessary to put the God first—so I had to go on, examining what the oracle meant by testing everyone with a reputation for knowledge. And by the Dog,[6] Gentlemen—I must tell you the truth—I swear that I had some such experience as this: it seemed to me, as I carried on inquiry in behalf of the God, that those most highly esteemed for wisdom fell little short of being most deficient, and that others reputedly inferior were men of more discernment.

But really, I must tell you of my wanderings, the labors I performed[7]—all to the end that I might not leave the oracle untested. From the politicians I went to the poets—tragic, dithyrambic, and the rest—thinking that there I would discover myself manifestly less wise by comparison. So I took up poems over which I thought they had taken special pains, and asked them what they meant, so as also at the same time to learn from them. Now, I am ashamed to tell you the truth, Gentlemen, but still, it must be told. There was hardly anyone present who could not give a better account than they of what they had themselves produced. So presently I came to realize that poets too do not make what they make by wisdom, but by a kind of native disposition or divine inspiration, exactly like seers and prophets. For the latter also utter many fine things, but know nothing of the things they speak. That is how the poets also appeared to me, while at the same time I realized that because of their poetry they thought themselves the wisest of men in other matters—and were not. Once again, I left thinking myself superior to them in just the way I was to the politicians.

Finally I went to the craftsmen. I was aware that although I knew scarcely anything, I would find that they knew many fine things. In this I was not mistaken: they

---

6. A humorous oath. The Dog is the Egyptian dog-headed god, Anubis.
7. I.e., like Heracles.

knew things that I did not, and in that respect were wiser. But, Gentlemen of Athens, it seemed to me that the poets and our capable public craftsmen had exactly the same failing: because they practiced their own arts well, each deemed himself wise in other things, things of great importance. This mistake quite obscured their wisdom. The result was that I asked myself on behalf of the oracle whether I would accept being such as I am, neither wise with their wisdom nor foolish with their folly, or whether I would accept then wisdom and folly together and become such as they are. I answered, both for myself and the oracle, that it was better to be as I am.

From this examination, Gentlemen of Athens, much enmity has risen against me, of a sort most harsh and heavy to endure, so that many slanders have arisen, and the name is put abroad that I am "wise." For on each occasion those present think I am wise in the things in which I test others. But very likely, Gentlemen, it is really the God who is wise, and by his oracle he means to say that "human nature is a thing of little worth, or none." It appears that he does not mean this fellow Socrates, but uses my name to offer an example, as if he were saying that "he among you, Gentlemen, is wisest who, like Socrates, realizes that he is truly worth nothing in respect to wisdom." That is why I still go about even now on behalf of the God, searching and inquiring among both citizens and strangers, should I think some one of them is wise; and when it seems he is not, I help the God and prove it. Due to this pursuit, I have no leisure worth mentioning either for the affairs of the City or for my own estate; I dwell in utter poverty because of my service to God.

Then too the young men follow after me—especially the ones with leisure, namely, the richest. They follow of their own initiative, rejoicing to hear men tested, and often they imitate me and undertake to test others; and next, I think, they find an ungrudging plenty of people who know little or nothing but think they have some knowledge. As a result, those whom they test become angry at me, not at themselves, and say that "this fellow Socrates is utterly polluted and corrupts the youth." And when someone asks them what it is this Socrates does, what it is he teaches, they cannot say because they do not know; but so as not to seem at a loss, they mutter the kind of things that lie ready to hand against anyone who pursues wisdom: "things in the Heavens and beneath the Earth," or "not acknowledging gods," or "making the weaker argument stronger." The truth, I suppose, they would not wish to state, namely, that it is become quite clear that they pretend to knowledge and know nothing. And because they are concerned for their pride, I think, and zealous, and numerous, and speak vehemently and persuasively about me, they have long filled your ears with zealous slander. It was on the strength of this that Meletus attacked me, along with Anytus and Lycon— Meletus angered on behalf of the poets, Anytus on behalf of the public craftsmen and the politicians, Lycon on behalf of the orators. So the result, as I said to begin with, is that I should be most surprised were I able to remove from you in this short time a slander which has grown so great. There, Gentlemen of Athens, you have the truth, and I have concealed or misrepresented nothing in speaking it, great or small. Yet I know quite well that it is just for this that I have become hated—which is in fact an indication of the truth of what I say—and that this is the basis of the slander and charges against me. Whether you inquire into it now or hereafter you will find it to be so.

REFUTATION OF MELETUS

SOCR.   Against the charges lodged by my first accusers, let this defense suffice. But for Meletus—the good man who loves his City, so he says—and for my later accusers, I shall attempt a further defense. Once more then, as before a different set of accusers, let us take up their sworn indictment.[8] It runs something like this: it says that Socrates is guilty of corrupting the youth, and of not acknowledging the gods the City acknowledges, but other new divinities. Such is the charge. Let us examine its particulars.

It claims I am guilty of corrupting the youth. But I claim, Gentlemen of Athens, that it is Meletus who is guilty—guilty of jesting in earnest, guilty of lightly bringing men to trial, guilty of pretending a zealous concern for things he never cared about at all. I shall try to show you that this is true.

Come here, Meletus. Now tell me. Do you count it of greatest importance that the young should be as good as possible?

---

8. The exact indictment is probably preserved in D.L. II.40; cf. Xenophon, *Memorabilia* I.i. 1.

MEL.   I do.

SOCR.   Then come and tell the jurors this: Who improves them? Clearly you know, since it is a matter of concern to you. Having discovered, so you say, that I am the man who is corrupting them, you bring me before these judges to accuse me. But now come and say who makes them better. Inform the judges who he is.

        You see, Meletus. You are silent. You cannot say. And yet, does this not seem shameful to you, and a sufficient indication of what I say, namely, that you never cared at all? Tell us, my friend. Who improves them?

MEL.   The laws.

SOCR.   But I did not ask you that, dear friend. I asked you what man improves them—whoever it is who in the first place knows just that very thing, the laws.

MEL.   These men, Socrates. The judges.

SOCR.   Really, Meletus? These men here are able to educate the youth and improve them?

MEL.   Especially they.

SOCR.   All of them? Or only some?

MEL.   All.

SOCR.   By Hera, you bring good news. An ungrudging plenty of benefactors! But what about the audience here. Do they improve them or not?

MEL.   They too.

SOCR.   And members of the Council?

MEL.   The Councilors too.

SOCR.   Well then, Meletus, do the members of the Assembly, the Ecclesiasts, corrupt the young? Or do they all improve them too?

MEL.   They too.

SOCR.   So it seems that every Athenian makes them excellent except me, and I alone corrupt them. Is that what you are saying?

MEL.   That is exactly what I am saying.

SOCR.   You condemn me to great misfortune. But tell me, do you think it is so with horses? Do all men improve them, while some one man corrupts them? Or quite to the contrary, is it some one man or a very few, namely horse-trainers, who are able to improve them, while the majority of people, if they deal with horses and use them, corrupt them? Is that not true, Meletus, both of horses and all other animals? Of course it is, whether you and Anytus affirm or deny it. It would be good fortune indeed for the youth if only one man corrupted them and the rest benefited. But the fact is, Meletus, that you sufficiently show that you never gave thought to the youth; you clearly indicate your own lack of concern, indicate that you never cared at all about the matters in which you bring action against me.

But again, dear Meletus, tell us this: Is it better to dwell among fellow citizens who are good, or wicked? Do answer, dear friend; surely I ask nothing hard. Do not wicked men do evil things to those around them, and good men good things?

MEL. Of course.

SOCR. Now, is there anyone who wishes to be harmed rather than benefited by those with whom he associates? Answer me, dear friend, for the law requires you to answer. Is there anyone who wishes to be harmed?

MEL. Of course not.

SOCR. Very well then, are you bringing action against me here because I corrupt the youth intentionally, or unintentionally?

MEL. Intentionally, I say.

SOCR. How can that be, Meletus? Are you at your age so much wiser than I at mine that you recognize that evil men always do evil things to those around them, and good men do good, while I have reached such a pitch of folly that I am unaware that if I do some evil to those with whom I associate, I shall very likely receive some evil at their hands, with the result that I do such great evil intentionally, as you claim? I do not believe you, Meletus, and I do not think anyone else does either. On the contrary: either I do not corrupt the youth, or if I do, I do so unintentionally. In either case, you lie. And if I corrupt them unintentionally, it is not the law to bring action here for that sort of mistake, but rather to instruct and admonish in private: for clearly, if I once learn, I shall stop what I unintentionally do. You, however, were unwilling to associate with me and teach me: instead, you brought action here, where it is law to bring those in need of punishment rather than instruction.

Gentlemen of Athens, what I said is surely now clear: Meletus was never concerned about these matters, much or little. Still, Meletus, tell us this: How do you say I corrupt the youth? Or is it clear from your indictment that I teach them not to acknowledge the gods the City acknowledges, but other new divinities? Is this what you mean by saying I corrupt by teaching?

MEL. Certainly. That is exactly what I mean.

SOCR. Then in the name of these same gods we are now discussing, Meletus, please speak a little more plainly still, both for me and for these gentlemen here. Do you mean that I teach the youth to acknowledge that there are gods, and thus do not myself wholly deny gods, and am not in that respect guilty—though the gods are not those the City acknowledges, but different ones, and that this is the cause of my indictment, that they are different? Or are you claiming that I do not myself acknowledge any gods at all, and that I teach this to others?

MEL.   I mean that. You acknowledge no gods at all.

SOCR.   Ah, my dear Meletus, why do you say such things? Do I not at least acknowledge Sun and Moon as gods, as other men do?

MEL.   No, no, Gentlemen and Judges, not when he says the Sun is a stone and the Moon earth.

SOCR.   My dear Meletus! Do you think it is Anaxagoras you are accusing? Do you so despise these judges here and think them so unlettered that they do not know it is the books of Anaxagoras of Clazomenae which teem with such statements? Are young men to learn these things specifically from me when they can buy them sometimes in the Orchestra for a drachma, if the price is high, and laugh at Socrates if he pretends they are his own—especially since they are so absurd? Well, dear friend, is that what you think? I acknowledge no gods at all?

MEL.   No, none whatever.

SOCR.   You cannot be believed, Meletus—even, I think, by yourself. Gentlemen of Athens. I think this man who stands here before you is insolent and unchastened, and has brought this suit precisely out of insolence and unchastened youth. He seems to be conducting a test by propounding a riddle: "Will Socrates, the wise man, realize how neatly I contradict myself, or will I deceive him and the rest of the audience?" For certainly it seems clear that he is contradicting himself in his indictment. It is as though he were saying. "Socrates is guilty of not acknowledging gods, and acknowledges gods." Yet surely this is to jest.

Please join me. Gentlemen, in examining why it appears to me that this is what he is saying. And you answer us, Meletus. The rest of you will please remember what I asked you at the beginning, and make no disturbance if I fashion arguments in my accustomed way.

Is there any man, Meletus, who acknowledges that there are things pertaining to men, but does not acknowledge that there are men? Let him answer for himself, Gentlemen—and let him stop interrupting. Is there any man who does not acknowledge that there are horses, but acknowledges things pertaining to horsemanship? Or does not acknowledge that there are flutes, but acknowledges things pertaining to flute playing? There is not, my good friend. If you do not wish to answer, I'll answer for you and for the rest of these people here. But do please answer my question, at least: Is there any man who acknowledges that there are things pertaining to divinities, but does not acknowledge that there are divinities?

MEL.   There is not.

SOCR.   How obliging of you to answer—reluctantly, and under compulsion from these gentlemen here. Now, you say that I acknowledge and teach things pertaining to divinities—whether new or old, still at least I acknowledge them, by your account; indeed you swore to that in your indictment. But if I acknowledge that there are things pertaining to divinities, must I surely not also acknowledge that there are divinities? Isn't that so? Of course it is—since you do not answer, I count you as agreeing. And divinities, we surely believe, are either gods or children of gods? Correct?

MEL.   Of course.

SOCR.   So if I believe in divinities, as you say, and if divinities are a kind of god, there is the jesting riddle I attributed to you; you are saying that I do not believe in gods, and again that I do believe in gods because I believe in divinities. On the other hand, if divinities are children of gods, some born illegitimately of nymphs,[9] or others of whom this is also told,[10] who could possibly believe that there are children of gods, but not gods? It would be as absurd as believing that there are children of horses and asses, namely, mules, without believing there are horses and asses. Meletus, you could not have brought this indictment except in an attempt to test us—or because you were at loss for any true basis of prosecution. But as to how you are to convince anyone of even the slightest intelligence that one and the same man can believe that there are things pertaining to divinities and gods, and yet believe that there are neither divinities nor heroes—there is no way.

---

9. Aesclepius. for example, son of Apollo and the nymph Coronis. Note that nymphs are themselves goddesses.

10. For example. Achilles, son of the nymph Thetis and Peleus, a mortal father; or Heracles, son of Zeus and Alomene, a mortal mother.

DIGRESSION:
SOCRATES' MISSION TO ATHENS

SOCR.   Gentlemen of Athens, I do not think further defense is
needed to show that, by the very terms of Meletus' indictment, I am not guilty; this, surely, is sufficient. But as I said
before, a great deal of enmity has risen against me among
many people, and you may rest assured this is true. And
that is what will convict me, if I am convicted—not Meletus, not Anytus, but the grudging slander of the multitude.
It has convicted many another good and decent man; I
think it will convict me: nor is there any reason to fear that
with me it will come to a stand. Perhaps someone may say,
"Are you not ashamed, Socrates, at having pursued such a
course that you now stand in danger of being put to death?"
To him I would make a just reply: You are wrong, Sir, if
you think that a man worth anything at all should take
thought for danger in living or dying. He should look when
he acts to one thing: whether what he does is just or unjust,
the work of a good man or a bad one. By your account,
those demigods and heroes who laid down their lives at
Troy would be of little worth—the rest of them, and the son
of Thetis. Achilles so much despised danger instead of submitting to disgrace that when he was intent on killing Hector his goddess mother told him, as I recall, "My son, if you
avenge the slaying of your comrade Patroclus with the
death of Hector, you yourself shall die; for straightway with
Hector is his fate prepared for you."[11] Achilles heard, and
thought little of the death and danger. He was more afraid
to live as a bad man, with friends left unavenged. "Straightway let me die," he said, "exacting right from him who did
the wrong, that I may not remain here as a butt of mockery
beside crook-beaked ships, a burden to the earth." Do you
suppose that he gave thought to death and danger?

Gentlemen of Athens, truly it is so: Wherever a man
stations himself in belief that it is best, wherever he is stationed by his commander, there he must I think remain and
run the risks, giving thought to neither death nor any other
thing except disgrace. When the commanders you chose
stationed me at Potidaea and Amphipolis and Delium,[12] I

---

11. This is not a wholly accurate quotation from the *Iliad*, but describes the
scene at XVIII 94*ff.*

12. All battles in which Socrates fought with conspicuous bravery. See *Symposium* 220d–221b, *Laches* 181b.

there remained as others did, and ran the risk of death; but I should indeed have wrought a fearful thing, Gentlemen of Athens, if then, when the God stationed me, as I thought and believed, obliging me to live in the pursuit of wisdom, examining myself and others—if then, at that point through fear of death or any other thing, I left my post. That would have been dreadful indeed, and then in truth might I be justly brought to court for not acknowledging the existence of gods, for willful disobedience to the oracle, for fearing death, for thinking myself wise when I am not.

For to fear death, Gentlemen, is nothing but to think one is wise when one is not; for it is to think one knows what one does not. No man knows death, nor whether it is not the greatest of all goods: and yet men fear it as though they well knew it to be the worst of evils. Yet how is this not folly most to be reproached, the folly of believing one knows what one does not? I, at least, Gentlemen, am perhaps superior to most men here and just in this: that as I have no satisfactory knowledge of things in the Place of the Dead, I do not think I do. I do know that to be guilty of disobedience to a superior, be he god or man, is shameful evil.

So as against evils I know to be evils, I shall never fear or flee from things which for aught I know may be good. Thus, even if you now dismiss me, refusing to do as Anytus bids—Anytus, who said that either I should not have been brought to trial to begin with or, since brought, must be put to death, testifying before you that if I were once acquitted your sons would pursue what Socrates teaches and all be thoroughly corrupted—if with this in view you were to say to me, "Socrates, we shall not at this time be persuaded by Meletus, and we dismiss you. But on this condition: that you no longer pass time in that inquiry of yours, or pursue philosophy. And if you are again taken doing it, you die." If, as I say, you were to dismiss me on that condition, I would reply that I hold you in friendship and regard, Gentlemen of Athens, but I shall obey the God rather than you, and while I have breath and am able I shall not cease to pursue wisdom or to exhort you, charging any of you I happen to meet in my accustomed manner: "You are the best of men, being an Athenian, citizen of a city honored for wisdom and power beyond all others. Are you then not ashamed to care for the getting of money, and reputation, and public honor, while yet having no thought or concern for truth and understanding and the greatest possible excellence of your soul?" And if some one of you disputes this, and says he does care, I shall not immediately dismiss him and go away. I shall question him and examine him and test him, and if he does not seem to me to possess virtue, and yet says he does, I shall rebuke him for counting of more importance things which by comparison are worthless. I shall do this to young and old, citizen and stranger, whomever I happen to meet, but I shall do it especially to citizens, in as much as they are more nearly related to me. For the God commands this, be well assured, and I believe that you have yet to gain in this City a greater good than my service to the God. I go about doing nothing but persuading you, young and old, to care not for body or money in place of, or so much as, excellence of soul. I tell you that virtue does not come from money, but money and all other human goods both public and private from virtue. If in saying this I corrupt the youth, that would be harm indeed. But anyone who claims I say other than this speaks falsehood. In these matters, Gentlemen of Athens, believe Anytus, or do not. Dismiss me, or do not. For I will not do otherwise, even if I am to die for it many times over.

Please do not make a disturbance, Gentlemen. Abide in my request and do not interrupt what I have to say, but listen. Indeed, I think you will benefit by listening. I am going to tell you certain things at which you may perhaps cry out; please do not do it. Be well assured that if you kill me, and if I am the sort of man I claim, you will harm me less than you harm yourselves. There is no harm a Meletus or Anytus can do me; it is not possible, for it does not, I think, accord with divine law that a better man should be harmed by a worse. Meletus perhaps can kill me, or exile me, or disenfranchise me; and perhaps he and others too think those things great evils. I do not. I think it a far greater evil to do what he is now doing, attempting to kill a man unjustly. And so, Gentlemen of Athens, I am far from making a defense for my own sake, as some might think; I make it for yours, lest you mistake the gift the God has given you and cast your votes against me. If you kill me, you will not easily find such another man as I, a man who—if I may put it a bit absurdly—has been fastened as it were to the City by the God as, so to speak, to a large and well-bred horse, a horse grown sluggish because of its size and in need of being roused by a kind of gadfly. Just so, I think, the God has fastened me to the City. I rouse you. I persuade you. I upbraid you. I never stop lighting on each one of you, everywhere, all day long. Such another will not easily come to you again. Gentlemen, and if you are persuaded by me, you will spare me. But perhaps you are angry, as men roused from sleep are angry, and perhaps you will swat me, persuaded by Meletus that you may lightly kill. Then will you continue to sleep out your lives, unless the God sends someone else to look after you.

That I am just that, a gift from the God to the City, you may recognize from this: It scarcely seems a human matter merely, that I should take no thought for anything of my own, endure the neglect of my house and its affairs for these long years now and ever attend to yours, going to each of you in private like a father or elder brother, persuading you to care for virtue. If I got something from it, if I took pay for this kind of exhortation, that would explain it. But as things are, you can see for yourselves that even my accusers, who have accused me so shamefully of everything else, could not summon shamelessness enough to provide witnesses to testify that I ever took pay or asked for it. For it is enough, I think, to provide my poverty as witness to the truth of what I say.

Perhaps it may seem peculiar that I go about in private advising men and busily inquiring, and yet do not enter your Assembly in public to advise the City. The reason is a thing you have heard me mention many times in many places, that something divine and godlike comes to me—which Meletus, indeed, mocked in his indictment.[13] I have had it from childhood. It comes as a kind of voice, and when it comes, it always turns me away from what I am about to do, but never toward it. That is what opposed my entering political life, and I think it did well to oppose. For be well assured, Gentlemen of Athens. that had I attempted to enter political affairs, I should long since have been destroyed—to the benefit of neither you nor myself.

Please do not be angry at me for telling the simple truth. It is impossible for any man to be spared if he publicly opposes you or any other democratic majority, and prevents many unjust and illegal things from occurring in his city. He who intends to fight for what is just, if he is to be spared even for a little time, must of necessity live a private rather than a public life.

---

13. The suggestion is that Meletus lodged his accusation of acknowledging new (or strange) gods because of the Sign. Cf. *Euthyphro* 3b.

I shall offer you a convincing indication of this—not words, but what you respect, deeds. Hear, then, what befell me, so that you may know that I will not through fear of death give way to any man contrary to what is right, even if I am destroyed for it. I shall tell you a thing which is tedious—it smacks of the law courts—but true. Gentlemen of Athens, I never held other office in the City, but I was once a member of the Council. And it happened that our Tribe, Antiochis, held the Prytany when you decided to judge as a group the cases of the ten generals who had failed to gather up the bodies of the slain in the naval battle—illegally, as later it seemed to all of you. But at the time, I alone of the Prytanies opposed doing a thing contrary to law, and cast my vote against it. And when the orators were ready to impeach me and have me arrested—you urging them on with your shouts—I thought that with law and justice on my side I must run the risk, rather than concur with you in an unjust decision through fear of bonds or death. Those things happened while the City was still under the Democracy. But when the oligarchy came, the Thirty in turn summoned me along with four others to the Rotunda and ordered us to bring back Leon the Salamanian from Salamis so that he might be executed, just as they ordered many others to do such things, planning to implicate as many people as possible in their own guilt. But I then showed again, not by words but deeds, that death, if I may be rather blunt, was of no concern whatever to me; to do nothing unjust or unholy—that was my concern. Strong as it was, that oligarchy did not so frighten me as to cause me to do a thing unjust, and when we departed the Rotunda, the other four went into Salamis and brought back Leon, and I left and went home. I might have been killed for that, if the oligarchy had not shortly afterward been overthrown. And of these things you will have many witnesses.

Now, do you think I would have lived so many years if I had been in public life and acted in a manner worthy of a good man, defending what is just and counting it, as is necessary, of first importance? Far from it, Gentlemen of Athens. Not I, and not any other man. But through my whole life I have shown myself to be that sort of man in public affairs, the few I've engaged in; and I have shown myself the same man in private. I never gave way to anyone contrary to what is just—not to others, and certainly not to those slanderously said to be my pupils. In fact, I have never been teacher to anyone. If, in speaking and tending to my own affairs, I found anyone. young or old, who wished to hear me, I never begrudged him: nor do I discuss for a fee and not otherwise. To rich and poor alike I offer myself as a questioner, and if anyone wishes to answer, he may then hear what I have to say. And if any of them turned out to be useful men, or any did not, I cannot justly be held responsible. To none did I promise instruction, and none did I teach; if anyone says that he learned from me or heard in private what others did not, you may rest assured he is not telling the truth.

Why is it, then, that some people enjoy spending so much time with me? You have heard, Gentlemen of Athens; I told you the whole truth. It is because they enjoy hearing people tested who think they are wise and are not. After all, it is not unamusing. But for my own part, as I say, I have been ordered to do this by God—in oracles, in dreams, in every way in which other divine apportionment orders a man to do anything.

These things, Gentlemen of Athens, are both true and easily tested. For if I am corrupting some of the youth, and have corrupted others, it must surely be that some among them, grown older, if they realize that I counseled them toward evil while young, would now come forward to accuse me and exact a penalty. And if they were unwilling, then some of their relatives—fathers, brothers, other kinsmen— would now remember, and exact a penalty, if their own relatives had suffered evil at my hands. Certainly there are many such men I see present. Here is Crito, first, of my own age and deme,[14] father of Critobulus: then there is Eysanias of Sphettos, father of Aeschines[15] here. Next there is Antiphon of Cephisus, father of Epigenes. Then there are others whose brothers engaged in this pastime. There is Nicostratus, son of Theozotides, brother of Theodotus—and Theodotus is dead, so he could not have swayed him—and Paralus here, son of Demococus, whose brother was Theages. And here is Adeimantus, son of Ariston, whose brother is Plato here; and Aeantodorus, whose brother is Apollodorus here. I could name many others, some of whom at least Meletus ought certainly have provided in his speech as witnesses. If he forgot it then, let him do it now—

---

14. Alopece. A deme was roughly the equivalent of a township.
15. Who, like Plato, went on to write Socratic dialogues.

I yield the floor—and let him say whether he has any witnesses of the sort. You will find that quite to the contrary, Gentlemen, every one of these men is ready to help me. I, who corrupt their relatives, as Meletus and Anytus claim. Those who are themselves corrupted might perhaps have reason to help me; but their relatives are older men who have not been corrupted. What reason could they have for supporting me except that it is right and just, because they know Meletus is lying and I am telling the truth?

PERORATION

SOCR. Very well, then, Gentlemen. This, and perhaps a few other things like it, is what I have to say in my defense. Perhaps some of you will remember your own conduct and be offended, if when brought to trial on a lesser charge than this, you begged your judges with tearful supplication and caused your children along with other relatives and a host of friends, to come forward so that you might be the more pitied, whereas I shall do none of these things, even though I am, as it would seem at least, in the extremity of danger. Perhaps someone with this in mind may become hardened against me; angered by it, he may cast his vote in anger. If this is true of any of you—not that I expect it, but if it is—I think it might be appropriate to say, "I too have relatives, my friend; for as Homer puts it, I am not 'of oak and rock,' but born of man, so I have relatives—yes, and sons too, Gentlemen of Athens, three of them, one already a lad and two of them children. Yet not one of them have I caused to come forward here, and I shall not beg you to acquit me." Why not? Not out of stubbornness, Gentlemen of Athens, nor disrespect for you. Whether or not I am confident in the face of death is another story; but I think that my own honor, and yours, and that of the whole City would suffer, if I were to behave in this way, I being of the age I am and having the name I have—truly or falsely it being thought that Socrates is in some way superior to most men. If those of you reputed to be superior in wisdom or courage or any other virtue whatever were men of this sort, it would be disgraceful; I have often seen such people behave surprisingly when put on trial, even though they had a reputation to uphold, because they were persuaded that they would suffer a terrible thing if they were put to death—as though they would be immortal if you did not kill them. I think they cloak the City in shame, so that a stranger might think that those men among the Athenians who are superior in virtue, and whom the Athenians themselves judge worthy of office and other honors, are not better than women. These are things, Gentlemen of Athens, which those of you who have a reputation to uphold ought not to do; nor if we defendants do them, ought you permit it. You ought rather make it clear that you would far rather cast your vote against a man who stages these pitiful scenes, and makes the City a butt of mockery, than against a man who shows quiet restraint. But apart from the matter of reputation, Gentlemen, it does not seem to me just to beg a judge, or to be acquitted by begging; it is rather just to teach and persuade. The judge does not sit to grant justice as a favor, but to render judgment; he has sworn no oath to gratify those whom he sees fit, but to judge according to law. We ought not accustom you, nor ought you become accustomed, to forswear yourselves; it is pious in neither of us. So do not consider it right, Gentlemen of Athens, that I do such things in your presence as I believe to be neither honorable nor just nor holy, especially since, by Zeus, it is for impiety that I am being prosecuted by this fellow Meletus here. For clearly, if I were to persuade and compel you by supplication, you being sworn as judges, I would teach you then indeed not to believe that there are gods, and in making my defense I would in effect accuse myself of not acknowledging them. But that is far from so; I do acknowledge them. Gentlemen of Athens, as none of my accusers does, and to you and to the God I now commit my case, to judge in whatever way will be best for me and also for you.

THE COUNTERPENALTY

I am not distressed, Gentlemen of Athens, at what has happened, nor angered that you have cast your votes against me. Many things contribute to this, among them the fact that I expected it. I am much more surprised at the number of votes either way; I did not think the censure would be by so little, but by more. As it is, it seems, if only thirty votes had fallen otherwise, I would have been acquitted.[16] And so far as Meletus at least is concerned, it seems to me, I am already acquitted—and more than acquitted, since it is clear that if Anytus and Lycon had not come forward to

---

16. Granting that there were 500 judges, the vote must have been 280 to 220.

accuse me, Meletus would have been fined a thousand drachmas for not obtaining a fifth part of the vote.

The man demands death for me. Very well. Then what counterpenalty shall I propose to you, Gentlemen of Athens?[17] Clearly something I deserve, but what? What do I deserve to pay or suffer because I did not through life keep quiet, and yet did not concern myself, as the multitude do, with money or property or military and public honors and other office, or the secret societies and political clubs which keep cropping up in the City, believing that I was really too reasonable and temperate a man to enter upon these things and survive? I did not go where I could benefit neither you nor myself; instead, I went to each of you in private, where I might perform the greatest service. I undertook to persuade each of you not to care for anything which belongs to you before first caring for yourselves, so as to be as good and wise as possible, nor to care for anything which belongs to the City before caring for the City itself, and so too with everything else in the same way. Now, what do I deserve to suffer for being this sort of man? Some good thing, Gentlemen of Athens, if penalty is really to be assessed according to desert. What then is fitting for a poor man who has served his City well, and needs leisure to exhort you? Why, Gentlemen of Athens, nothing is more fitting for such a man than to be fed in the Prytaneum,[18] at the common table of the City—yes, and far more fitting than for one of you who has been an Olympic victor in the single-horse or two- or four-horse chariot races. For he makes you seem happy, whereas I make you happy in truth; and he does not need subsistence, and I do. If then I must propose a penalty I justly deserve, I propose that, public subsistence in the Prytaneum.

Perhaps some of you will think that in saying this I speak much as I spoke of tears and pleading, out of stubborn pride. That is not so, Gentlemen of Athens, though something of this sort is: I am persuaded that I have not intentionally wronged any man, but I cannot persuade you of it; we have talked so short a time. Now, I believe if you had

---

17. Under Athenian law, the prosecutor proposed a penalty, and the convicted defendant a counterpenalty; the jury was required to choose between them without alteration. The usual practice was for a convicted person to propose a penalty as heavy as he could bear short of that which the prosecutor demanded, in hope that the jury might accept it.

18. Public subsistence in the Prytaneum was a great honor, traditionally given to Olympic victors in major events.

a law, as other men do, that cases involving death shall not be decided in a single day, that you would be persuaded; but as things are, it is not easy in so short a time to do away with slanders grown so great. Being persuaded, however, that I have wronged no one, I am quite unwilling to wrong myself, or to claim that I deserve some evil and propose any penalty of the kind. What is there to fear? That I may suffer the penalty Meletus proposes, when as I say, I do not know whether it is good or evil? Shall I choose instead a penalty I know very well to be evil? Imprisonment, perhaps? But why should I live in prison, a slave to men who happen to occupy office as the Eleven? A fine, then, and prison till I pay it? But that comes to the same thing, since I have no money to pay it. Shall I then propose exile? Perhaps you would accept that. But I must indeed love life and cling to it dearly, Gentlemen, if I were so foolish as to think that although you, my own fellow-citizens, cannot bear my pursuits and discussions, which have become so burdensome and hateful that you now seek to be rid of them, others will bear them lightly. No, Gentlemen. My life would be fine indeed, if at my age I went to live in exile, always moving from city to city, always driven out. For be well assured that wherever I go, the young men will listen to what I say as they do here; if I turn them away, their fathers and relations will drive me out in their behalf.

Perhaps someone may say, "Would it not be possible for you to live in exile, Socrates, if you silently kept quiet?" But this is the hardest thing of all to make some of you believe. If I say that to do so would be to disobey the God, and therefore I cannot do it, you will not believe me because you will think that I am being sly and dishonest.[19] If on the other hand I say that the greatest good for man is to fashion arguments each day about virtue and the other things you hear me discussing when I examine myself and others, and that the unexamined life is not for man worth living, you will believe what I say still less. I claim these things are so, Gentlemen; but it is not easy to convince you. At the same time, I am not accustomed to think myself deserving of any evil. If I had money, I would propose a fine as great as I could pay—for there would be no harm in that. But as things stand, I have no money, unless the amount I can pay is the amount

---

19. That is, an *eiron*. "Irony" was regarded as a defect of character, not a virtue, as Theophrastus's portrait in the *Characters* of the ironical man makes clear.

you are willing to exact of me. I might perhaps be able to pay a mina of silver.[20] So I propose a penalty in that amount. But Plato here, Gentlemen of Athens, and Crito and Critobulus and Apollodorus bid me propose thirty minae, and they will stand surety. So I propose that amount. You have guarantors sufficient for the sum.

EPILOGUE

For the sake of only a little time, Gentlemen of Athens, you are to be accused by those who wish to revile the City of having killed Socrates, a wise man—for those who wish to reproach you will say I am wise even if I am not. And if you had only waited a little, the thing would have come of its own initiative. You see my age. You see how far spent my life already is, how near I am to death.

I say this, not to all of you, but to those of you who voted to condemn me. To them I also say this: Perhaps you think, Gentlemen of Athens, that I have been convicted for lack of words to persuade you, had I thought it right to do and say anything to be acquitted. Not so. It is true I have been convicted for a lack; not a lack of words, but lack of bold shamelessness, unwillingness to say the things you would find it pleasant to hear—weeping and wailing, saying and doing many things I claim to be unworthy of me, but things of the sort you are accustomed to hear from others. I did not then think it necessary to do anything unworthy of a free man because of danger; I do not now regret so having conducted my defense; and I would far rather die with that defense than lie with the other. Neither in court of law nor in war ought I or any man contrive to escape death by any means possible. Often in battle it becomes clear that a man may escape death by throwing down his arms and turning in supplication to his pursuers; and there are many other devices for each of war's dangers, so that one can avoid dying if he is bold enough to say and do anything whatever. It is not difficult to escape death, Gentlemen; it is more difficult to escape wickedness, for wickedness runs faster than death. And now I am old and slow, and I have been caught by the slower runner. But my accusers are

---

20. It is useless to try to give modern money equivalents, but the ultimate fine proposed is substantial: Aristotle gives one mina as the conventional ransom for a prisoner of war (*Nicomachean Ethics* V 1134b21). Why did Socrates propose a fine at all, or accept his friends' offer of suretyship? See 29d–30b, 30d–e.

clever and quick,. and they have been caught by the faster runner, namely Evil. I now take my leave, sentenced by you to death: they depart, convicted by Truth for injustice and wickedness. I abide in my penalty, and they in theirs. That is no doubt as it should be, and I think it is fit.

I desire next to prophesy to you who condemned me. For I have now reached that point where men are especially prophetic—when they are about to die. I say to you who have decreed my death that to you there will come hard on my dying a punishment far more difficult to bear than the death you have visited upon me. You have done this thing in the belief that you would be released from submitting to examination of your lives. I say that it will turn out quite otherwise. Those who come to examine you will be more numerous, and I have up to now restrained them, though you perceived it not. They will be more harsh inasmuch as they are younger, and you shall be the more troubled. If you think by killing to hold back the reproach due you for not living rightly, you are profoundly mistaken. That release is neither possible nor honorable. The release which is both most honorable and most easy is not to cut down others, but to take proper care that you will be as good as possible. This I utter as prophecy to you who voted for my condemnation, and take my leave.

But with you who voted for my acquittal, I should be glad to discuss the nature of what has happened, now, while the authorities are busy and I am not yet gone where, going, I must die. Abide with me, Gentlemen, this space of time; for nothing prevents our talking with each other while we still can. To you, as my friends, I wish to display the meaning of what has now fallen to my lot. A remarkable thing has occurred, Gentlemen and Judges—and I correctly call you Judges. My accustomed oracle, which is divine, always came quite frequently before in everything, opposing me even in trivial matters if I was about to err. And now a thing has fallen to my lot which you also see, a thing which some might think, and do in fact believe, to be ultimate among evils. But the Sign of the God did not oppose me early this morning when I left my house, or when I came up here to the courtroom, or at any point in my argument in anything I was about to say. And yet frequently in other arguments, it has checked me right in the middle of speaking: but today it has not opposed me in any way, in none of my deeds, in none of my words. What do I take to be the reason? I will tell you. Very likely what has fallen to me is good, and those among us who think that death is an evil are wrong. There has been convincing indication of this. For the accustomed Sign would surely have opposed me, if I were not in some way acting for good.

Let us also consider a further reason for high hope that death is good. Death is one of two things. Either to be dead is not to exist, to have no awareness at all, or it is, as the stories tell, a kind of alteration, a change of abode for the soul from this place to another. And if it is to have no awareness, like a sleep when the sleeper sees no dream, death would be a wonderful gain; for I suppose if someone had to pick out that night in which he slept and saw no dream, and put the other days and nights of his life beside it, and had to say after inspecting them how many days and nights he had lived in his life which were better and sweeter, I think that not only any ordinary person but even the Great King[21] himself would find them easily numbered in relation to other days, and other nights. If death is that, I say it is gain; for the whole of time then turns out to last no longer than a single night. But if on the contrary death is like taking a journey, passing from here to another place, and the stories told are true, and all who have died are there—what greater good might there be, my Judges? For if a man once goes to the place of the dead, and takes leave of those who claim to be judges here, he will find the true judges who are said to sit in judgment there—Minos, Rhadamanthus, Aeacus, Triptolemus, and the other demigods and heroes who lived just lives. Would that journey be worthless? And again, to meet Orpheus and Musaeus, Hesiod and Homer—how much would any of you give? I at least would be willing to die many times over, if these things are true. I would find a wonderful pursuit there, when I met Palamedes, and Ajax, son of Telemon, and any others among the ancients done to death by unjust verdicts, and compared my experiences with theirs. It would not, I think, be unamusing. But the greatest thing, surely, would be to test and question there as I did here: Who among them is wise? Who thinks he is and is not? How much might one give, my Judges, to examine the man who led the great army against Troy, or Odysseus, or Sisyphus, or a thousand other men and women one might mention—to converse with

21. Of Persia. a proverbial symbol of wealth and power.

them, to associate with them, to examine them—why, it would be inconceivable happiness. Especially since they surely do not kill you for it there. They are happier there than men are here in other ways, and they are already immortal for the rest of time, if the stories told are true.

But you too, my Judges, must be of good hope concerning death. You must recognize that this one thing is true: there is not evil for a good man either in living or in dying, and the gods do not neglect his affairs. What has now come to me did not occur of its own initiative. It is clear to me that to die now and be released from my affairs is better for me. That is why the Sign did not turn me back, and I bear no anger whatever toward those who voted to condemn me, or toward my accusers. And yet, it was not with this in mind that they accused and convicted me. They thought to do harm, and for that they deserve blame. But this much would I ask of them: When my sons are grown, Gentlemen, exact a penalty of them; give pain to them exactly as I gave pain to you, if it seems to you that they care more for wealth or anything else than they care for virtue. And if they seem to be something and are nothing, rebuke them as I rebuked you, because they do not care for what they ought, because they think themselves something and are worth nothing. And should you do that, both I and my sons will have been justly dealt with at your hands.

But it is now the hour of parting—I to die and you to live. Which of us goes to the better is unclear to all but the God.

HENRY DAVID THOREAU
Civil Disobedience

HENRY DAVID THOREAU (1817–1862) began keeping a journal when he graduated from Harvard in 1837. The journal was preserved and published, and it shows us the seriousness, determination, and elevation of moral values characteristic of all his work. He is best known for *Walden* (1854), a record of his departure from the warm congeniality of Concord, Massachusetts, and the home of his close friend Ralph Waldo Emerson (1803–1882), for the comparative "wilds" of Walden Pond, where he built a cabin, planted a garden, and lived simply. In *Walden* Thoreau describes the deadening influence of ownership and extols the vitality and spiritual uplift that comes from living close to nature. He also argues that civilization's comforts sometimes rob a person of independence, integrity, and even conscience.

Thoreau and Emerson were prominent among the group of writers and thinkers who were referred to as the Transcendentalists. They believed in something that transcended the limits of sensory experience—in other words, something that transcended materialism. Their philosophy was based on the works of Immanuel Kant (1724–1804), the German idealist philosopher; Samuel Taylor Coleridge (1772–1834), the English poet; and Johann Wolfgang von Goethe (1749–1832), the German dramatist and thinker. These writers praised human intuition and the capacity to see beyond the limits of common experience.

Their philosophical idealism carried over into the social concerns of the day, expressing itself in works such as *Walden* and "Civil Disobedience," which was published with the title "Resistance to Civil Government" in 1849, a year after the publication of *The Communist Manifesto*. Although Thoreau all but denies his idealism in "Civil Disobedience," it is obvious that after spending a night in the Concord jail, he realizes he cannot quietly accept his government's behavior in regard to slavery. He begins to feel that it is not only appropriate but imperative to disobey unjust laws.

In Thoreau's time the most flagrantly unjust laws were those that supported slavery. The Transcendentalists strongly opposed slavery and spoke out against it. Abolitionists in Massachusetts harbored escaped slaves and helped them move to Canada and freedom. The Fugitive Slave Act, enacted in 1850, the year after "Civil Disobedience" was published, made Thoreau a criminal because he refused to comply with Massachusetts civil authorities when in 1851 they began returning escaped slaves to the South as the law required.

"Civil Disobedience" was much more influential in the twentieth century than it was in the nineteenth. Mohandas Gandhi (1869–1948) claimed that while he was editor of an Indian newspaper in South Africa, it helped to inspire his theories of nonviolent resistance. Gandhi eventually implemented these theories against the British empire and helped win independence for India. In the 1960s, Martin Luther King Jr. applied the same theories in the fight for racial equality in the United States. Thoreau's essay once again found widespread adherents among the many young men who resisted being drafted into the military to fight in Vietnam because they believed that the war was unjust.

"Civil Disobedience" was written after the Walden experience (which began on July 4, 1845, and ended on September 6, 1847). Thoreau quietly returned to Emerson's home and "civilization." His refusal to pay the Massachusetts poll tax — a "per head" tax imposed on all citizens to help support what he considered an unjust war against Mexico — landed him in the Concord jail. He spent just one day and one night there — his aunt paid the tax for him — but the experience was so extraordinary that he began examining it in his journal.

Thoreau's Rhetoric

Thoreau maintained his journal throughout his life and eventually became convinced that writing was one of the few professions by which he could earn a living. He made more money, however, from lecturing on the lyceum circuit. The lyceum, a New England institution, was a town adult education program, featuring important speakers such as the very successful Emerson and foreign lecturers. Admission fees were very reasonable, and in the absence of other popular entertainment, the lyceum was a popular proving ground for speakers interested in promoting their ideas.

"Civil Disobedience" was first outlined in rough-hewn form in the journal, where the main ideas appear and where experiments in phrasing began. (Thoreau was a constant reviser.) Then in February 1848, Thoreau delivered a lecture on "Civil Disobedience" at the Concord Lyceum urging people of conscience to actively resist a government that acted badly. Finally, the piece was prepared for publication in *Aesthetic Papers,* an intellectual journal edited by Elizabeth Peabody (1804–1894), the sister-in-law of another important New England writer, Nathaniel Hawthorne (1804–1864). There it was refined again, and certain important details were added.

"Civil Disobedience" bears many of the hallmarks of the spoken lecture. For one thing, it is written in the first person and addresses an audience that Thoreau expects will share many of his sentiments but certainly not all his conclusions. His message is to some extent anarchistic, virtually denying an unjust government any authority or respect.

Modern political conservatives generally take his opening quote—"That government is best which governs least"—as a rallying cry against governmental interference in everyday affairs. Such conservatives usually propose reducing government interference by reducing the government's capacity to tax wealth for unpopular causes. In fact, what Thoreau opposes is simply any government that is not totally just, totally moral, and totally respectful of the individual.

The easiness of the pace of the essay also derives from its original form as a speech. Even such locutions as "But to speak practically and as a citizen" (para. 3) connect the essay with its origins. Although Thoreau was not an overwhelming orator—he was short and somewhat homely, an unprepossessing figure—he ensured that his writing achieved what some speakers might have accomplished by means of gesture and theatrics.

Thoreau's language is marked by clarity. He speaks directly to every issue, stating his own position and recommending the position he feels his audience, as reasonable and moral people, should accept. One impressive achievement in this selection is Thoreau's capacity to shape memorable, virtually aphoristic statements that remain "quotable" generations later, beginning with his own quotation from the words of John L. O'Sullivan: "That government is best which governs least." Thoreau calls it a motto, as if it belonged on the great seal of a government or on a coin. It contains an interesting and impressive rhetorical flourish—the device of repeating "govern" and the near rhyme of "best" with "least."

His most memorable statements show considerable attention to the rhetorical qualities of balance, repetition, and pattern. "The only obligation which I have a right to assume is to do at any time what I think right" (para. 4) uses the word *right* in two senses: first, as a matter of personal volition; second, as a matter of moral rectitude. One's right, in other words, becomes the opportunity to do right. "For it matters not how small the beginning may seem to be: what is once well done is done forever" (para. 21) also relies on repetition for its effect and balances the concept of a beginning with its capacity to reach out into the future. The use of the rhetorical device of *chiasmus,* a criss-cross relationship between key words, marks "Under a government which imprisons any unjustly, the true place for a just man is also a prison" (para. 22). Here is the pattern:

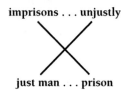

imprisons . . . unjustly

just man . . . prison

Such attention to phrasing is typical of speakers whose expressions must catch and retain the attention of listeners. Audiences do not have the advantage of referring to a text, so the words they hear must be forceful.

Thoreau relies also on analogy — comparing men with machines, people with plants, even the citizen with states considering secession from the Union. His analogies are effective and thus worth examining in some detail. He draws on the analysis of circumstance throughout the essay, carefully examining government actions to determine their qualities and their results. His questions include comments on politics (para. 1), on the Bible (para. 23), on Confucius (para. 24), and finally on his contemporary, Daniel Webster (1782–1852) (para. 42), demonstrating a wide range of influence but avoiding the pedantic tone that can come from using quotations too liberally or from citing obscure sources. This essay is simple, direct, and uncluttered. Its enduring influence is in part due to the clarity and grace that characterize Thoreau's writing at its best. Its power derives from Thoreau's demand that citizens act on the basis of conscience.

PREREADING QUESTIONS: WHAT TO READ FOR

The following prereading questions may help you anticipate key issues in the discussion on Henry David Thoreau's "Civil Disobedience." Keeping them in mind during your first reading of the selection should help focus your reactions.

• What kind of government does Thoreau feel would be most just?

• What is the individual's responsibility regarding supporting the government when it is wrong?

• How does Thoreau deal with unjust laws?

Civil Disobedience

I heartily accept the motto—"That government is best which   1
governs least,"[1] and I should like to see it acted up to more rapidly and systematically. Carried out, it finally amounts to this, which also I believe—"That government is best which governs not at all"; and when men are prepared for it, that will be the kind of government which they will have. Government is at best but an expedient; but most governments are usually, and all governments are sometimes, inexpedient. The objections which have been brought against a standing army, and they are many and weighty, and deserve to prevail, may also at last be brought against a standing government. The standing army is only an arm of the standing government. The government itself, which is only the mode which the people have chosen to execute their will, is equally liable to be abused and perverted before the people can act through it. Witness the present Mexican war,[2] the work of comparatively a few individuals using the standing government as their tool; for in the outset the people would not have consented to this measure.

This American government—what is it but a tradition, a recent   2
one, endeavoring to transmit itself unimpaired to posterity but each instant losing some of its integrity? It has not the vitality and force of a single living man; for a single man can bend it to his will. It is a

---

[1] **"...governs least"** John L. O'Sullivan (1813–1895) wrote in the *United States Magazine and Democratic Review* (1837) that "all government is evil, and the parents of evil.... The best government is that which governs least." Thomas Jefferson wrote, "That government is best which governs the least, because its people discipline themselves." Both comments echo the *Tao-te Ching*.

[2] **the present Mexican war (1846–1848)** The war was extremely unpopular in New England because it was an act of a bullying government anxious to grab land from a weaker nation. The United States had annexed Texas in 1845, precipitating a retaliation from Mexico.

sort of wooden gun to the people themselves. But it is not the less necessary for this; for the people must have some complicated machinery or other, and hear its din, to satisfy that idea of government which they have. Governments show thus how successfully men can be imposed on, even impose on themselves, for their own advantage. It is excellent, we must all allow. Yet this government never of itself furthered any enterprise but by the alacrity with which it got out of its way. *It* does not keep the country free. *It* does not settle the West. *It* does not educate. The character inherent in the American people has done all that has been accomplished; and it would have done somewhat more if the government had not sometimes got in its way. For government is an expedient by which men would fain succeed in letting one another alone; and, as has been said, when it is most expedient the governed are most let alone by it. Trade and commerce, if they were not made of India-rubber, would never manage to bounce over the obstacles which legislators are continually putting in their way; and, if one were to judge these men wholly by the effects of their actions and not partly by their intentions, they would deserve to be classed and punished with those mischievous persons who put obstructions on the railroads.

But to speak practically and as a citizen, unlike those who call   3
themselves no-government men, I ask for, not at once no government, but *at once* a better government. Let every man make known what kind of government would command his respect, and that will be one step toward obtaining it.

After all, the practical reason why, when the power is once in   4
the hands of the people, a majority are permitted, and for a long period continue, to rule is not because they are most likely to be in the right, nor because this seems fairest to the minority but because they are physically the strongest. But a government in which the majority rule in all cases cannot be based on justice, even as far as men understand it. Can there not be a government in which majorities do not virtually decide right and wrong but conscience?—in which majorities decide only those questions to which the rule of expediency is applicable? Must the citizen ever for a moment, or in the least degree, resign his conscience to the legislator? Why has every man a conscience then? I think that we should be men first and subjects afterward. It is not desirable to cultivate a respect for the law, so much as for the right. The only obligation which I have a right to assume is to do at any time what I think right. It is truly enough said that a corporation has no conscience; but a corporation of conscientious men is a corporation *with* a conscience. Law never made men a whit more just; and, by means of their respect for it, even the well-disposed are daily made the agents of injustice. A common and nat-

ural result of an undue respect for law is that you may see a file of soldiers, colonel, captain, corporal, privates, powder-monkeys,[3] and all, marching in admirable order over hill and dale to the wars, against their wills, ay, against their common sense and consciences, which makes it very steep marching indeed and produces a palpitation of the heart. They have no doubt that it is a damnable business in which they are concerned; they are all peaceably inclined. Now, what are they? Men at all? or small movable forts and magazines at the service of some unscrupulous man in power? Visit the Navy-Yard,[4] and behold a marine, such a man as an American government can make, or such as it can make a man with its black arts — a mere shadow and reminiscence of humanity, a man laid out alive and standing, and already, as one may say, buried under arms with funeral accompaniments, though it may be —

> Not a drum was heard, not a funeral note,
> As his corse to the rampart we hurried;
> Not a soldier discharged his farewell shot
> O'er the grave where our hero we buried.[5]

The mass of men serve the state thus, not as men mainly, but as   5
machines, with their bodies. They are the standing army, and the militia, jailers, constables, posse comitatus,[6] &c. In most cases there is no free exercise whatever of the judgment or of the moral sense; but they put themselves on a level with wood and earth and stones; and wooden men can perhaps be manufactured that will serve the purpose as well. Such command no more respect than men of straw or a lump of dirt. They have the same sort of worth only as horses and dogs. Yet such as these even are commonly esteemed good citizens. Others — as most legislators, politicians, lawyers, ministers, and office-holders — serve the state chiefly with their heads; and, as they rarely make any moral distinctions, they are as likely to serve the Devil, without *intending* it, as God. A very few, as heroes, patriots, martyrs, reformers in the great sense, and *men*, serve the state with their consciences also and so necessarily resist it for the most part; and they are commonly treated as enemies by it. A wise man will only be useful as a man and will not submit to be "clay" and "stop a hole to keep the wind away," but leave that office to his dust at least:

---

[3] **powder-monkeys** The boys who delivered gunpowder to cannons.

[4] **Navy-Yard** This is apparently the U.S. naval yard at Boston.

[5] These lines are from "Burial of Sir John Moore at Corunna" (1817) by the Irish poet Charles Wolfe (1791–1823).

[6] **posse comitatus** Literally, the power of the county; the term means a law-enforcement group made up of ordinary citizens.

> I am too high-born to be propertied,
> To be a secondary at control,
> Or useful serving-man and instrument
> To any sovereign state throughout the world.[7]

He who gives himself entirely to his fellow-men appears to them 6
useless and selfish; but he who gives himself partially to them is pro-
nounced a benefactor and philanthropist.

How does it become a man to behave toward this American 7
government today? I answer, that he cannot without disgrace be associated with it. I cannot for an instant recognize that political organization as *my* government which is the *slave's* government also.

All men recognize the right of revolution; that is, the right to 8
refuse allegiance to, and to resist the government when its tyranny
or its inefficiency are great and unendurable. But almost all say that
such is not the case now. But such was the case, they think, in the
Revolution of '75. If one were to tell me that this was a bad government because it taxed certain foreign commodities brought to its
ports, it is most probable that I should not make an ado about it, for
I can do without them. All machines have their friction; and possibly this does enough good to counterbalance the evil. At any rate, it
is a great evil to make a stir about it. But when the friction comes to
have its machine, and oppression and robbery are organized, I say
let us not have such a machine any longer. In other words, when a
sixth of the population of a nation which has undertaken to be the
refuge of liberty are slaves, and a whole country is unjustly overrun
and conquered by a foreign army and subjected to military law, I
think that it is not too soon for honest men to rebel and revolutionize. What makes this duty the more urgent is the fact that the country so overrun is not our own, but ours is the invading army.

Paley,[8] a common authority with many on moral questions, in 9
his chapter on the "Duty of Submission to Civil Government," re-
solves all civil obligation into expediency; and he proceeds to say,
"that so long as the interest of the whole society requires it, that is,
so long as the established government cannot be resisted or charged
without public inconveniency, it is the will of God that the established government be obeyed, and no longer.... This principle being

---

[7] **"clay," "stop a hole... wind away," I am too high-born...** These lines are
from Shakespeare; the first is from *Hamlet,* V.i.226–227. The verse is from *King
John,* V.ii.79–82.

[8] **William Paley (1743–1805)** An English theologian who lectured widely
on moral philosophy. Paley is famous for *A View of the Evidences of Christianity*
(1794). "Duty of Submission to Civil Government Explained" is Chapter 3 of Book 6
of *The Principles of Moral and Political Philosophy* (1785).

admitted, the justice of every particular case of resistance is reduced to a computation of the quantity of the danger and grievance on the one side, and of the probability and expense of redressing it on the other." Of this, he says, every man shall judge for himself. But Paley appears never to have contemplated those cases to which the rule of expediency does not apply, in which a people, as well as an individual, must do justice, cost what it may. If I have unjustly wrested a plank from a drowning man, I must restore it to him though I drown myself. This, according to Paley, would be inconvenient. But he that would save his life, in such a case, shall lose it. This people must cease to hold slaves and to make war on Mexico, though it cost them their existence as a people.

In their practice, nations agree with Paley; but does anyone   10
think that Massachusetts does exactly what is right at the present crisis?

> A drab of state, a cloth-o'-silver slut,
> To have her train borne up, and her soul trail in the dirt.[9]

Practically speaking, the opponents to a reform in Massachusetts are not a hundred thousand politicians at the South but a hundred thousand merchants and farmers here, who are more interested in commerce and agriculture than they are in humanity, and are not prepared to do justice to the slave and to Mexico, cost what it may. I quarrel not with far-off foes but with those who, near at home, co-operate with, and do the bidding of, those far away, and without whom the latter would be harmless. We are accustomed to say that the mass of men are unprepared; but improvement is slow because the few are not materially wiser or better than the many. It is not so important that many should be as good as you as that there be some absolute goodness somewhere; for that will leaven the whole lump. There are thousands who are in opinion opposed to slavery and to the war who yet in effect do nothing to put an end to them; who, es-teeming themselves children of Washington and Franklin, sit down with their hands in their pockets and say that they know not what to do, and do nothing; who even postpone the question of freedom to the question of free trade, and quietly read the prices-current along with the latest advices from Mexico after dinner and, it may be, fall asleep over them both. What is the price-current of an honest man and patriot today? They hesitate and they regret and sometimes they

---

[9] **A drab...** From Cyril Tourneur (1575?–1626), *Revenger's Tragedy* (1607), IV.iv.70–72. "Drab" is an obsolete term for a prostitute. Thoreau quotes the lines to imply that Massachusetts is a "painted lady" with a defiled soul.

petition; but they do nothing in earnest and with effect. They will wait, well disposed, for others to remedy the evil, that they may no longer have it to regret. At most, they give only a cheap vote, and a feeble countenance and God-speed, to the right, as it goes by them. There are nine hundred and ninety-nine patrons of virtue to one virtuous man. But it is easier to deal with the real possessor of a thing than with the temporary guardian of it.

All voting is a sort of gaming, like checkers or backgammon, 11 with a slight moral tinge to it, a playing with right and wrong, with moral questions; and betting naturally accompanies it. The character of the voters is not staked. I cast my vote, perchance, as I think right; but I am not vitally concerned that that right should prevail. I am willing to leave it to the majority. Its obligation, therefore, never exceeds that of expediency. Even voting *for the right* is *doing* nothing for it. It is only expressing to men feebly your desire that it should prevail. A wise man will not leave the right to the mercy of chance, nor wish it to prevail through the power of the majority. There is but little virtue in the action of masses of men. When the majority shall at length vote for the abolition of slavery, it will be because they are indifferent to slavery, or because there is but little slavery left to be abolished by their vote. *They* will then be the only slaves. Only *his* vote can hasten the abolition of slavery who asserts his own freedom by his vote.

I hear of a convention to be held at Baltimore,[10] or elsewhere, 12 for the selection of a candidate for the Presidency, made up chiefly of editors, and men who are politicians by profession; but I think, what is it to any independent, intelligent, and respectable man what decision they may come to? Shall we not have the advantage of his wisdom and honesty nevertheless? Can we not count upon some independent votes? Are there not many individuals in the country who do not attend conventions? But no: I find that the responsible man, so called, has immediately drifted from his position, and despairs of his country when his country has more reason to despair of him. He forthwith adopts one of the candidates thus selected as the only *available* one, thus proving that he is himself *available* for any purposes of the demagogue. His vote is of no more worth than that of any unprincipled foreigner or hireling native who may have been bought. O for a man who is a *man* and, as my neighbor says has a bone in his back which you cannot pass your hand through! Our

---

[10] **Baltimore** In 1848 the political environment was particularly intense; it was a seedbed for theoreticians of the Confederacy, which was only beginning to be contemplated seriously.

statistics are at fault: the population has been returned too large. How many *men* are there to a square thousand miles in this country? Hardly one. Does not America offer any inducement for men to settle here? The American has dwindled into an Odd Fellow[11]—one who may be known by the development of his organ of gregariousness and a manifest lack of intellect and cheerful self-reliance; whose first and chief concern, on coming into the world, is to see that the Almshouses are in good repair; and, before yet he has lawfully donned the virile garb, to collect a fund for the support of the widows and orphans that may be; who, in short, ventures to live only by the aid of the Mutual Insurance Company, which has promised to bury him decently.

It is not a man's duty, as a matter of course, to devote himself to   13
the eradication of any, even the most enormous wrong; he may still properly have other concerns to engage him; but it is his duty, at least, to wash his hands of it and, if he gives it no thought longer, not to give it practically his support. If I devote myself to other pursuits and contemplations, I must first see, at least, that I do not pursue them sitting upon another man's shoulders. I must get off him first, that he may pursue his contemplations too. See what gross inconsistency is tolerated. I have heard some of my townsmen say, "I should like to have them order me out to help put down an insurrection of the slaves, or to march to Mexico—see if I would go"; and yet these very men have each directly by their allegiance and so indirectly, at least, by their money, furnished a substitute. The soldier is applauded who refuses to serve in an unjust war by those who do not refuse to sustain the unjust government which makes the war; is applauded by those whose own act and authority he disregards and sets at naught; as if the State were penitent to that degree that it hired one to scourge it while it sinned, but not to that degree that it left off sinning for a moment. Thus, under the name of Order and Civil Government, we are all made at last to pay homage to and support our own meanness. After the first blush of sin comes its indifference; and from immoral it becomes, as it were, *un*moral, and not quite unnecessary to that life which we have made.

The broadest and most prevalent error requires the most disin-   14
terested virtue to sustain it. The slight reproach to which the virtue of patriotism is commonly liable, the noble are most likely to incur. Those who, while they disapprove of the character and measures of

---

[11]**Odd Fellow** The Independent Order of Odd Fellows, a fraternal and benevolent secret society, founded in England in the eighteenth century and first established in the United States in 1819 in Baltimore.

a government, yield to it their allegiance and support, are undoubtedly its most conscientious supporters, and so frequently the most serious obstacles to reform. Some are petitioning the State to dissolve the Union, to disregard the requisitions of the President. Why do they not dissolve it themselves—the union between themselves and the State—and refuse to pay their quota into its treasury? Do not they stand in the same relation to the State that the State does to the Union? And have not the same reasons prevented the State from resisting the Union which have prevented them from resisting the State?

How can a man be satisfied to entertain an opinion merely, and   15
enjoy *it?* Is there any enjoyment in it if his opinion is that he is aggrieved? If you are cheated out of a single dollar by your neighbor, you do not rest satisfied with knowing that you are cheated, or with saying that you are cheated, or even with petitioning him to pay you your due; but you take effectual steps at once to obtain the full amount and see that you are never cheated again. Action from principle, the perception and the performance of right, changes things and relations; it is essentially revolutionary and does not consist wholly with anything which was. It not only divides states and churches, it divides families; ay, it divides the *individual,* separating the diabolical in him from the divine.

Unjust laws exist: shall we be content to obey them, or shall we   16
endeavor to amend them and obey them until we have succeeded, or shall we transgress them at once? Men generally, under such a government as this, think that they ought to wait until they have persuaded the majority to alter them. They think that if they should resist the remedy would be worse than the evil. *It* makes it worse. Why is it not more apt to anticipate and provide for reform? Why does it not cherish its wise minority? Why does it cry and resist before it is hurt? Why does it not encourage its citizens to be on the alert to point out its faults and *do* better than it would have them? Why does it always crucify Christ and excommunicate Copernicus and Luther[12] and pronounce Washington and Franklin rebels?

One would think that a deliberate and practical denial of its au-   17
thority was the only offence never contemplated by government; else why has it not assigned its definite, its suitable and proportionate penalty? If a man who has no property refuses but once to earn nine shillings for the State, he is put in prison for a period unlimited

---

[12]**Nicolaus Copernicus (1473–1543) and Martin Luther (1483–1546)** Copernicus revolutionized astronomy and the way humankind perceives the universe; Luther was a religious revolutionary who began the Reformation and created the first Protestant faith.

by any law that I know, and determined only by the discretion of those who placed him there; but if he should steal ninety times nine shillings from the State, he is soon permitted to go at large again.

If the injustice is part of the necessary friction of the machine of government, let it go, let it go: perchance it will wear smooth—certainly the machine will wear out. If the injustice has a spring or a pulley or a rope or a crank exclusively for itself, then perhaps you may consider whether the remedy will not be worse than the evil; but if it is of such a nature that it requires you to be the agent of injustice to another, then I say break the law. Let your life be a counter friction to stop the machine. What I have to do is to see, at any rate, that I do not lend myself to the wrong which I condemn.   18

As for adopting the ways which the State has provided for remedying the evil, I know not of such ways. They take too much time, and a man's life will be gone. I have other affairs to attend to. I came into this world, not chiefly to make this a good place to live in, but to live in it, be it good or bad. A man has not everything to do, but something; and because he cannot do *everything*, it is not necessary that he should do *something* wrong. It is not my business to be petitioning the Governor or the Legislature any more than it is theirs to petition me; and if they should not hear my petition what should I do then? But in this case the State has provided no way: its very Constitution is the evil. This may seem to be harsh and stubborn and unconciliatory; but it is to treat with the utmost kindness and consideration the only spirit that can appreciate or deserves it. So is all change for the better, like birth and death, which convulse the body.   19

I do not hesitate to say that those who call themselves Abolitionists should at once effectually withdraw their support, both in person and property, from the government of Massachusetts, and not wait till they constitute a majority of one before they suffer the right to prevail through them. I think that it is enough if they have God on their side, without waiting for that other one. Moreover, any man more right than his neighbors constitutes a majority of one already.   20

I meet this American government or its representative, the State government, directly and face to face once a year—no more—in the person of its tax-gatherer; this is the only mode in which a man situated as I am necessarily meets it; and it then says distinctly, Recognize me; and the simplest, the most effectual and, in the present posture of affairs, the indispensablest mode of treating with it on this head, of expressing your little satisfaction with and love for it, is to deny it then. My civil neighbor, the tax-gatherer, is the very man I have to deal with—for it is, after all, with men and not with parchment that I quarrel—and he has voluntarily chosen to be an agent   21 of the government. How shall he ever know well what he is and does as an officer of the government, or as a man, until he is obliged to consider whether he shall treat me, his neighbor, for whom he has respect, as a neighbor and well-disposed man, or as a maniac and disturber of the peace, and see if he can get over this obstruction to his neighborliness without a ruder and more impetuous thought or speech corresponding with his action. I know this well, that if one thousand, if one hundred, if ten men whom I could name — if ten *honest* men only — ay, if *one* HONEST man in this State of Massachusetts, *ceasing to hold slaves,* were actually to withdraw from this copartnership and be locked up in the county jail therefor, it would be the abolition of slavery in America. For it matters not how small the beginning may seem to be: what is once well done is done forever. But we love better to talk about it: that we say is our mission. Reform keeps many scores of newspapers in its service but not one man. If my esteemed neighbor,[13] the State's ambassador, who will devote his days to the settlement of the question of human rights in the Council Chamber, instead of being threatened with the prisons of Carolina, were to sit down the prisoner of Massachusetts, that State which is so anxious to foist the sin of slavery upon her sister — though at present she can discover only an act of inhospitality to be the ground of a quarrel with her — the Legislature would not wholly waive the subject the following winter.

Under a government which imprisons any unjustly, the true   22
place for a just man is also a prison. The proper place today, the only place which Massachusetts has provided for her freer and less desponding spirits is in her prisons, to be put out and locked out of the State by her own act, as they have already put themselves out by their principles. It is there that the fugitive slave and the Mexican prisoner on parole and the Indian come to plead the wrongs of his race should find them; on that separate but more free and honorable ground where the State places those who are not *with* her but *against* her — the only house in a slave State in which a free man can abide with honor. If any think that their influence would be lost there, and their voices no longer afflict the ear of the State, that they would not be as an enemy within its walls, they do not know by how much truth is stronger than error, nor how much more eloquently and effectively he can combat injustice who has experienced a little in his

---

[13] **esteemed neighbor** Thoreau refers to Samuel Hoar (1778–1856), a Massachusetts congressman, who went to South Carolina to protest that state's practice of seizing black seamen from Massachusetts ships and enslaving them. South Carolina threatened Hoar and drove him out of the state. He did not secure the justice he demanded.

own person. Cast your whole vote, not a strip of paper merely, but your whole influence. A minority is powerless while it conforms to the majority; it is not even a minority then; but it is irresistible when it clogs by its whole weight. If the alternative is to keep all just men in prison or give up war and slavery, the State will not hesitate which to choose. If a thousand men were not to pay their tax-bills this year, that would not be a violent bloody measure, as it would be to pay them, and enable the State to commit violence and shed innocent blood. This is, in fact, the definition of a peaceable revolution, if any such is possible. If the tax-gatherer or any other public officer asks me, as one has done, "But what shall I do?" my answer is, "If you really wish to do anything, resign your office." When the subject has refused allegiance and the officer has resigned his office, then the revolution is accomplished. But even suppose blood should flow. Is there not a sort of blood shed when the conscience is wounded? Through this wound a man's real manhood and immortality flow out, and he bleeds to an everlasting death. I see this blood flowing now.

I have contemplated the imprisonment of the offender rather   23 than the seizure of his goods—though both will serve the same purpose—because they who assert the purest right, and consequently are most dangerous to a corrupt State, commonly have not spent much time in accumulating property. To such the State renders comparatively small service, and a slight tax is wont to appear exorbitant, particularly if they are obliged to earn it by special labor with their hands. If there were one who lived wholly without the use of money, the State itself would hesitate to demand it of him. But the rich man—not to make any invidious comparison—is always sold to the institution which makes him rich. Absolutely speaking, the more money, the less virtue; for money comes between a man and his objects, and obtains them for him; and it was certainly no great virtue to obtain it. It puts to rest many questions which he would otherwise be taxed to answer; while the only new question which it puts is the hard but superfluous one, how to spend it. Thus his moral ground is taken from under his feet. The opportunities of living are diminished in proportion as what are called the "means" are increased. The best thing a man can do for his culture when he is rich is to endeavor to carry out those schemes which he entertained when he was poor. Christ answered the Herodians[14] according to their condition. "Show me the tribute-money," said he—and one

---

[14]**Herodians** Followers of King Herod who were opposed to Jesus Christ (see Matthew 22:16).

took a penny out of his pocket—if you use money which has the image of Caesar on it, and which he has made current and valuable, that is, if *you are men of the State* and gladly enjoy the advantages of Caesar's government, then pay him back some of his own when he demands it; "Render therefore to Caesar that which is Caesar's, and to God those things which are God's"—leaving them no wiser than before as to which was which; for they did not wish to know.

When I converse with the freest of my neighbors, I perceive that   24 whatever they may say about the magnitude and seriousness of the question, and their regard for the public tranquillity, the long and the short of the matter is that they cannot spare the protection of the existing government, and they dread the consequences to their property and families of disobedience to it. For my own part, I should not like to think that I ever rely on the protection of the State. But if I deny the authority of the State when it presents its tax-bill, it will soon take and waste all my property and so harass me and my children without end. This is hard. This makes it impossible for a man to live honestly, and at the same time comfortably, in outward respects. It will not be worth the while to accumulate property; that would be sure to go again. You must hire or squat somewhere and raise but a small crop and eat that soon. You must live within yourself and depend upon yourself always tucked up and ready for a start, and not have many affairs. A man may grow rich in Turkey even, if he will be in all respects a good subject of the Turkish government. Confucius[15] said: "If a state is governed by the principles of reason, poverty and misery are subjects of shame; if a state is not governed by the principles of reason, riches and honors are the subjects of shame." No; until I want the protection of Massachusetts to be extended to me in some distant Southern port, where my liberty is endangered, or until I am bent solely on building up an estate at home by peaceful enterprise, I can afford to refuse allegiance to Massachusetts and her right to my property and life. It costs me less in every sense to incur the penalty of disobedience to the State than it would to obey. I should feel as if I were worth less in that case.

Some years ago the State met me in behalf of the Church and   25 commanded me to pay a certain sum toward the support of a clergyman whose preaching my father attended, but never I myself. "Pay," it said, "or be locked up in the jail." I declined to pay. But, unfortu-

---

[15]**Confucius (551–479 B.C.)** The most important Chinese religious leader. His *Analects* (collection) treated not only religious but moral and political matters as well.

nately, another man saw fit to pay it. I did not see why the school-master should be taxed to support the priest, and not the priest the schoolmaster; for I was not the State's schoolmaster, but I supported myself by voluntary subscription. I did not see why the lyceum should not present its tax-bill and have the State to back its demand, as well as the Church. However, at the request of the selectmen, I condescended to make some such statement as this in writing: —
"Know all men by these presents, that I, Henry Thoreau, do not wish to be regarded as a member of any incorporated society which I have not joined." This I gave to the town clerk; and he has it. The State, having thus learned that I did not wish to be regarded as a member of that church, has never made a like demand on me since; though it said that it must adhere to its original presumption that time. If I had known how to name them, I should then have signed off in detail from all the societies which I never signed on to; but I did not know where to find a complete list.

I have paid no poll-tax[16] for six years. I was put into a jail once   26
on this account, for one night; and, as I stood considering the walls of solid stone, two or three feet thick, the door of wood and iron, a foot thick, and the iron grating which strained the light, I could not help being struck with the foolishness of that institution which treated me as if I were mere flesh and blood and bones, to be locked up. I wondered that it should have concluded at length that this was the best use it could put me to and had never thought to avail itself of my services in some way. I saw that if there was a wall of stone between me and my townsmen, there was a still more difficult one to climb or break through before they could get to be as free as I was. I did not for a moment feel confined, and the walls seemed a great waste of stone and mortar. I felt as if I alone of all my towns-men had paid my tax. They plainly did not know how to treat me but behaved like persons who are underbred. In every threat and in every compliment there was a blunder; for they thought that my chief desire was to stand the other side of that stone wall. I could not but smile to see how industriously they locked the door on my meditations, which followed them out again without let or hin-drance, and *they* were really all that was dangerous. As they could not reach me, they had resolved to punish my body; just as boys, if they cannot come at some person against whom they have a spite, will abuse his dog. I saw that the State was half-witted, that it was

---

[16]**poll-tax** A tax levied on every citizen living in a given area; *poll* means "head," so it is a tax per head. The tax Thoreau refers to, about $2, was used to sup-port the Mexican War.

timid as a lone woman with her silver spoons, and that it did not know its friends from its foes, and I lost all my remaining respect for it and pitied it.

Thus the State never intentionally confronts a man's sense, intel- 27 lectual or moral, but only his body, his senses. It is not armed with superior wit or honesty but with superior physical strength. I was not born to be forced. I will breathe after my own fashion. Let us see who is the strongest. What force has a multitude? They only can force me who obey a higher law than I. They force me to become like themselves. I do not hear of *men* being *forced* to live this way or that by masses of men. What sort of life were that to live? When I meet a government which says to me, "Your money or your life," why should I be in haste to give it my money? It may be in a great strait and not know what to do: I cannot help that. It must help itself; do as I do. It is not worth the while to snivel about it. I am not responsible for the successful working of the machinery of society. I am not the son of the engineer. I perceive that, when an acorn and a chestnut fall side by side, the one does not remain inert to make way for the other, but both obey their own laws and spring and grow and flourish as best they can till one, perchance, overshadows and destroys the other. If a plant cannot live according to its nature, it dies; and so a man.

The night in prison was novel and interesting enough. The pris- 28 oners in their shirt-sleeves were enjoying a chat and the evening air in the doorway when I entered. But the jailer said, "Come, boys, it is time to lock up"; and so they dispersed, and I heard the sound of their steps returning into the hollow apartments. My room-mate was introduced to me by the jailer as "a first-rate fellow and a clever man." When the door was locked, he showed me where to hang my hat and how he managed matters there. The rooms were white-washed once a month; and this one, at least, was the whitest, most simply furnished, and probably the neatest apartment in the town. He naturally wanted to know where I came from and what brought me there; and when I had told him, I asked him in my turn how he came there, presuming him to be an honest man, of course; and, as the world goes, I believe he was. "Why," said he, "they accuse me of burning a barn; but I never did it." As near as I could discover, he had probably gone to bed in a barn when drunk and smoked his pipe there; and so a barn burnt. He had the reputation of being a clever man, had been there some three months waiting for his trial to come on, and would have to wait as much longer; but he was quite domesticated and contented, since he got his board for nothing and thought that he was well treated.

He occupied one window, and I the other; and I saw that if one   29
stayed there long, his principal business would be to look out the
window. I had soon read all the tracts that were left there and examined where former prisoners had broken out and where a grate had
been sawed off and heard the history of the various occupants of
that room; for I found that even here there was a history and a gos-
sip which never circulated beyond the walls of the jail. Probably this
is the only house in the town where verses are composed, which afterward printed in a circular form but not published. I was shown
quite a long list of verses which were composed by some young men
who had been detected in an attempt to escape, who avenged themselves by signing them.

I pumped my fellow-prisoner as dry as I could, for fear I should   30
never see him again; but at length he showed me which was my bed
and left me to blow out the lamp.

It was like travelling into a far country, such as I had never ex-   31
pected to behold, to lie there for one night. It seemed to me that I
never had heard the town-clock strike before, nor the evening
sounds of the village; for we slept with the windows open, which
were inside the grating. It was to see my native village in the light of
the Middle Ages, and our Concord was turned into a Rhine stream,
and visions of knights and castles passed before me. They were the
voices of old burghers that I heard in the streets. I was an involuntary spectator and auditor of whatever was done and said in the
kitchen of the adjacent village-inn—a wholly new and rare experience to me. It was a closer view of my native town. I was fairly inside of it. I never had seen its institutions before. This is one of its
peculiar institutions; for it is a shire town.[17] I began to comprehend
what its inhabitants were about.

In the morning our breakfasts were put through the hole in the   32
door, in small oblong-square tin pans, made to fit, and holding a
pint of chocolate, with brown bread and an iron spoon. When they
called for the vessels again, I was green enough to return what bread
I had left; but my comrade seized it and said that I should lay that
up for lunch or dinner. Soon after he was let out to work at haying
in a neighboring field, whither he went every day, and would not be
back till noon; so he bade me good-day, saying that he doubted if he
should see me again.

When I came out of prison—for someone interfered and paid   33
that tax—I did not perceive that great changes had taken place on the

---

[17] **shire town** A county seat, which means the town had a court, county offices, and jails.

common, such as he observed who went in a youth and emerged a tottering and gray-headed man; and yet a change had to my eyes come over the scene — the town and State and country — greater than any that mere time could effect. I saw yet more distinctly the State in which I lived. I saw to what extent the people among whom I lived could be trusted as good neighbors and friends; that their friendship was for summer weather only; that they did not greatly propose to do right; that they were a distinct race from me by their prejudices and superstitions, as the Chinamen and Malays are; that, in their sacrifices to humanity, they ran no risks, not even to their property; that, after all, they were not so noble but they treated the thief as he had treated them and hoped, by a certain outward observance and a few prayers, and by walking in a particular straight though useless path from time to time, to save their souls. This may be to judge my neighbors harshly; for I believe that many of them are not aware that they have such an institution as the jail in their village.

It was formerly the custom in our village, when a poor debtor 34 came out of jail, for his acquaintances to salute him, looking through their fingers, which were crossed to represent the grating of a jail window, "How do ye do?" My neighbors did not thus salute me but first looked at me and then at one another as if I had returned from a long journey. I was put into jail as I was going to the shoemaker's to get a shoe which was mended. When I was let out the next morning I proceeded to finish my errand, and having put on my mended shoe, joined a huckleberry party who were impatient to put themselves under my conduct; and in half an hour — for the horse was soon tackled — was in the midst of a huckleberry field on one of our highest hills two miles off, and then the State was nowhere to be seen.

This is the whole history of "My Prisons." 35

I have never declined paying the highway tax, because I am as 36 desirous of being a good neighbor as I am of being a bad subject; and as for supporting schools I am doing my part to educate my fellow countrymen now. It is for no particular item in the tax-bill that I refuse to pay it. I simply wish to refuse allegiance to the State, to withdraw and stand aloof from it effectually. I do not care to trace the course of my dollar, if I could, till it buys a man or a musket to shoot one with — the dollar is innocent — but I am concerned to trace the effects of my allegiance. In fact, I quietly declare war with the State, after my fashion, though I will still make what use and get what advantage of her I can, as is usual in such cases.

If others pay the tax which is demanded of me from a sympathy 37 with the State, they do but what they have already done in their own case, or rather they abet injustice to a greater extent than the State requires. If they pay the tax from a mistaken interest in the individual taxed, to save his property, or prevent his going to jail, it is because they have not considered wisely how far they let their private feelings interfere with the public good.

This, then, is my position at present. But one cannot be too much on his guard in such a case, lest his action be biassed by obstinacy or an undue regard for the opinions of men. Let him see that he does only what belongs to himself and to the hour. 38

I think sometimes, Why, this people mean well; they are only ignorant; they would do better if they knew how: why give your neighbors this pain to treat you as they are not inclined to? But I think again, this is no reason why I should do as they do or permit others to suffer much greater pain of a different kind. Again, I sometimes say to myself, When many millions of men, without heat, without ill will, without personal feeling of any kind, demand of you a few shillings only, without the possibility, such is their constitution, of retracting or altering their present demand, and without the possibility, on your side, of appeal to any other millions, why expose yourself to this overwhelming brute force? You do not resist cold and hunger, the winds and the waves, thus obstinately; you quietly submit to a thousand similar necessities. You do not put your head into the fire. But just in proportion as I regard this as not wholly a brute force but partly a human force, and consider that I have relations to those millions as to so many millions of men, and not of mere brute or inanimate things, I see that appeal is possible, first and instantaneously, from them to the Maker of them, and secondly, from them to themselves. But if I put my head deliberately into the fire, there is no appeal to fire or to the Maker of fire, and I have only myself to blame. If I could convince myself that I have any right to be satisfied with men as they are, and to treat them accordingly, and not according, in some respects, to my requisitions and expectations of what they and I ought to be, then, like a good Mussulman[18] and fatalist, I should endeavor to be satisfied with things as they are and say it is the will of God. And, above all, there is this difference between resisting this and a purely brute or natural force, that I can resist this with some effect; but I cannot expect, like Orpheus,[19] to change the nature of the rocks and trees and beasts. 39

---

[18] **Mussulman** Muslim; a follower of the religion of Islam.
[19] **Orpheus** In Greek mythology Orpheus was a poet whose songs were so plaintive that they affected animals, trees, and even stones.

I do not wish to quarrel with any man or nation. I do not wish 40
to split hairs, to make fine distinctions, or set myself up as better
than my neighbors. I seek rather, I may say, even an excuse for con-
forming to the laws of the land. I am but too ready to conform to
them. Indeed, I have reason to suspect myself on this head; and each
year, as the tax-gatherer comes round, I find myself disposed to review the acts and position of the general and State governments, and
the spirit of the people, to discover a pretext for conformity.

> We must affect our country as our parents;
> And if at any time we alienate
> Our love or industry from doing it honor,
> We must respect effects and teach the soul
> Matter of conscience and religion,
> And not desire of rule or benefit.[20]

I believe that the State will soon be able to take all my work of this
sort out of my hands, and then I shall be no better a patriot than my
fellow-countrymen. Seen from a lower point of view, the Constitution, with all its faults, is very good; the law and the courts are very
respectable; even this State and this American government are, in
many respects, very admirable and rare things, to be thankful for,
such as a great many have described them; but seen from a point of
view a little higher, they are what I have described them; seen from a
higher still, and the highest, who shall say what they are, or that
they are worth looking at or thinking of at all?

However, the government does not concern me much, and I 41
shall bestow the fewest possible thoughts on it. It is not many mo-
ments that I live under a government, even in this world. If a man is
thought-free, fancy-free, imagination-free, that which is *not* never for
a long time appearing *to be* to him, unwise rulers or reformers cannot fatally interrupt him.

I know that most men think differently from myself; but those 42
whose lives are by profession devoted to the study of these or kindred subjects content me as little as any. Statesmen and legislators,
standing so completely within the institution, never distinctly and
nakedly behold it. They speak of moving society but have no
resting-place without it. They may be men of a certain experience
and discrimination and have no doubt invented ingenious and even

---

[20] **We must affect...** From George Peele (1556–1596), *The Battle of Alcazar*
(acted 1588–1589, printed 1594), II.ii. Thoreau added these lines in a later printing
of the essay. They emphasize the fact that one is disobedient to the state as one is to
a parent—with love and affection and from a cause of conscience. Disobedience is
not taken lightly.

useful systems, for which we sincerely thank them; but all their wit and usefulness lie within certain not very wide limits. They are wont to forget that the world is not governed by policy and expediency. Webster[21] never goes behind government and so cannot speak with authority about it. His words are wisdom to those legislators who contemplate no essential reform in the existing government; but for thinkers, and those who legislate for all time, he never once glances at the subject. I know of those whose serene and wise speculations on this theme would soon reveal the limits of his mind's range and hospitality. Yet, compared with the cheap professions of most re-formers, and the still cheaper wisdom and eloquence of politicians in general, his are almost the only sensible and valuable words, and we thank Heaven for him. Comparatively, he is always strong, origi-nal, and, above all, practical. Still his quality is not wisdom but pru-dence. The lawyer's truth is not Truth but consistency, or a consis-tent expediency. Truth is always in harmony with herself and is not concerned chiefly to reveal the justice that may consist with wrong-doing. He well deserves to be called, as he has been called, the De-fender of the Constitution. There are really no blows to be given by him but defensive ones. He is not a leader but a follower. His leaders are the men of '87.[22] "I have never made an effort," he says, "and never propose to make an effort; I have never countenanced an ef-fort, and never mean to countenance an effort, to disturb the arrangement as originally made, by which the various States came into the Union." Still thinking of the sanction which the Constitu-tion gives to slavery, he says, "Because it was a part of the original compact—let it stand." Notwithstanding his special acuteness and ability, he is unable to take a fact out of its merely political relations and behold it as it lies absolutely to be disposed of by the intellect—what, for instance, it behooves a man to do here in America today with regard to slavery but ventures, or is driven, to make some such desperate answer as the following, while professing to speak ab-solutely, and as a private man—from which what new and singular code of social duties might be inferred? "The manner," says he, "in which the governments of those States where slavery exists are to regulate it, is for their own consideration, under their responsibility to their constituents, to the general laws of propriety, humanity, and

---

[21] **Daniel Webster (1782–1852)** One of the most brilliant orators of his time. He was secretary of state from 1841 to 1843, which is why Thoreau thinks he cannot be a satisfactory critic of government.

[22] **men of '87** The men who framed the Constitution in 1787.

justice, and to God. Associations formed elsewhere, springing from a feeling of humanity, or any other cause, have nothing whatever to do with it. They have never received any encouragement from me, and they never will."[23]

They who know of no purer sources of truth, who have traced 43 up its stream no higher, stand, and wisely stand, by the Bible and the Constitution, and drink at it there with reverence and humility; but they who behold where it comes trickling into this lake or that pool gird up their loins once more and continue their pilgrimage toward its fountain-head.

No man with a genius for legislation has appeared in America. 44 They are rare in the history of the world. There are orators, politicians, and eloquent men by the thousand; but the speaker has not yet opened his mouth to speak who is capable of settling the much-vexed questions of the day. We love eloquence for its own sake and not for any truth which it may utter or any heroism it may inspire. Our legislators have not yet learned the comparative value of free-trade and of freedom, of union, and of rectitude, to a nation. They have no genius or talent for comparatively humble questions of taxation and finance, commerce and manufacturers and agriculture. If we were left solely to the wordy wit of legislators in Congress for our guidance, uncorrected by the seasonable experience and the effectual complaints of the people, America would not long retain her rank among the nations. For eighteen hundred years, though perchance I have no right to say it, the New Testament has been written; yet where is the legislator who has wisdom and practical talent enough to avail himself of the light which it sheds on the science of legislation?

The authority of government, even such as I am willing to sub- 45 mit to—for I will cheerfully obey those who know and can do better than I, and in many things even those who neither know nor can do so well—is still an impure one: to be strictly just, it must have the sanction and consent of the governed. It can have no pure right over my person and property but what I concede to it. The progress from an absolute to a limited monarchy, from a limited monarchy to a democracy, is a progress toward a true respect for the individual. Even the Chinese philosopher[24] was wise enough to regard the individual as the basis of the empire. Is a democracy such as we know it the last improvement possible in government? Is it not possible to

---

[23] These extracts have been inserted since the Lecture was read. [Thoreau's note]

[24] **Chinese philosopher** Thoreau probably means Confucius.

take a step further towards recognizing and organizing the rights of man? There will never be a really free and enlightened State until the State comes to recognize the individual as a higher and independent power, from which all its own power and authority are derived, and treats him accordingly. I please myself with imagining a State at last which can afford to be just to all men and to treat the individual with respect as a neighbor; which even would not think it inconsistent with its own repose if a few were to live aloof from it, not meddling with it, nor embraced by it, who fulfilled all the duties of neighbors and fellow-men. A State which bore this kind of fruit and suffered it to drop off as fast as it ripened would prepare the way for a still more perfect and glorious State, which also I have imagined but not yet anywhere seen.

QUESTIONS FOR CRITICAL READING

1. How would you characterize the tone of Thoreau's address? Is he chastising his audience? Is he praising it? What opinion do you think he has of his audience?
2. Explain what Thoreau means when he says, "But a government in which the majority rule in all cases cannot be based on justice, even as far as men understand it" (para. 4).
3. How is injustice "part of the necessary friction of the machine of government" (para. 18)?
4. Why does Thoreau provide us with "the whole history of 'My Prisons'" (paras. 28–35)? Describe what being in jail taught Thoreau. Why do you think Thoreau reacted so strongly to being in a local jail for a single day?
5. Choose an example of Thoreau's use of irony, and comment on its effectiveness. (One example appears in para. 25.)
6. How might Thoreau view the responsibility of the majority to a minority within the sphere of government?
7. How clear are Thoreau's concepts of justice? On what are they based?

SUGGESTIONS FOR WRITING

1. Thoreau insists, "Law never made men a whit more just" (para. 4). He introduces the concept of conscience as a monitor of law and government. Explain his views on conscience and the conscientious person. How can conscience help create justice? Why is it sometimes difficult for law to create justice?

2. Do you agree with Thoreau when he says, "All voting is a sort of gaming" (para. 11)? Examine his attitude toward elections and the relationship of elections to the kind of justice one can expect from a government.

3. Answer Thoreau's question: "Unjust laws exist: shall we be content to obey them, or shall we endeavor to amend them and obey them until we have succeeded, or shall we transgress them at once?" (para. 16). Thoreau reminds us that the law has been created by the majority and to disobey would put him in a minority—a "wise minority." Why should the wise minority have the right to disobey laws created by the majority?

4. In what ways was the United States government of Thoreau's time built on the individual or on the individual's best interests? In what way is our current government based on the individual's best interests? How can satisfying the individual's best interests be reconciled with satisfying the community's interest? Which would produce more justice?

5. Examine quotations from Thoreau that focus on justice for the individual, and write an essay that establishes the values of the government Thoreau describes. How might that government see its obligations to the governed? How would it treat matters of justice and moral issues? Describe Thoreau's view of the American government of his time in enough detail to give a clear sense of the essay to someone who has not read it.

6. Reread Thoreau's question in item 3 above. Answer it in an essay that focuses on issues that are significant to you. Be as practical and cautious as you feel you should be, and provide your own answer—not the one you feel Thoreau might have given. Then describe the forms that Thoreau's disobedience would be likely to take. What probably would be the limits of his actions?

Acknowledgments

Aristotle, "A Definition of Justice" Book III, Chapters 9–12, pages 116–127 of *Aristotle's Politics* Translated Benjamin Jowett. Dover Thrift Edition, 2000.

James Baldwin, "Stranger in the Village." From *Notes of a Native Son* by James Baldwin. Copyright © 1955, renewed 1983, by James Baldwin. Reprinted by permission of Beacon Press, Boston.

Simone De Beauvoir, "Women, Myth and Reality." From *The Second Sex* by Simone de Beauvoir, translated by H. M. Parshley. Copyright © 1942 and renewed 1980 by Alfred A. Knopf, Inc. Reprinted by permission of the publisher.

Martin Luther King Jr., "Letter from Birmingham Jail." Copyright © 1963 by Martin Luther King Jr., copyright renewed 1991 by Coretta Scott King. Reprinted by arrangement with The Heirs to the Estate of Martin Luther King Jr., c/o Writers House Inc., as agent for the proprietor.

Plato, "Crito." From *The Last Days of Socrates* by Plato, translated by Hugh Tredennick and Harold Tarrant (Penguin, 1954). Copyright Hugh Tredennick, 1954, 1959, 1969. Copyright Harold Tarrant 1993.

Plato, "The Apology." From The dialogues of Plate/translated with analysis by R. E. Allen. Imprint New Haven: Yale University Press, copyright 1984.